The Parables
Of Our Savior

by
William M. Taylor

© **Guardian of Truth Foundation 2004.** All rights reserved. No part of this book may be reproduced in any form without written permission from the publisher. Printed in the United States of America.

ISBN 1-58427-073-X

Guardian of Truth Foundation
P.O. Box 9670
Bowling Green, Kentucky 42102

PREFACE

THE parables of our Lord have always had a special attraction for students of the Gospels, and there are probably more works devoted to their exposition than to that of any other portion of the Saviour's teachings. In adding another to the number, I can claim only such originality as may be fairly accounted for by what astronomers have called the "personal equation;" and the result may be a further illustration of the many-sidedness of these exquisite stories. To Archbishop Trench, who more than any other English writer has brought Patristic lore to bear upon the illustration of the parables, every later author must express his peculiar obligations; but the recent works of Professor Bruce and Siegfried Goebel have broken new ground in this department, and my aim has been to turn their fruitful suggestions to good homiletical account. The little volumes of Dr. Dods — only the first of which was in my hands when these discourses were prepared — are full of golden nuggets; and the Expositions of William Arnot are characterized by the masculine sense, rich Christian experience, and striking illustrations for which he was so remarkable. But the present work, while more or less indebted in different respects to all these authors, will be found to be in others independent of them all. It is given to the press at the urgent request of many who heard the discourses when delivered; and, such as it is, it is laid at the feet of Him whose sayings it is designed to illustrate, with the prayer that he would use it for the glory of his name, in the edification of his Church, and the conversion of men.

WM. M. TAYLOR.

CONTENTS

		PAGE
Preface		iii
1.	Introduction	1
2.	The Four Kinds of Soil	17
3.	The Tares, and The Drag-net	38
4.	The Mustard Seed, and The Leaven	54
5.	The Hidden Treasure, and The Pearl of Great Price	70
6.	The Unmerciful Servant	86
7.	The Laborers in the Vineyard	104
8.	The Two Sons	121
9.	The Wicked Husbandmen	137
10.	The Royal Marriage Feast	149
11.	The Ten Virgins	164
12.	The Intrusted Talents	180
13.	The Growth of the Seed	196
14.	The Two Debtors	210
15.	The Good Samaritan	226
16.	The Friend at Midnight	243
17.	The Foolish Rich Man	259
18.	The Barren Fig Tree	276

Contents

		PAGE
19.	The Great Supper	290
20.	The Lost Sheep	305
21.	The Lost Coin	320
22.	The Prodigal Son	337
23.	The Elder Brother	356
24.	The Prudent Steward	371
25.	The Rich Man and Lazarus	387
26.	The Ploughing Servant	402
27.	The Importunate Widow, and The Pharisee and the Publican	415
28.	The Pounds	431

THE PARABLES OF OUR SAVIOUR

I
INTRODUCTION

As we enter upon the exposition of the Saviour's parables, we are met by two or three preliminary questions, the answers to which will determine, to a considerable extent, the character and quality of our work. To the consideration and settlement of these, therefore, we shall devote this introductory discourse.

I. First, what is a parable? In the New Testament, two Greek words have been rendered by this one English term. The one of these, παροιμία, is almost peculiar to the fourth Evangelist, seeing that he uses it four times, while it occurs only once elsewhere; to wit, in 2 Pet. ii. 22, where it is translated "proverb." Literally it signifies "something by the way;" and in its secondary sense it denotes a figurative discourse or dark saying, in which more is meant than meets the ear, and into which much valuable though hidden meaning has been closely packed. The other and more common term, παραβολή, which, curiously enough, is never used by John, while it is the only one employed by the

THE PARABLES OF OUR SAVIOUR

other Evangelists, is simply the English word in Greek letters. It comes from a verb which signifies to throw or place side by side, and denotes a placing of one thing beside another for the purpose of comparison, or, more generally, an utterance which involves a comparison. It is used by the sacred writers both in a wider and in a narrower sense. In the wider sense, it is employed sometimes to denote an adage, or proverb properly so called;[1] sometimes to signify a sentiment so briefly and darkly worded as not to be easily understood;[2] sometimes to designate a pithy instruction couched in the form of an aphorism;[3] and sometimes to describe a lesson which is confirmed by a simile drawn from nature.[4] But, in its more restricted sense, it is the name given to a connected narrative, whether of events in human life or of a process in nature, by which some great spiritual truth is illustrated or enforced. It is not a mere simile, which may be expressed in a single clause; or even a detailed comparison of one thing to another: but a little history, which might be read merely for its own sake, but which, as used by the Great Teacher, was made the vehicle of instruction or warning, of comfort or condemnation. The little girl was very near the mark, when she said that a parable is "an earthly story with a heavenly meaning;" and we may not be far wrong if we define it to be a narrative true to nature or to life, used for the purpose of conveying spiritual truth to the mind of the hearer. Its force depends on the analogy which exists between God's works in nature and providence, and his operations in grace. The world of nature came at first from, and is still sustained by, the hand of Him who formed the human soul; and the administration of

[1] Luke iv. 23.   [2] Matt. xv. 15.   [3] Luke xiv. 7.   [4] Matt. xxiv. 32.

providence is carried on by Him who gave to us the revelation of his will in the Sacred Scriptures, and provided for us salvation through his Son. We may expect, therefore, to find a principle of unity running through all these three departments of his administration; and a knowledge of his operations in any one of them may be helpful to us in our investigation of the others.

The use which was made of this truth by Bishop Butler, in his great work on "The Analogy of Religion, Natural and Revealed, to the Constitution and Course of Nature," is known to every student of the Christian evidences. Postulating that the course and constitution of nature are maintained by God, he shows that the difficulties which emerge in revelation are precisely parallel to those which meet us in nature and in providence, and draws these two conclusions: namely, that, as we have met difficulties in these other departments, we ought not to be surprised to meet similar difficulties in revelation, coming as that does from the same divine Author; and that, as in the one case the difficulties are not regarded as sufficient to invalidate our belief that the constitution and course of nature are from God, so in the other they ought not to be allowed to stand in the way of our acceptance of the Scriptures as from him. The argument is irrefutable by those who admit the postulate with which he sets out; and they who reject it at all can do so consistently, only by accepting, as unhappily James Mill did, the dreary, unrelieved darkness of absolute atheism.

The existence of this analogy lies also at the root of the finest poetry, and accounts for the effect produced upon us by the revelation of those hidden harmonies which genius has discovered and revealed. Not seldom, too, the physical philosopher has been led by the same principle to some of his grandest discoveries; and, as in the case of the great German, the insight of the poet has been combined with — has, indeed, contributed to — the eminence of the man of science. Thus all things are double, one against another. The external is the mirror in which we may behold the internal and spiritual; and Milton was not wrong when he said, —

> "What if earth
> Be but the shadow of heaven and things therein,
> Each to the other like, more than on earth is thought?"

Hence a true parable is something more than a mere felicitous illustration. It is an outward symbol of an inward reality. It is not the creation of a new similarity, but the revelation of a similarity that has always existed; not the putting into nature or into life of that which was not formerly in them, but the bringing-out from them of that which they have always contained, and which is indeed their deepest and their truest significance. Trench is not overstating the case, therefore, when he says of the Saviour's parables, that "their power lies in the harmony unconsciously felt by all men, and which all deeper minds have delighted to trace, between the natural and spiritual worlds, so that analogies from the first are felt to be something more than illustrations happily but yet arbitrarily chosen. They are arguments, and may be alleged as witnesses; the world of nature being throughout a witness for the world of spirit, proceeding from the same hand, growing out of the same root, and being constituted for that very end."[1]

[1] Notes on the Parables, by Archbishop Trench, pp. 12, 13.

Herein, too, lies the root of the difference between the parable, strictly so called, and the fable. No doubt, as has been often pointed out, the fable finds its sphere in the lower department of merely worldly prudence, while that of the parable is in the enforcement of the highest spiritual truths. But that to which I direct attention more particularly now is the fact that the author of the fable puts into nature something that is not originally there, in order that he may draw out again the lesson which he designs to teach; while the setter-forth of a parable relates a narrative which in all its parts is true to nature, and finds in that nature, when rightly interpreted, the higher principle which he seeks to enforce. The fabulist does violence to nature, by transferring human motives and actions to trees and animals, in order that he may make them the mouthpieces of that shrewdness which he does not care to utter in his own proper personality. Thus, in Jotham's fable of the trees choosing a king,[1] he attributes the actions of human beings to the vine, the olive, and the fig-tree; and the lesson which he brings out of the whole story is one which he had himself first put into it. In a parable, on the other hand, there is nothing contrary to the truth of nature: every thing is in character; and the moral is not one which has been thrust into it for the time being and for a particular purpose, but one which has all along been in that aspect of human life, and that process of nature, and which waited only for the eye that could see it, and the voice that could reveal it to the world. So as science advances, and history rolls on in its course, the materials for parable are increased; and those who keep abreast of their times may find ever-new analogies wherewith to attract

[1] Judg. ix. 8–20.

the attention of their fellows, and illustrate to them the eternal verities of the gospel.

But observe: to do all this, the parable must be true to nature and to life. If it be not, then it is no proper parable; the analogy is forced, and the lesson conveyed is not one which God meant to teach, but only one which the human speaker has himself devised. This must never be lost sight of; and yet, at the same time, it must never be misunderstood. For it does not imply that the narrative in a parable must be the history of an actual occurrence. It may or it may not be so. The essential thing is, that, whether fact or fiction, it shall be *true*. It may indeed seem paradoxical when I speak of fiction as being true; but the proper antithesis to fiction is fact, not truth, and a thing may be true without being fact. Thus, to take a modern instance, we may find mistakes in matters of fact in some of the historical plays of Shakspeare; but still no mere chronicler of facts has given us any thing like such a truthful idea of the life of the periods which he has delineated, as he has furnished in these dramas. So the story of the Prodigal Son may have been a history of literal facts. There is nothing in it that renders that impossible. But it may also be, as I believe it is, a fiction; and as such it has the truth of an ideal which corresponds to many different reals. Every thing in it is to the life; and as each person reads it, he may have some case in his mind, distinct from that in the mind of every other, to which the description exactly answers. Putting together, then, the different things which we have emphasized, we may say that a parable is the narrative — fictitious or otherwise — of a scene in human life or a process in nature; yet true in its representations either of the one or of the other, and having under it a spiritual lesson : or, to repeat the little girl's definition, it is "an earthly story with a heavenly meaning."

II. But now let us ask, in the second place, why the Lord Jesus used parables in his discourses. And to that we may answer, first of all, that he employed this form of instruction as a means of attracting attention. Every one knows how the interest of young people is awakened and sustained by the telling of "a story." We can all remember how in our early days our minds were fascinated and our imaginations were filled by those classics of the nursery, as I may call them, which were read to us by our seniors, and which we eagerly received, without any questioning on our part as to their truth, or any consciousness, either in the reader or the hearers, of any hidden meaning lurking beneath their incidents. But in this respect we are all only children of a larger growth, as is made abundantly evident by the fact that when a public speaker descends from abstract reasoning to concrete illustration, and clinches his argument by a pat and parallel anecdote, an immediate hush of eager interest stills his audience into a breathless silence, which is broken only at the close by the outburst of irrepressible applause. Now, knowing well this peculiarity of our nature, the Lord secured the attention of his hearers by the beautiful parables which he introduced into his discourses. And the effect was heightened by his selection, for this purpose, of the scenes, incidents, and objects with which men were familiar in common life. He never introduced recondite subjects, or went out of the region with which his hearers were acquainted; but he lifted up that which lay at his hand, making it magnetic in its attractiveness, and luminous in its application. **This,** indeed, was one of the reasons of his popularity as a teacher. The sower going forth to sow; the fisherman casting his net into the lake; the woman kneading her dough, or sweeping her house in search of a piece of money which she had lost; the growth of the mustard-plant from a tiny seed; the shepherd going after his sheep; the father receiving back his long-lost son; the details and incidents of a marriage procession; the hiring of laborers in the market-place, — all were turned by him to profitable account. And this helps to explain how it came, that, with a Joseph and a Nicodemus among his disciples, it was also true that "the common people heard him gladly;" for here, in their liking for "a story" lying in the sphere of daily life, "the rich and the poor meet together," and both alike are attracted by the spell of its influence.

But another reason why our Lord used parables in his teaching was to prevent his auditors from being repelled by a too sudden revelation, either of his purpose or of his message. His hearers were largely prejudiced against the truth which he came to teach; and by means of these delightful stories he secured the presentation of it to their minds in a form which, for the time at least, disarmed antagonism. He had to reveal his truth to men "as they were able to bear it," and so he gave it to them first under the guise of parables. The same reason which underlies the fact that the gospel dispensation as a whole was preceded by the Jewish — which with its types and shadows was just one great parable — is to be found at the heart of our Saviour's employment of this mode of instruction. The race had to be prepared for the fuller revelation which was coming, by the pictorial representation which went before. And what was true of the race as a whole is true also of the individual. The old heathen myth which represented that the sight of the unveiled image of Truth, at Saïs, would smite a man into death or into blindness, has its full interpretation here; and parable was the veil which Jesus put over the face of truth, to secure its safer perception by those who listened to his words. Had he spoken plainly, they would have been largely repelled; but by his use of analogy he prepared the way for their ultimate reception of his teaching. Thus, to take but one illustration: the Jews of his day had set their hearts upon a literal restoration of their earthly kingdom. Indeed, they fully expected that as the fulfilment of their ancient oracles. Now, if Jesus, at the beginning of his ministry, had affirmed as plainly as he did at its close, to Pilate, who had no such prejudice, that "his kingdom was not of this world," they would have given him no further heed. But in his wisdom he veiled that fact beneath the many parables which tell of "the kingdom of heaven;" and in that form it was preserved for his genuine disciples, while it was hidden for the time from his antagonists. This seems to me to be the true explanation of the somewhat difficult passage wherein the Lord himself describes his purpose in the use of parables, to his followers. He says, "Therefore speak I to them in parables, because they seeing see not, and hearing they hear not, and do not understand."[1] Had he spoken plainly, they would have been stirred to immediate antagonism, and the crisis of the cross would have come before his personal ministry had been well begun. But by the adoption of the parabolic method he postponed the inevitable catastrophe, and so secured time for the education of his apostles, and for the communication to

[1] Matt. xiii. 13.

them, and through them to the world at large, of the true principles of his gospel.

But, as another illustration of the same sort, I may refer to his parables of reproof. By his employment of the story, he made the severest exposure of the conduct of his antagonists, before they were aware of his design; and so secured that they were put to confusion, nay, oftentimes convicted out of their own mouths. You remember how Nathan did with David in the matter of the Psalmist's great iniquity.[1] Had the prophet gone in to the king, and directly and immediately denounced his guilt, while at the same time he attempted to pronounce sentence upon him, and to declare that punishment would surely follow, it is at least questionable if he would have been listened to at all; and it is certain, I think, that he would have provoked the monarch to anger, rather than led him to repentance. But by the telling of the touching story of the ewe lamb, he awoke the better nature of the king: and when, after his lord had given his judgment in an outburst of honest indignation, he turned and said, "*Thou art the man,*" the effect was tremendous; for in the ejaculation, "*I have sinned,*" there was the germ of the entire Fifty-first Psalm, and the beginning of a penitence which was as sincere as the transgression had been aggravated.

Now, we can see a similar purpose in some of our Lord's parables; although unhappily, owing to the hardened state of the hearts of his opponents, they were not brought to a similar acknowledgment of their guilt. Thus in the story of the wicked husbandmen (Matt. xxii. 33-46), the chief priests and Pharisees at the end, but not till then, perceived that he had spoken of them; and it is recorded, that they sought to lay hands on

[1] 2 Sam. xii. 1-7.

him, but were prevented only by fear of the multitude. Still he had secured his object; for he had so held up the mirror before them, that they recognized themselves, and were self-condemned. Thus the parable was a veil which both revealed and concealed the truth. It was, if you will allow me to coin a word, an *inverbation* of the truth, corresponding in some sort to the incarnation of Deity in Christ himself. To those who had the spirit to discern, the outward covering brought the truth nearer, even as the incarnation has been, to the spiritually minded, the clearest revelation of God the world has ever seen; but to those who lacked that spirit, there was nothing but the story, even as, to the materialists among us, there is nothing but mere humanity in the person of the Christ. With all his usual acuteness, but with a sublimity that is somewhat unwonted in his comments, Matthew Henry has said that parable was "the cloud" wherein the Great Teacher "descended."[1] Yea, a cloud luminous to some, yet dark to others; the envelment, but also the unveiling, of the truth to men.

Now, if this view of the matter be correct, we shall see how two other objects were served by this use of parables by our Lord. For I remark, in the third place, that he employed them to stimulate inquiry. The man who saw in the story nothing but a story, would turn away from it as trifling and unimportant; but those who had the insight to perceive that the narrative was rehearsed for a high moral and spiritual purpose, would be stirred up to inquire into that, and would be rewarded by the discovery of its hidden meaning. Thus we learn, that after the Lord had related the story of the sower, and that of the tares and the wheat, his disciples

---

[1] Commentary on Matt. xiii. 1-23.

came to him, and asked an explanation of his words.
To that he responded by giving the interpretation of
the parables; and so he exemplified the meaning, as well
as the truth, of his own words, "Whosoever hath, to
him shall be given, and he shall have more abundance;
but whosoever hath not, from him shall be taken away
even that he hath." [1]

And that leads directly and immediately to the last
purpose which the Lord had in view in his employment
of this method of discourse; which was, to test the characters of his hearers. Nothing better on this subject has
ever been written than the following suggestive sentences
by Neander, in that "Life of Jesus Christ," which was
the first of the answers to the notorious work of Strauss,
and which, in my judgment, is still — with some drawbacks incidental to the author's theory of inspiration —
incomparably the best of all the works under that title
which have been published in modern times. He says,
"The form of his expressions, whether he uttered parables, proverbs, maxims, or apparent paradoxes, was intended to spur men's minds to profounder thought, to
awaken the divine consciousness within, and so to teach
them to *understand* that which at first served only as a
mental stimulus. It was designed to impress indelibly
upon the memory of his hearers, truths perhaps as yet
not fully intelligible, but which would grow clear as
the divine life was formed within them, and become an
ever-increasing source of spiritual light. His doctrine
was not to be propagated as a lifeless stock of tradition,
but to be received, as a living Spirit, by willing minds,
and brought out into full consciousness, according to its
import, by free spiritual activity. Its individual parts,
too, were only to be apprehended in their first propor

Matt. xiii. 12.

tions, in the complete connection of that higher consciousness which he was to call forth in man. The form of teaching which repelled the stupid, and passed unheeded and misunderstood by the unholy, roused susceptible minds to deeper thought, and rewarded their inquiries by the discovery of ever-increasing treasures. But the attainment of this end depended on the susceptibility of the hearers. So far as they hungered for true spiritual food, so far the parable stimulated them to deeper thought, and so far only it revealed new riches. Men with whom this really was the case were accustomed to wait until the throng had left their Master, or, gathering round him in a narrow circle in some retired spot, to seek clearer light on points which the parable had left obscure. The scene described in Mark iv. 10 shows us that *others besides the twelve apostles* were named among those who remained behind to ask him questions after the crowd had dispersed. Not only did such questions afford the Saviour an opportunity of imparting more thorough instruction, but those who felt constrained to offer them were thereby drawn into closer fellowship with him. He became better acquainted with the souls that were longing for salvation. The greater number, however, in their stupidity, did not trouble themselves to penetrate the shell in order to reach the kernel. Yet they must have perceived that they had *understood nothing;* they could not learn separate phrases from Christ, as they might from other religious teachers, and *think* they comprehended them, when they did not. And so, in proportion to the susceptibility of his hearers, the parables of Christ revealed sacred things to some, and veiled them from others, who were destined, through their own fault, to remain in darkness. Thus, like those 'hard sayings,' which were to some an insupportable 'offence,' the parables served to sift and purge the throng of Christ's hearers."[1] They tested character, while they symbolized truth.

III. But now a word or two as to how parables are to be interpreted. The Lord himself has given us a pattern here, and in his expositions of the parables of the sower and the tares he has shown us how we ought to proceed. Each is told for the enforcement of one main truth; and to that attention is to be particularly devoted, without seeking to run into minute details, or giving a significance to every little thing that is introduced. Now, what the main purpose of the parable is, we may in general discover easily, either from the manner in which it is introduced, or from the circumstances in connection with which it was delivered. Not seldom, indeed, the purpose is indicated in the very first words, as in the numerous parables beginning with "The kingdom of heaven is like;" while occasionally we have it definitely announced, as in the words prefixed to that of the Pharisee and the publican: "He spake this parable unto certain which trusted in themselves that they were righteous, and despised others."[2] Sometimes, too, as in the case of that of the Good Samaritan, the parable is given as an answer to the question either of a caviller or of an inquirer; and then there can be little hesitation as to its meaning. When we have found out, then, what the main drift and purpose is, we have the key for the opening-up of its significance. Still, just as, in the interpretation of the symbolism of the Jewish tabernacle, we run into trifling and conceit when we attempt to give a spiritual significance to every pillar, and curtain, and coupling,

---

[1] Neander's Life of Christ, Bohn's edition, pp. 106, 107.
[2] Luke xviii. 9.

and pin; so we miss the full force of a parable when we try to find a meaning in every fold of its drapery. In such a case, we divide the river of its teaching into so many little branches that it finally disappears, like one of those streams which flow through many channels into the Australian desert, and lose themselves in the sand. Thus, in regard to the parable of the Good Samaritan, which Christ himself interpreted by saying, "Go and do thou likewise," we have had such laborious trifling as this: The man who fell among thieves was Adam; the thieves were the Devil and his angels; the priest and Levite were the Mosaic dispensation; the Good Samaritan was Christ himself; the oil and the wine were the comforts and blessings of the gospel; the beast on which he rode was the humanity of Christ; the setting of the wounded man thereon was his vicarious salvation; the inn was the Church; and the two pence, the life that now is, and the life that is to come. But where, meanwhile, is the great lesson of practical beneficence which the Lord designed to teach? or how, from such a multitude of conceits, will one deduce an answer to the question, "Who is my neighbor?"

This may serve as a beacon of warning, and keep us from striking against the rock of over-minuteness. But, while we guard against that danger, let us not forget the thought which has been already before us; namely, that the impression produced on us, and the instruction conveyed to us, by the parables, depend on our own spiritual character and susceptibility. We must bring something to them before we can get any thing out of them. We must have the docile spirit of disciples, a willingness to hear, an eagerness to learn, and a readiness to accept what comes to us from the Great Teacher's lips; and for those qualities we must apply to Him from whom all good counsels flow. Let us first, and before all things else, then, seek after these; and, having these, our study will be at once instructive, stimulating, and helpful to us in the prosecution of the Christian life.

Different classifications of the Saviour's parables have been suggested by different authors; and there are, undoubtedly, some advantages to be derived from the following of such a course as that which has been taken by Bruce and Goebel. But, on the other hand, the adoption of such a method is apt to make us lose sight of the very marked difference in structure and in theme between the parables recorded by Matthew, and those preserved by Luke; and we may best discover the "personal equation" of the Evangelists by taking them in the order in which we find them in the Gospels, while, at the same time, we shall secure variety of topic, and so conserve our interest in the series from first to last. Without attempting any systematic classification of the parables, therefore, we shall examine them in the order in which we come upon them in the narratives of the Evangelists.

II

THE FOUR KINDS OF SOIL
Matthew 13:1-9, 18-23

THIS thirteenth chapter of Matthew's Gospel contains seven parables, all of which, apparently, were spoken on the same occasion, and each of which was designed to give distinctness to one special aspect of the same subject. That subject is "the kingdom of heaven," by which is meant, not the glorified state of the future life, but that presently existing spiritual community of which Christ is the head, and which is composed of those whose hearts and lives are subject to him as their sovereign. The theme is thus the same as that which is dealt with in the Sermon on the Mount, and the discourse in which these parables are found may almost be regarded as an illustrative appendix to that matchless address. In the Sermon, the Saviour treats the subject abstractly and impersonally: in the parables, he uses familiar figures for its illustration, and has special reference to the different effects produced by its presentation, on men of different dispositions. In the Sermon, he is mainly retrospective, and sets forth the points of contrast between the Mosaic system, and that which he came to introduce: in the parables, he is almost entirely prospective, and unfolds the manner of the progress of his kingdom, and the nature of its consummation. In the Sermon, he lays down principles, and proclaims laws: in the parables, he gives prominence to individual cases and peculiar features. But both have an important bearing on the one great topic; and, to have a right understanding of that as a whole, both must be studied together.

This being the case, it is not wonderful that certain expositors have imagined that they saw a parallelism between the beatitudes of the Sermon and the parables of this chapter; but their attempts to establish this position in detail are as fanciful as those which others have made to prove that there is a similar relation between these seven parables, and the epistles to the seven churches of Asia, in the beginning of the Book of Revelation. There is a certain fascination, for some minds, in the tracing of these minute resemblances between different portions of the Scriptures; but all such attempts are more or less artificial, and in following them out we may miss the great lessons which the parables were meant to enforce. Accordingly I shall not allow myself to be diverted from my main purpose by the consideration of any such similarities, but content myself with the general statement that these parables were meant to set before us the origin, hinderances, progress, preciousness, and consummation of the kingdom of God among men, and that they really accomplish that object in such a way as to be clearly intelligible and strikingly impressive to every attentive reader.

But, while we rule out fancies, it is our duty with all reverence to take note of facts. Now, the careful student will be struck with two things about these parables. He will not fail to observe, in the first place, that while those of the sower, — so called, — the tares, the mustard-seed, and the leaven, were spoken to the people promiscuously, those of the hidden treasure, the pearl of great price, and the drag-net, were given to the disciples alone. And it is, perhaps, a fair inference from that fact, to say, that, while the former four deal with those aspects of the kingdom which are public and patent to all, the latter three are concerned with the deeper things which are matter of personal history, and which are fully appreciated only by those who become subjects of the kingdom. The first four may be verified by observation, but the last three have to be interpreted by experience.

Again, it will be apparent to the attentive reader, that there is a certain beauty of arrangement in the order of these parables. After that of the four sorts of soil, which stands alone as illustrating the general effects produced by the preaching of the gospel anywhere, the other six come in pairs; and in these three couplets each member is the complement and companion of the other. Thus the parables of the tares and of the dragnet illustrate the same thing; but the one gives prominence to the origin of the mixture of evil with the good in the kingdom, while the other directs attention to the means by which that state of things is to be brought to an end. Again, those of the hidden treasure, and the pearl of great price, do both illustrate the acceptance of the gospel by the individual believer; but the one sets before us the case of a man finding what he was not, at the moment, looking for, while the other depicts the success of the earnest seeker. Once more, those of the mustard-seed and the leaven both illustrate the progress of the gospel in the world, but, while the one represents its outward and visible manifestation, the other suggests its hidden and mysterious operation.

These general statements are all that is required to point out the drift of the parables in this chapter, and the relation of any one of them to all the rest, so that we may now proceed to the more particular consideration of that of the four kinds of ground.

We need not spend much time on the mere externals of the story. It was springtime by the Lake of Galilee, and a crowd of eager listeners were pressing round the Great Teacher as he sat upon the shore. To escape the crush, he stepped into a boat, which he caused to be pushed out a few yards; and from that novel pulpit he spoke to the multitudes that lined the beach. They were numerous, and apparently very enthusiastic just then; but they were very far from being permanently attached to his cause. A winnowing time was coming, and in a few days the great majority of them would "go back, and walk no more with him." The thought was fraught with solemnity to himself, and therefore it gave shape and purpose to his discourse. Why was that crowd so soon to melt away? Would it not be well to look at that question now, before their defection occurred, so that, if possible, some among them might be shaken up to such seriousness as should prevent their withdrawal; while his permanent followers might, at the same time, be prepared for what might otherwise be most discouraging? These were, as I believe, the motives which led the Saviour to tell this simple but suggestive story.

There is nothing in its literal aspect that is at all difficult to apprehend. The sower going forth to sow is a familiar figure in all agricultural districts; and in most places, there is the same difference in the soils on which the seed falls as we find here described. The "wayside," however, is not the margin of the highway with which we are so well acquainted, but rather the footpath through the field, like that on which the Lord and his disciples walked when the latter plucked the ears of corn. The seed that fell by the wayside, therefore, is not that which incidentally dropped from the sower as he was going to the field, but rather that which inevitably fell on the hard path through the field when he was passing over it at his proper work. He could not so nicely adjust his "cast," as that nothing should fall on the walk which many feet had hardened, and his plough had left unturned. The "stony ground" was not soil mixed with stones, but rather a thin layer of earth on the top of underlying rock. The thorny ground was not soil in which thorns were already grown rank and strong, but rather ground which had not been thoroughly "cleaned," as the farmer phrases it, and in which the seeds of thorns were present in abundance. The good soil was that which was neither trodden into hardness, nor lying in shallowness on the top of rocks, nor full of the roots of weeds that had not been carefully removed; but ground which had been well prepared for the reception of the seed. And the results corresponded in each case to the character of the soil. That which fell on the footpath never grew at all. Indeed, it never got into the soil at all, but became the food of birds. That which fell on the rocky soil grew rapidly for a season, and then withered away; that which fell on the ground in which the roots of thorns existed grew, but with difficulty, for the thorns choked it, and prevented it from coming to maturity; while even in the good soil there were degrees of fertility, and in some places the crop was larger than in others. Here, then, is the main thought of the parable in its literal sense: *the growth of the seed depends always on the quality of the soil.* The stress of the story lies not on the character of the sower, or even on the quality of the seed, — though that must not be lost sight of, — but on the nature of the soil. The crop depends upon the character of the ground. That is a universal natural law. What is here described may never have happened literally, in all its incidents, in a single case; but always and everywhere the law of which these incidents are illustrations holds good. The growth of the seed depends on the nature of the soil. I emphasize that as the one great thought of the parable, because, naming it as we do, the parable of the sower, though we are following therein the example of the narrative itself, we are apt to imagine that we must look for its significance in something about the sower, rather than in the differences in the ground. The Germans call it the parable of "the four sorts of soil;" and perhaps we should do well to follow their example, for by so denominating it we should bring into prominence the particular department in which its lesson lies.

What, then, is that lesson? The Saviour has given us the answer in his own interpretation of the story. The seed is the word of God, or the word of the kingdom; and the soil is human hearts: so that, reduced to a general law, the teaching of the parable is, that the results of the hearing of the gospel always and everywhere depend on the condition of heart of those to whom it is addressed. The character of the hearer determines the effect of the word upon him. That which a man takes from the word depends on what he first brings to the word. This is the one lesson of the parable, and it is illustrated by four sorts of examples. Elsewhere in the Scriptures, attention is drawn very strongly to the character of the preacher, and to the nature of the instruction which he communicates; but here the emphasis is laid on the character of the hearer, and the whole teaching of the parable is concentrated into the command of the Lord with which, by Luke, the parable is combined, "*Take heed, therefore, how ye hear.*"[1]

Now, as it seems to me, this is a lesson which the men of our generation need very much to learn. For while, in the broadest and highest sense, the sower here is the greatest of all preachers, even the Lord Jesus himself, and the field is the world, yet the same great law which is here exemplified holds of every preacher of the gospel, and of every company of hearers to whom the gospel message is proclaimed. It is just as true here and now as it was when the Saviour sat, that day, in the boat on the Lake of Galilee, that the effects of the preaching of the gospel depend on the characters of the hearers. But that is an aspect of the matter which is too largely lost sight of in this generation. For, if the services of the sanctuary are uninteresting or unedifying, the blame is too generally and too exclusively laid upon the preacher, and little or nothing is either said or thought about the dispositions of the hearers. I do not wish to say, of course, that no responsibility rests upon the preacher. On the contrary, it is his duty to adapt the presentation of the truth to the circumstances and necessities of those who wait upon his ministrations, and to take all proper means for commending it to the acceptance of his fellow-men; but it ought not to be forgotten, that a corresponding obligation rests on them, and that it is their duty to cultivate spiritual susceptibility, so that they may be interested and profited by what they hear. Criticism of the pulpit is very common, and not always very wise; but criticism of the pews is rarely, if ever, heard: and while many lectureships have been founded in our theological seminaries of late years, for

[1] Luke viii. 18.

the treatment of the best methods of preaching, it might not be amiss to have some similar means of bringing before the people generally some important home truths on the best way of cultivating the habit of profitable hearing. It is well that our students should be instructed how to preach, but it is equally important that the people should be taught how to hear; for if it be true, as is sometimes cynically said, that good preaching is one of the lost arts, it is to be feared that good hearing also has too largely disappeared; and, wherever the fault may have begun, the two act and re-act on each other. A good hearer makes a lively preacher, just as really as a poor preacher makes a dull hearer; and eloquence is not all in the speaker. To use Mr. Gladstone's illustration, he gets from his hearers in vapor that which he returns to them in flood, and a receptive and responsive audience adds fervor and intensity to his utterance. Eloquent hearing, therefore, is absolutely indispensable to effective preaching; and so it is quite as necessary that listeners should be taught to hear, as it is that preachers should be taught what and how to speak.

Now, it is just here that the lessons of this parable are in place; and, when we come to examine, we shall find that they range themselves under two heads, — the negative and the positive; or, to put it in another way, the things to be guarded against, and the things to be cultivated, in connection with the hearing of the gospel.

I. 1. Taking, then, first, the things to be guarded against, we find foremost among these the danger of preventing the truth from getting any entrance into the soul at all. The seed that fell upon the pathway lay on the outside of the soil. The ground had been so hardened by the tread of many feet, that the grain could not get into it, and it remained ungerminating and exposed until the birds devoured it. So, sometimes, the soul of the hearer has been indurated and made impenetrable to the truth by the traffic over it of many different things. What these are, it might be difficult to enumerate; but a sample or two will make good our statement. One of them, strangely enough, may be the constant hearing of the truth itself, as a mere religious form. The soul may be sermon-hardened, as well as sin-hardened. One may get so into the habit of having the verities of the gospel presented to him, and resisted by him, that by and by he takes no note whatever of what is said by the preacher, and it falls on the outside of him, like rain upon a rock, or snow upon a roof. There is little danger of this, perhaps, in an age or in a place in which gospel privileges are rare, but it becomes very real and insidious in days like our own, when these blessings are so commonly and so regularly enjoyed; and there are too many in all our congregations like Tennyson's "Northern Farmer" of the old school, who said about the parson, —

"And I always came to his church, before my Sally were dead,
And heard him a-bumming away like a buzzard-clock over my head;
And I never knew what he meant, but I thought he had something to say,
And I thought he said what he ought to have said, and I came away."

This is a very serious peril, and has to be strenuously looked after, especially by those who have from their early years been constant attendants on the sanctuary. The preacher may do much to counteract it, indeed, by cultivating fresh methods of presenting and enforcing the truth, and by abjuring all stereotyped phraseology in his discourses; but the hearer, also, must use means to neutralize it, and should seek to stir up his attention when he enters the place of worship, by pausing a little to ask himself why he is there, and to lift up his heart in prayer to God, for the open ear to hear, and the open heart to receive, the message which his Lord has, in his providence, prepared for him.

But another thing which makes a foot-walk over the soul is an evil habit. Ah! how many men's hearts have become thoroughfares for sins, which have trafficked to and fro over them, until they have become as hard as the pavements of our streets, and the truth has no more chance of finding an entrance into them than corn would have to grow upon an asphaltic roadway! Think of Judas in this regard, and you have a concrete instance of the sort which I would describe. How tenderly, and yet how faithfully, the Lord spoke to him on the night of the betrayal! One would have thought that he must have been moved. But no: the sin of covetousness, the habit of dishonesty, had so overcrusted his heart, that the Master's words found no entrance; and "he went out," cold and callous, to do his perfidious deed. So, many in our modern churches have let defalcation, or secret sin, or habitual self-indulgence, freeze over their spirits with such a hard covering of icy callousness, that the truth which otherwise would have descended to the very depths of their being, lies all frosted and uncared-for on the surface. Then the natural result follows; for the casual talk of others like themselves as they retire from the house of God, on topics of frivolous or even worse description, takes all remembrance of it away, and they get no good from the service. O my friends, take good heed here! The habits of the week will either open or stop the ears on the Lord's Day; and if you would be good hearers of the word, you must also be faithful doers of the same.

2. But a second danger to be avoided is that of shallow impulsiveness. The seed which fell on the soil which lay in a thin layer on the top of the rock sprang up at once; but it had no permanent result, for when the sun was up it withered because it had no depth of earth. So the man of shallow nature makes a great show at first. He is all enthusiasm. He "never heard such a sermon in all his life." He seems greatly moved, and for a time it looks as if he were really converted; but it does not last. It is but an ague-fever, which is succeeded by a freezing chill; and by and by some new excitement follows, to give place in its turn to another alternation into cold neglect. He lacks depth of character, for he has nothing but rock beneath the surface. He seems to have much feeling, indeed, and his religion is all emotional; but, in reality, he has no proper feeling. It is all superficial. That which is only feeling, will not even be feeling long. For, as Robertson has profoundly remarked, "the superficial character is connected with the hard heart." Violent emotion is a sign of shallowness, and never lasts. But the tender heart disposes to moral thoughtfulness; and, where *that* is, the feeling is permanent. So the heart must be kept from rockiness if the word heard is to go deep down into it, and remain rooted there: otherwise the first difficulty will drive all sentiment away, — even as Pliable was daunted, and turned back, at the sight of the Slough of Despond.

But you ask how all this is to be helped, if the defect be in character? and though that is not treated of in the parable at all, for it confines itself rigidly to one theme, we yet may indicate the direction in which the remedy is to be sought. The Lord himself, indeed, has elsewhere done it to our hand, when he says,[1] "Whosoever doth not bear his cross, and come after me, cannot be my disciple. For which of you, intending to build a tower, sitteth not down first and counteth the cost, whether he have sufficient to finish it? Lest haply, after he hath laid the foundation, and is not able to finish it, all that behold it begin to mock him, saying, This man began to build, and was not able to finish. Or what king, going to make war against another king, sitteth not down first, and consulteth whether he be able with ten thousand to meet him that cometh against him with twenty thousand? or else, while he is yet a great way off, he sendeth an ambassage, and desireth conditions of peace. So likewise, whosoever he be of you that forsaketh not all that he hath, cannot be my disciple." And we have an instance of this class in him who said, "Lord, I will follow thee whithersoever thou goest;" to whom the Master made reply, "Foxes have holes, and birds of the air have nests; but the Son of man hath not where to lay his head;" as also to some degree in Peter, who alleged that though all men should deny Christ, yet he never would, and who was found at length doing the very thing which he so strongly reprobated. Now, the fault in all this lies in a lack of thoughtfulness, or a neglecting to "count the cost." The man of depth looks before he leaps. He will not commit himself until he has carefully examined all that is involved; but when he does thus commit himself, he does so irrevocably. He who signs a document without reading it will be very likely to repudiate it when any trouble comes of it; but the man who knew what he

[1] Luke xiv. 27-33.

was doing when he appended his name to it, if he be a true man, will stand to his bond at all hazards. Now, the merely impulsive, shallow, flippant hearer acts without deliberation, signs his bond without reading it, and is therefore easily discouraged. When he is called to suffer any thing unpleasant for his confession, he backs down. He had not calculated on such a contingency. He enlisted only for the review, and not for the battle; and so, on the first alarm of war, he disappears from the ranks. He did not stop to consider all that his enlistment involved; he was allured only by the uniform, and the gay accessories of military life: but, when it came to fighting, he deserted. Ah! but the Christian has to *bear his cross;* and he who understands what that means, when he takes his place among Christ's disciples, is a disciple until death. With that before him, he will be too thoughtful to be impulsive; for the very depth of his nature will keep him from demonstrativeness. How apt we are, in the light of these facts, to misjudge others! The enthusiastic convert is often preferred to the calm and apparently unimpassioned disciple. The growth in the one seems so much more rapid than in the other, that he is put far above him. But when affliction or persecution arises, what a revelation it makes! for then the enthusiasm of the one *goes* out, and that of the other *comes* out. That which causes apostasy in the one develops constancy in the other, and permanence is the proof of genuineness. See to it, then, oh! see to it, that you count the cost when you commit yourself to Christ. Be not content with mere sincerity, but cultivate depth along with it. Let intelligent conviction be the root of impulse; for unless it be so rooted, it will wither away.

3. But we must look now briefly at the third thing

to be guarded against, which we may call the pre-occupation of the heart by other objects than the word heard by the man. This is symbolized in the parable by the unclean soil, wherein secretly lurked the seeds of many thorny weeds, which grew up with the grain, and at length overtopped and overmastered it, taking to themselves all the sap that was needed for its nourishment, so that it never came to maturity. Here, you see, there was a real growth so far; but it was not the exclusive growth of the good seed, for other things sprang up by which it was ultimately choked. Now, in his interpretation of the story, the Lord tells us what these thorns represent in the heart of the gospel hearer. In Matthew he describes them as "the cares of this world, and the deceitfulness of riches;" in Mark he calls them "the cares of this world, the deceitfulness of riches, and the lusts of other things;" while in Luke he summarizes them as "cares, and riches, and pleasures of this life." Now, putting them all together, we get these four things symbolized by the thorns, — namely, cares, riches, ambition, and pleasure; and we may surely say that he who sees no dangers in these as competitors in the human heart with the word of God does not know his own heart, and has learned little from the observation of his fellow-men.

Take the cares; and how often have we seen the maiden who in her young life gave great promise of a lofty Christian character, grow stunted and narrowed spiritually, under the influence of mere domestic trivialities! "Careful and troubled about many things," she has dwindled into a mere housekeeper, on whose heart the management of home sits so heavily as to overlay all higher things. She can talk of nothing but her children; she has no vision beyond her dwelling; the great things of the kingdom are shut out from her perception by the nearness with which she holds the little things of her daily life to her eyes; and the dust upon her furniture lies more heavily on her conscience than any sense of sin. She has ceased to be a companion to her husband in the highest sense, because she takes no interest in what he regards as of pre-eminent importance; and matters public, intellectual, and spiritual are all choked in her by the undue development of family cares. Her character shrivels, just because she has allowed these meaner things to get her entire devotion. This may seem to some a caricature, but I am convinced that there is enough of truth in it to point the moral of this part of the parable. And the danger can be obviated only through cleansing the heart of all such cares, by casting them on God and leaving them with him; while, at the same time, the mind is turned to the consideration of the infinitely more momentous matters that Christ in his word has brought before its attention.

Take riches, again, and how frequently we have seen a case like this! A young man runs fairly well the Christian life, and is even helped thereby into his first business success; but, as his prosperity extends, his moral thoughtfulness contracts. He gives ever less and less time to private devotion. Meditation on sacred themes gradually disappears from his life. One after another his practical engagements in the field of Christian usefulness are given up. His business spreads, and spreads, and spreads. He lets it grow upon him so that it is impossible for him to manage it all without overtaxing his strength. Then after a while there is a hopeless break-down in health, but not before there has been a far more serious deterioration in his spiritual life; and he who gave such promise of bringing forth much fruit ends his days without bringing any to perfection. Do I exaggerate in all this? Have I overdrawn the picture? And, if I have not, what a loud call is there in this description, to our business men, to study moderation, and to be on their guard against that deceitfulness in prosperity which would lure them on with the promise of greater things, into the ultimate loss of the greatest of all things! How many, who in their earliest days were earnest Christian young men, have dwindled down, through their successes, into careless and indifferent, half-day, half-hearted hearers, who contend that religion never should interfere with business, though they themselves have let their business very seriously interfere with their religion! "What, then," you ask, "must we go out of business?" I answer, No; but do not give your whole heart to it. Rule it, but never let it rule you. Transact it for God, and so consecrate it to God. Let God send you to your business, but beware of letting your business send you away from God.

Take, again, ambition, the desires of other things, and you may see the same thing illustrated. It makes no matter whether the department be literature, or science, or politics: the determination *at all hazards* and at every sacrifice to be eminent in any of them is fraught with danger to the Christian life, and may choke the growth of the word in the heart. It is the sucker which draws away the sap from the tree, and so robs it of its vitality, that it immediately begins to decay. What happens, commonly, when a man among us goes into politics, and becomes absorbingly desirous of getting the position of a senator or a governor, or what not? If the office seeks him, he may be all safe, and may keep himself in the line of spiritual growth; but if he seeks the office with overmastering ambition, let him beware, for, if he persist in such a course, he may choke out his Christian life. Christ must be supreme, or he retires altogether from the soul.

Finally take pleasure, and then tell me what a poor, paltry, butterfly Christianity (if, indeed, we should call it Christianity at all) theirs is who try to combine with their profession a life in and for fashion and frivolity. We cannot withdraw from society, indeed; but they who delight in it as the supreme good have already overlaid the germs of spiritual life within them, and will soon become worldlings.

Am I wrong, my friends, when I say that in these thorns we have the great dangers against which gospel hearers in this day and in this place need most of all to guard? They are too largely choking the growth of the word in the city as a whole. They have encroached on our week-day Christianity, and they are gradually invading the sanctuary of the Lord's Day itself; while among individuals they are growing so strong and rank, that the closet is too much neglected; family worship has almost disappeared; the weekly prayer and conference meeting is ignored; and every thing is made to give way to business or pleasure or ambition. I am no pessimist; but I see in all this a great peril, not only to individuals, but to the Church as a whole, and to the community at large.

II. I ought now to go on to the consideration of the qualities to be cultivated by gospel hearers, as these are indicated in the Saviour's explanation of the seed which fell into good soil; but the length to which my remarks have already extended, as well as the fact that I have already incidentally anticipated much that might be said on this branch of the subject, must constrain me to be brief. Our Lord, as reported by Luke, says, "That on the good ground are they which in an honest and good heart, having heard the word, keep it, and bring forth fruit with patience." "An honest and good heart,"— that is what we need when we come to listen to the word; a heart whose aim is noble, and which is entirely devoted to that aim; such a heart as Cornelius had when he said to Peter, "Now therefore are we all here present, to hear all things that are commanded us of God;"[1] such a heart as the Bereans had, of whom it is said that after listening to Paul they "searched the Scriptures daily, whether these things were so."[2]

Now, the qualities which such hearts bring to the hearing of the gospel are these: Attention: they hear. Meditation: they keep. Obedience: they bring forth fruit with patience.

1. There is, first, attention. The good hearer stirs himself up to listen. He trains himself to follow the speaker. He will not be allured, by any association, to take his mind away from the truths which are brought before him. He will leave his business behind him for the time. He will let the dress and appearance of his fellow-hearers alone. He will recognize, that, in the providence of God's Spirit, there is something in the daily ministration for him; and he will be eagerly on the watch lest he should miss that. His hearing is an opportunity, and he is determined to make the most of it in that aspect of the case.

2. There is, second, meditation. I use that term, rather than "remembrance," as the equivalent of "keeping" the word: for some have such memories that they can recall an address verbatim, while yet it does them no

---

[1] Acts x. 23.   [2] Ibid., xvii. 11.

apparent good; and others have no verbal remembrance of what has been said, while yet somehow the subject seems to have permeated their spirits and greatly benefited them, because they have caught the drift of the thought, and have carried out independent meditation thereon. Not, therefore, the memory of what we hear, but reflective thought upon it, is of essential service here; and we must not imagine that what we cannot recall does us no good, any more than that, because we can recall it, we must surely be the better for it. Meditation is to hearing what digestion is to eating: it assimilates what we hear, for our own edification and growth in grace. And the good and honest heart will always seek to have some time for its exercise after the hearing of the word. But alas! meditation as a Christian exercise is rapidly disappearing from among us. A great English preacher has said, "I, for my part, believe that there are few Christian duties more neglected than that of meditation, the very name of which has fallen of late into comparative disuse that augurs ill for the frequency of the thing. We are so busy discussing, defending, inquiring, or preaching, and teaching, and working, that we have no time and no leisure of heart for quiet contemplation, without which the exercise of the intellect upon Christ's truth will not feed, and busy activity in Christ's cause may starve the soul. There are few things which the Church of this day in all its parts needs more than to obey the invitation, "Come ye yourselves apart into a lonely place, and rest a while.'"[1] This witness is true. Let us learn, therefore, from these words, to cultivate this neglected grace. Willmot says, in his hints on reading, "Proportion an hour's re-

[1] Alex. Maclaren, D.D., The Secret of Power, and other Sermons, p. 35.

flection to an hour's reading, and so dispirit the book into the student."[1] So I would say, Let every time of hearing be followed by a time of meditation; that the seed which has fallen on the soil may, as it were, be "harrowed" into it by the process.

3. Then there is, finally, obedience: they bring forth fruit with patience. To hear without obeying is to harden the heart; for, as Bishop Butler says, "passive impressions grow weaker by being repeated."[2] So the man who, being affected by what he hears, takes no action thereon, only makes himself thereby more impervious to the truth when it is again presented, and he will need more to bring these feelings back another time, than he did to have them produced at first; until at last he becomes "past feeling" altogether. But the acting on what we hear prepares us for being better hearers next time, and quickens the receptivity of the soul. Even among good hearers, however, there will be differences, and some will make more of their opportunities than others; just as in the good soil some brought forth thirty-fold, some sixty-fold, and some an hundred-fold. But these discrepancies may be owing to inherent and original differences of disposition, and should neither make us envious of others, nor dispose us to think ourselves superior to them.

To sum up, then, the great lesson of this parable is, that, to get all the good out of the hearing of the word that we possibly can, we must bring to it an honest heart, that will attend to, meditate on, and act out the truth which is presented to it. And we must be on our guard against a heart that is hardened into imperviousness, or characterized by superficial impulsiveness, or

---

[1] Willmot's Pleasures of Literature, p. 38.
[2] Butler's Analogy, Part I., chap. v.

foul with the germs of care or covetousness or ambition or pleasure. And if you want to know where and how to get such a heart, go home, and ponder and pray over these words of the sacred historian regarding the first Christian convert in Philippi: "whose heart the Lord opened, that she attended to the things that were spoken of Paul."[1]

[1] Acts xvi. 13.

III

THE TARES, AND THE DRAG-NET
Matthew 13:24-30, 36-43, 47-50

THESE two parables must be taken together. They form one of the "pairs" which we named in our last discourse, when we classified the parables contained in this chapter. They illustrate different shades of the same general truth. Both alike deal with the co-existence of good and evil within the same enclosure, and both of them look at the question of the absolute separation of the evil from the good; but the one gives prominence to the impracticability of attaining that before a certain period, while the other emphasizes the assurance that such a separation will be ultimately secured.

In the parable of the tares, we have a field, which, after due preparation, the husbandman sows with good wheat. But after a while, and before that seed has sprouted, an enemy steals along in the night, when all honest people are asleep, and sows the field over again with tares. There is therefore, you observe, no censure even so much as implied, on men generally for being asleep. It was the time for sleep, and they were taking only their regular and proper rest. But the enemy, knowing that, took advantage of it to carry out his malicious purpose, and contrived to do a very mean and troublesome thing. For the tare — which is not

to be confounded with the vetch that is often called by
that name in England — was really the bearded darnel,
which is a very noxious weed. In the earlier stages of
its growth, it is almost impossible for any one to distinguish it from wheat or barley; although, when both it
and the wheat have "headed out," the one is easily
known from the other. Says Dr. Thomson, "Even the
farmers, who in Palestine generally weed their fields,
do not pretend to distinguish the one from the other.
They would not only mistake good grain for tares, but
very commonly the roots of the two are so intertwined
that it is impossible to separate them without plucking
out both."[1] The same author assures us that he had
never heard of Arab malice having tried to injure an
enemy in this particular way: but it must have been
known in the time of our Saviour; and Dean Alford[2]
tells us that even in England, in this enlightened age, a
field that belonged to himself was thus wilfully and
enviously sown with charlock over the wheat, and heavy
damages were obtained against the offender. In course
of time, both wheat and tares grew up; and when the
tares revealed themselves, the servants of the husbandman asked whether they should pull them up; but he,
knowing the nature of the darnel, and unwilling to
endanger the wheat, forbade them to do any thing, saying, "Let both grow together until the harvest." When
the reaping-time came, however, and the thing could be
done without detriment to the wheat, the tares were
gathered into bundles and burned, and the wheat was
housed in the barn. Here, then, as we have already
hinted, we have the separation between the good and
the evil deferred, for a good reason too, till the com-

---

[1] Central Palestine and Phœnicia, pp. 395, 396.
[2] Greek Testament, *in loco.*

pletion of growth and the ripening of both; **and then** it is absolutely and forever effected.

In the parable of the net, we see fishermen, such as some of the apostles themselves were, casting their long seine-net into the lake, and then dragging it by boats at either end to the shore. It brings in a heterogeneous collection of all sorts of things that swim the deep, and much that is of no use whatever to anybody. But by and by order is brought out of the confusion; for the fishermen gather that which is good into vessels, and cast the bad away. Here, again, we have good and bad in the same enclosure. The mixture in this case could not have been prevented by any ordinary fisherman, but there was a separation at the last.

So far all is plain. But what is the spiritual significance of all this? The Lord himself has given us a partial answer, in his interpretation of the parable of the tares, when he tells us that the field is the world; that the sower of the good seed is the Son of man; that the sower of the tares is the Devil; and that the wheat represents the children of the kingdom, and the tares the children of the wicked one. We have also much light shed on the whole matter, when we learn that the harvest is the end of the world, and that the separation between the good and the bad shall take place at the final judgment, — all of which is confirmed by the words with which the Lord concludes the parable of the net: "So shall it be at the end of the world: the angels shall come forth, and sever the wicked from among the just, and shall cast them into the furnace of fire; there shall be wailing, and gnashing of teeth."

But all this, I said, is only a *partial* answer, and some may wonder at my using such an expression in regard to any interpretation given by the Lord himself. Yet it is the literal truth; for there has been immense difficulty, from the earliest days of the Church until now, in coming at the meaning of his words, "the field is the world;" and you will observe that he has himself left out of his interpretation of the parable all reference whatever to the proposal of the servants to go and gather up the tares, as also to the answer of the husbandman to this effect: "Nay, lest while ye gather up the tares, ye root up also the wheat with them. Let both grow together until the harvest." And there has been much discussion as to the spiritual significance of that conversation. We can hardly suppose that so prominent a colloquy had no hidden meaning; and yet the silence of the Saviour regarding it has left the matter open, and that has provoked considerable controversy.

The main questions are these: What does Christ precisely mean when he says, "the field is the world"? And did he desire it to be inferred from the conversation between the husbandman and his servants, that no means whatever are to be taken for keeping the good from being contaminated and injured by the evil?

First, what precisely does he mean when he says that "the field is the world"? Does he mean the world in its most extensive sense, as including the human race as a whole? Or does he mean what we in these days would call the Church visible, which consists of the aggregation of all the Christian organizations in the world? Since the days of the Donatist controversy, in the beginning of the fifth century, that has been a much-contested question. On the one hand, it has been contended that the parable refers to the history of the human race, and that it was simply intended to forbid

every thing like persecution for religious opinion or
belief. No attempt should be made, either by civil
magistrate or by church dignitary or by ecclesiastical
court, to get rid of error or unbelief by putting the
heretic or the infidel to death. Let both believer and
unbeliever live. Both alike are accountable for all such
things to God alone, and he will send every one to his
own place at the last. So said the Donatists when
they were pressed with this parable by Augustine, who
inferred from it that the absolutely pure church for
which they were contending was to be found alone in
heaven; and so virtually say still such commentators as
Arnot and Abbot. Such also was my own opinion when
I went to study the parable with a view to the preparation of this discourse. But the longer time I have
given to the consideration of the subject, the less am I
inclined to hold by this view as correct. For the parable is designed to illustrate the kingdom of heaven,
"which signifies the new order of things which Christ
came to establish, and which is conveniently described
as the church which owns him as its Lord."[1] It will
hardly do, therefore, to adopt an interpretation which
sends us away back to the creation of man, when all
in him as well as around him was very good, and which
sees in the temptation of our first parents the sowing of
the field with tares. The sower of the good seed is
the Son of man: therefore it is clear that we must look
in the church, and after the incarnation, for the growth
of that seed; and there, too, we must look for the tares
which sprang up among the wheat. This view is cor-
roborated by the parable of the net; for, if the net is
not the church, what is it? Mr. Arnot virtually — at
least, so it seems to me — answers, Death; but that

[1] Plumptre, *in loc.*

is surely a far-fetched view of the case, and the consciousness that it is so seems almost to betray itself in the vague phraseology which he has employed. Here are his words: "The net, almost or altogether invisible at first to those whom it surrounds, is that unseen bond, which, by an invisible ministry, is stretched over the living, drawing them gradually, secretly, surely, toward the boundary of this life, and over it into another."[1] It is a long periphrasis, but I can make nothing else out of it than Death, with his stealthy march, gathering all on to the shore of the beyond, preparatory to final judgment. But what has that to do with the kingdom of heaven, — the new system which Christ set up, and to which the net is here likened? Was not all that just as true of death and the race before Christ came? And must we not seek for the interpretation in something peculiar to the kingdom of heaven as such? These considerations outweigh all others. And so we regard the net here as representing the church, and that finds its parallel in the field in the parable of the tares. In the church, therefore, as in the net and in the field, there will be both good and bad.

Well, but, if that is the case, what are we to make of the command given to the servants, "Let both grow together until the harvest"? — do not attempt just now to uproot the tares, lest ye pull up the wheat with them. Does not that look like a formal prohibition of any thing like discipline in the visible Church? And can an interpretation which leads to such a conclusion be correct? No doubt, on the first blush of the matter, there appears to be great force in these objections; and it was on account of them, I believe, that Mr. Arnot

[1] The Parables of Our Lord, by Rev. William Arnot, p. 170.

was so strenuous in advocating the other view. But in
reply to them I would advance the following considerations: First, That church discipline is clearly enjoined
by many plain passages of the New Testament, and
that no interpretation of any parable may be put against
that. It is a recognized canon of interpretation, that
nothing in a parable is to be made, simply in and of
itself, the foundation of a doctrine or a practice. So,
whatever may be the meaning of this parable, it will
not invalidate what is elsewhere plainly laid down as to
discipline. Second, Discipline rightly understood is for
the saving of a man to the church, and not for the casting of him out of it. The end of discipline is not so
much the purity of the church, — though that of course
is not to be lost sight of, — as the restoration of the
offender. Third, What the parable here recommends is
not so much the following of a certain course, as the
cultivating of a certain spirit. As Bruce has said in
this very connection, "Christ is not here laying down
a rule for the regulation of ecclesiastical practice, but
inculcating the cultivation of a certain spirit, the spirit
of a wise patience." And again, "The parable neither
prohibits nor fixes limits to ecclesiastical discipline, but
teaches a spirit that will affect that part as well as all
other parts of religious conduct, and which, if it had
prevailed in the church more than it ever has prevailed,
would have made the church's history very different
from what it is."[1] Do as we will, we shall never get
evil entirely out of the church in this world; and the
attempt to uproot it at all hazards is sure to end in
something worse than that which was sought to be removed.

These are the two truths which to me now are sug-

[1] The Parabolic Teaching of Christ, by A. B. Bruce, D.D., pp. 54, 55.

gested by the principal portion of the parable of the tares; while the concluding part of it, and the whole parable of the net, give solemn emphasis to the fact, that what is impracticable here will be accomplished at last, when "the righteous shall shine forth as the sun in the kingdom of their Father; and all that offend, and they which do iniquity, shall be cast into the place of torment, where shall be wailing and gnashing of teeth."

Let us seek to illustrate briefly each of these three points, and so get at the combined essence of these two parables.

I. Do as we will, we shall never get evil entirely out of the church. The ideal church is in heaven. Of that, and that alone, can it be said with truth, "And there shall in no wise enter into it any thing that defileth, neither whatsoever worketh abomination or maketh a lie; but they which are written in the Lamb's book of life."[1] Even the Donatists were obliged to admit, that, with all their efforts to obtain purity of communion, they were unable absolutely to gain that on which their hearts were set. In the Philippian church there were many of whom Paul, weeping, wrote that they were "the enemies of the cross of Christ;" and among the twelve who were the first apostles of the Lord, we cannot forget that there was Judas, the son of perdition. Always there has been this mixture of good and evil, even in the visible Christian Church; and there always will be, till the time of the end.

Now, this truth, sad in itself, has a twofold lesson in it. First, it is well fitted to give comfort to those who are laboring in the ministry of the gospel, and to all who are tenderly solicitous for the honor of the church.

[1] Rev. xxi. 27.

As a faithful pastor's ministry lengthens out, few things tend more to sadden him than the perception of imperfections, positive blemishes, and evils in the characters and conduct of those who are members of the church. In the beginning of his career, he is all on fire for the conversion of sinners; so much so, indeed, that the Christians among his hearers are apt to feel as if they were almost neglected in his daily ministrations. But after a while they who ran well are seen to be somehow hindered, and ever and anon, it may be, to fall into serious sins; so that he is in danger of becoming discouraged, and learns that he must give a little more of his attention to the watch and guidance of those who have been converted and are already in the church. These feelings, too, are largely shared by the office-bearers who are associated with him; and they all enter into the spirit which must have dictated the words of Keble:—

> "Lord, in thy field I work all day,
> I read, I preach, I warn and pray;
> And yet these wilful, wandering sheep,
> Within thy fold I cannot keep." [1]

Now, at such a time, the thought emphasized by the first of these parables comes as a relief. The pastor learns from it, that tares are to be expected among the wheat, and that never on earth shall the one be entirely separated from the other. He discovers that no new thing has happened to him, but that the trial which has come upon him is one which has been common to all who have labored in the service of the Church from the beginning; and while he never thinks of becoming the less earnest in his declaration of the whole counsel

---

[1] The Christian Year: Tuesday in Whitsun week.

of God, or the less desirous for the purity of the church, he moderates his expectations, and begins to look for things which otherwise would have been serious disappointments and discouragements. Now, that is a great matter; and it is well for all who are pastors or office-bearers or members of the church, and seriously concerned for its purity, to remember it. Especially it is well that the younger brethren in the ministry should take note of it; for, while it will not abate their zeal, it will keep them from looking for impossibilities, and from courting disappointment.

But, secondly, this truth is well calculated to correct the error of those who decline to enter into the membership of the church because it is not absolutely pure. There are multitudes everywhere who make the faults of some who are in the church an excuse for their remaining unconnected with any church. They cannot get a church pure enough to satisfy them. But have these friends ever reflected, that even if they could get, on the earth, a perfectly pure church, it would be at once defiled by their connection with it? For they themselves surely cannot claim to be absolutely perfect, and therefore by joining such a church they would at once contaminate it. But, more to our present purpose, they are looking for what they cannot find upon the earth. For admissions into the membership of the church are regulated by men who cannot see into the heart, so that it is inevitable that they should be sometimes deceived; and, the more of value that there comes to be attached to church-membership in a community, the more frequently will such deception be practised upon them, just as a forger seeks most frequently to counterfeit the notes of highest figure. Let no man, therefore, plead the impurity of the church as an excuse for his not joining it; for the pure church is in heaven, and the true conception of the earthly church is that of a school for the training of imperfect Christians toward that perfection which is to be found at last above. The church is not a great exhibition-hall for the display of perfect Christians, but an educational institution for the development of imperfect believers. Men do not go to school because they know what is to be taught in it, but that they may learn that of which they are ignorant; and the true spirit in which one should enter the church is that of a humble disciple, who confesses his weakness and ignorance and imperfection, and is willing to take Christ as his teacher, that he may learn of him.

II. But the second great lesson taught by the parable of the tares is that the rash attempt to separate the good from the bad in the church may result in a state of things that is worse than that which is sought to be amended. The premature effort to secure the absolute best may result in the positive worst. This holds in every department of life; and wherever you go, or in whatever sphere you may be called to labor, you will find that you will have patiently to put up, for a time, with things of which you cannot, in the abstract, approve; lest, by trying hastily to mend them, you make them worse than ever. Moses even, as a lawgiver, suffered many things for the hardness of men's hearts. He did not approve of the practices which he found existing among the Hebrews in regard to marriage, blood-revenge, and the like; but so deeply rooted were these in the habits of the people, that any effort on his part to remove them at once and altogether might have led to the repudiation of the law as a whole; so he was content with something short of the best, in order to obtain the better. We find the same principle underlying the proverb, which is so frequently quoted in politics, that "half a loaf is better than no bread;" and there are many among us who think we see that the enthusiastic prohibitionists, who oppose every restriction short of the absolute best which they advocate, are losing sight of the wisdom which the lesson of this parable inculcates. But it is not otherwise in the church. We have to do with things as they are; and we must patiently bear with some matters which we cannot approve, because we cannot reform them without seriously imperilling other and more important interests. Take the matter of music, for example. A young pastor coming to a church may feel that the existing state of "the service of song in the house of the Lord" is far from being what it ought to be. What must he do? Let me answer by quoting a short section from my lectures to the students at Yale: "Accept the situation, and make the very best possible out of it, for the glory of God and the edification of the people. Only [let him] remember this, that nothing will more interfere with his usefulness or his happiness, than the stirring-up of a musical quarrel. The best all round is often lost by attempting to have the absolute best in any one department. In the organ, if every note be separately tuned up to the scale, discord will be the effect when one attempts to play upon it; for it is an imperfect instrument, and most of the fifths must be left somewhat flat, and the few others made somewhat sharp, the octaves alone being put in perfect unison. So, if we attempt to bring up the music to the point of perfection, we shall most likely put the whole church out of tune. We must make the best of things as a whole, and be content sometimes with a little less in some departments, and a little more in others, in order that we may have harmony in all. Peace in a church is essential to progress. The dew is not shed forth in a storm, but in the gentle calm of the summer's eve it distils on every blade of grass. So the Spirit comes not down amid controversy and debate; but where brethren are dwelling in unity, there the Lord commandeth the blessing, even life forevermore. No music, however perfect, is for a moment to be preferred to those higher matters of spiritual life, for the fostering of which the church exists. 'The life is more than meat, and the body than raiment.' The church is more than music,"[1] and the gaining of the finest music that was ever rendered is not worth a church quarrel.

Now, it is quite similar with discipline. Discipline is for the church, not the church for discipline; and that uncompromising purism which will insist on casting every little peccadillo out of the church, and disciplining a man for matters of small moment, concerning which many of the members have no conscientious scruples whatever, will end in the absolute annihilation of the church itself. In this connection, there comes to my memory a fact narrated to me by a brother minister in England to this effect. He had been visiting a Scottish town, and called on a friend there who belonged to one of the little denominations which had broken off from a larger one on some scruple of conscience. "How is your church getting on?" he asked. "Oh," replied his friend, with a kind of humor for which he was noted, "our church seems to me to have been born for the illustration of the infinite divisibility of matter, for there are now forty-five members and seven churches." We recall, too, the story — true or

[1] The Ministry of the Word, pp. 234, 235.

false, I have no means of knowing, but it may well enough have been true — of a small church whose members went on excommunicating and excommunicating each other for every little thing, until there was left, as a remnant, only a man and his wife. "Well," said one to her, "you must have got a pure church at last." "'Deed," was the answer, with inimitable self-complacency, "'deed, and I am not so sure of John." That is the *reductio ad absurdum* of this rash and premature attempt to get the absolute best. The boy thought it was a good device, when, after being well pecked by the hen for seeking to find how many eggs were beneath her, he said, "Oh, I know how to get her out: I will burn her out." And he did so, but he burned the barn down with her. So it has frequently happened in far more serious matters, and a church has been destroyed in the effort simply made by some imprudent men to get what they supposed was the absolute best. A quarrel about communion-wine has before now closed up a church, and quenched a light that could not be rekindled. So true it is, that, in the effort to root up the tares, the wheat also has been plucked with them.

Again, however, I am anxious that you should not misunderstand all this. It is *not* a condemnation of discipline wisely administered, but it is the recommendation of a spirit of forbearance akin to that which the Master showed when he allowed Judas, after his knowledge of his dishonesty, to remain for years among his disciples. And the full reason for this forbearance no parable can furnish, for it lies in this: that, by the influence of that patience, the evil members may become good, and the tares — a natural impossibility, but a spiritual possibility — be transmuted into wheat. On the one hand, then, there is in this rashness a danger of destroying the good that is in a church: on the other, there is a prospect and hope, by the patience which I have been enforcing, of changing the evil into the good; and so on all grounds it ought to be preferred. As Goebel has said, "The prohibition in this parable is not opposed to any kind of church discipline, exercised on individual members for their training, or as an atonement (?) for a special public scandal; but it is simply directed against the fundamental attempt, by summary and absolute exclusion of all false members, to establish the Church of God's kingdom in complete purity and sanctity during the stadium of its development on the ground of the world."[1]

III. But now, finally, both the parables, and especially that of the net, emphasize the fact that there will be, at the last judgment, an absolute separation between the good and the bad. "The Son of man shall send forth his angels; and they shall gather out of his kingdom all things that offend, and them which do iniquity, and shall cast them into a furnace of fire: there shall be wailing and gnashing of teeth. Then shall the righteous shine forth as the sun in the kingdom of their Father." And again: "At the end of the world the angels shall come forth, and sever the wicked from among the just, and shall cast them into the furnace of fire: there shall be wailing and gnashing of teeth." The judgment shall make that separation for all men. But here the solemn part of the lesson is, that those who are to be separated from each other were together in the Church of Christ upon the earth. And so the warning comes with terrible power, to the effect that

[1] The Parables of Jesus, by Siegfried Goebel, translated by Professor Banks, p. 73.

mere membership in the church gives no guaranty of everlasting felicity. Read the concluding sections of the Sermon on the Mount, and you will understand better, perhaps, the Saviour's meaning here. It is not enough that you have eaten and drunk in Christ's presence, and that you have been active in working in and for the church: the question is, Are you in Christ? It is not enough that you are growing in the field of the church: the question is, Are you wheat, or tares? are you Christ's in heart and soul and character, as well as by profession and position? It is not enough that you are enclosed in the net of the church: the question, after all, is, Are you good or bad in it? I shall not undertake to answer that for you; but I will urge you to take it with you to the closet, and ask God to help you to find the truth about it for yourselves there.

And if, at last, judgment is to begin thus at the house of God, what shall the end be of them that "obey not the gospel of God"? If the impure member of the church is to be cast out forever into the place where shall be wailing and gnashing of teeth, what shall be the portion of the open sinner? Let him not congratulate himself that he is innocent of insincerity or hypocrisy; for, though that be true, it is only a confession that he is sincerely God's enemy, and that is a terrible thing. Beware, therefore, lest you break yourself against the thick bosses of the Almighty's buckler, and be everlastingly cut off.

IV

THE MUSTARD SEED, AND THE LEAVEN
Matthew 13:31-33

IN the parables belonging to this chapter which we have already considered, the Lord has dealt mainly with the obstacles which his kingdom had to meet alike in the hearts of men and in the malice of Satan; but in those now before us he proceeds to speak of its final triumph. These also constitute a pair, and must be studied together if at least we would get at the full truth regarding the subject of which they both treat. That subject is the progress of the kingdom of heaven upon the earth; but the one gives prominence to the external contrast between its small beginning and its ultimate magnitude, while the other emphasizes the method of its internal operation, and the universality of its diffusion at the last.

In the former the kingdom is compared to a mustard-seed planted by a man, which grew up to be so large that the birds of the air found a lodging in its branches. Among the rabbins, "a grain of mustard-seed" was a familiar phrase for any thing exceedingly small, just as we sometimes speak of a "peppercorn;" and with this fact in our minds it is idle, as Dr. James Hamilton has said,[1] to seek for a seed more tiny, or to press the words, "which is indeed the least of all seeds," into literal

---

[1] Fairbairn's Imperial Bible Dictionary, art. "Mustard-seed."

exactness, and cavil at the accuracy of the representation, because it may turn out that the seed of a poppy or the spore of a fungus is smaller. When this little germ is planted, it grows up to become one of the largest of herbs. It does not develop into a size like that of the oak or the cedar tree; but it overtops other herbs, and becomes sufficiently high and expansive for birds to find shelter in its branches. *A great result from a small beginning*, a large growth from a little germ, — that is the one thought of the parable, and of that the Lord declares that the kingdom of heaven upon the earth is an instance. It is simply absurd, therefore, to endeavor to find a hidden meaning in the field in which the seed was planted, in the man who planted it, in the pungency of the mustard, or in the little birds that seek shelter beneath its leaves. All these are over-refinements and irrelevant, tending only to withdraw attention from the main point for the bringing-out of which the parable was employed, and which in these later days needs only to be stated to be recognized. The kingdom of heaven on the earth had a beginning, which, when compared with its present condition, is as the mustard-seed is to the herb that grows therefrom.

The Christian Church was almost insignificant, externally at least, in its origin. Two of the disciples of John the Baptist having heard their master say, as he pointed to Jesus, " Behold the Lamb of God, that taketh away the sin of the world," followed him with the inquiry, " Rabbi, where dwellest thou ? " spent the night with him, became convinced that he was the Christ, and determined to take him as their master. That was all. Then one of these brought his brother; and a third who had been meanwhile called brought one of his friends, who in turn enlisted his fellow-townsman; and so it went on until after the lapse of two or three centuries it had overspread the Roman Empire, and now its adherents are numbered by millions, dwelling on all the quarters of the globe, and on the islands of all the seas. It is another version of Daniel's prophecy that the stone cut out of the mountain, without hands, should become a great mountain, and fill the whole earth; and another illustration of Zechariah's words, "Who hath despised the day of small things?" The parable gives no indication how this result was to be brought about. It rather implies than mentions the vitality of the seed; and it has nothing to say about the philosophy of its growth, or about the nature of the effects which it produces. It simply points the contrast between the smallness of the beginning, and the magnitude of the result.

This is a thought with which in many other departments we are familiar; but there is none of them all which can furnish such an exemplification of it as that which is given by the Christian Church. In its origin it was all but unnoticed by the great ones of the earth. Hardly a secular historian alludes to it, and the two who do make mention of it speak of the gospel as a wretched superstition; but to-day it is the most conspicuous fact in the civilized world, and it is still pushing its conquests into the uttermost parts of the earth. The handful of corn scattered upon the tops of the mountains now shakes like the cedars of Lebanon. The fishermen disciples of the despised Nazarene have multiplied into twelve million fold. "The stone which the builders despised has become the head stone of the corner: this is the Lord's doing, and it is marvellous in our eyes."

The parable of the mustard-seed is taken from the garden or the field; that of the leaven is derived from the household. There is nothing, therefore, in the homely work of this woman which needs any explanation at my hands. Probably every house-mother here knows more about it than I could tell her; and we can all see that it is employed to illustrate that active and aggressive principle in the kingdom of heaven which assimilates men to Christ, and which is to continue at work on the earth until "the kingdoms of this world are become the kingdom of our Lord and of his Christ, and he shall reign for ever and ever."

It has been thought by some, indeed, that as leaven is generally — we may even say almost invariably — used as a symbol of evil, we must take this parable as designed to set before us the progress of corruption, rather than of regeneration, in the world. This view has been specially advocated by many brethren whose opinions regarding the second advent of Christ lead them to believe that things must become worse and worse upon the earth until he shall personally appear for their renewal. But, whatever may be said on the question whether the second advent of Christ shall be pre-millennial or post-millennial, it is absolutely clear to me, that the leaven in this place cannot be taken as an emblem of evil. I admit that in Scripture and as a figure it is most commonly employed in that sense, and that the literal leaven was generally excluded from offerings under the Mosaic law. But there was one exception; namely, in the case of the two wave-loaves (Lev. xxiii. 17) that formed part of the offering of first-fruits; and it is possible that in the figurative use of the term there may be a similar exception to the general rule, in the parable before us. For there is no rigid uniformity in the symbolism of the Bible, and sometimes the same thing is used in different places as an emblem of different, I would even say of opposite, persons or principles. Thus, by one sacred writer the Devil is described as a lion, while by another Christ is spoken of as the Lion of the tribe of Judah; and in one of the Psalms, a flourishing tree is used as a symbol of a righteous man, while in another it is employed to illustrate the prosperity of the wicked. If, therefore, the context here seems to require us to take the leaven in a sense different from or even opposite to that in which as a symbol it is generally used by the sacred writers, we are at perfect liberty so to do. And this, as it seems to me, is very clearly demanded of us, both by the terms of the parable itself, and by its relation to the whole series of parables of which here it forms a part. "The kingdom of heaven is like unto leaven," so the words run; but is it any true or proper description of the kingdom of heaven, to say that evil will go on corrupting the human race until the whole be corrupted? Was not that the case, rather, before the Son of God came to earth to found his kingdom? Was it not, indeed, the very prevalence of the corruption, that necessitated the intervention of God in Christ to arrest its progress, and overcome its influence? To take the leaven as representing evil, therefore, would make this parable a correct description of the progress of the kingdom of Satan, and an accurate epitome of the history of the race, for the most part, up till the time of the coming of Christ; but it would render it absurdly inaccurate as a delineation of the kingdom of heaven.

But our interpretation is demanded also by the relation of this parable to the others in the series of which it is a member. They all illustrate, in one way or another, the effect of the preaching of Christ among men. The good seed, alike in the stories of the sower and of the tares, is *the word;* and, by all the laws of analogy, it should be that also, which is represented by the leaven. Moreover, in those parables here in which evil appears, the good is seen to be in conflict with it, and is ultimately separated from it. Thus the tares were at the harvest taken out from among the wheat; and the bad fish caught in the net were taken out from among the good, and cast away. If, therefore, it had been the Saviour's purpose to illustrate the progress of evil in the world by this parable, we are warranted, from the tenor of the others, to conclude that he would have represented the leaven as in conflict with something which symbolized his gospel, and as being eventually separated from or overcome by it; for it cannot be that he should give any countenance to the idea, everywhere else repudiated, that the gospel is to be ultimately vanquished, and that Satan is to be left to have universal and undisputed dominion over the world.

Besides, I remind you of the dualism in the arrangement of these parables, and ask if we are not warranted to expect, that in this couplet, composed of the mustard-seed and the leaven, we have the same subject looked at from different angles, just as we had in those of the tares and the net, and as we are yet to have in those of the pearl of great price and the hidden treasure.

Nor is this all: we must not allow it to be forgotten, that while in itself leaven is incipient corruption, and therefore an abstractly evil thing, it is yet used by the housewife as a good thing for her purpose, which purpose was also good; namely, the production of light and wholesome bread. For the object which the woman had in view, therefore, the leaven was a good thing, and may warrantably enough be taken as a symbol of that whose effect in the world is beneficial.

For these reasons, then, and without allowing ourselves to be drawn into the discussion of millennarian theories, which have no more to do with this parable than with the others in whose immediate connection it is found, we feel bound to take the leaven here as a symbol of the good, wholesome, aggressive influence which Christ introduced into the world when he came to earth, and lived and died, and rose again, as the Saviour of sinners.

But here, too, we must beware of running into merely fanciful conceits. We cannot press into significance the three measures of meal, as if they denoted either the three continents into which the ancients divided the world as it was known to them; or the three sons of Noah, by whose descendants the world was peopled after the flood; or the three constituent parts of man, — body, soul, and spirit: though each of these interpretations has had its advocates among expositors. The simple fact is, that three measures of meal was a usual quantity for a single home-baking; and so they are most naturally specified.

Neither may we extract any mystical meaning from the circumstance that a woman put the leaven into the meal, as if thereby the Lord had designed to set before us either the work of the Holy Spirit, or the agency of the Church; for, as Arnot has well remarked, "A man took the mustard-seed, and sowed it in his field: a woman took the leaven, and hid it in three measures of meal. The two parables are in this respect strictly parallel: in both, an ordinary act is performed, and in each it is performed by a person of the appropriate sex."[1] The great truth here illustrated, then, is that

[1] The Parables of Our Lord, as before, p. 114.

the Lord Jesus Christ, by his coming and work, introduced into humanity an element which works a change on it, that shall continue to operate until the whole is transformed, — therein resembling leaven, hidden by a woman in three measures of meal until the whole was leavened.

Thus regarded, some very important things are suggested by the parable.

In the first place, it tells us that the coming of Christ into the world brought an entirely new influence to bear upon it. The leaven was not in the meal by nature: it had to be put into it. In like manner, the gospel is not a merely natural product. It was not a latent quality in the heart of man, needing only favorable circumstances for its development. It is not a human invention, but a divine remedy provided for the counteracting and overcoming of that evil nature which is inherent in the human race.

We cannot get rid of the fact that men are depraved. Explain it as we may, there is moral evil in the world. Humanity is tainted, and men of themselves have never been able to eradicate the spiritual malady by which they are all alike afflicted. So far from that, they have never been able to keep themselves from becoming worse. How suggestive in this regard are the two great visions to which prominence is given in the Book of Daniel! You remember how the image, which had its head of gold, deteriorated, as it descended, through breast of silver, belly and thighs of brass, and legs of iron, to feet part of iron and part of clay.[1] You cannot have forgotten either, how, in the vision of the four beasts, there was first the lion, then the bear, then the

---

[1] Dan. ii.

panther, and then that huge, composite, unnamed monster, with great iron teeth, devouring and breaking in pieces, and stamping the residue with the feet of it.[1] We have heard a great deal lately of theories of development; and this is neither the time nor the place to enter upon the consideration of these, so far as they are used to explain or account for the present condition of the physical universe. But, morally, the only development of man, when left to himself, which history has seen, has been downwards; and the ancient civilization, as you may see from the writings of those who have described it, was little better than a veneered brutality. If, therefore, the progress of evil was to be arrested, and men were to be delivered from its influence, it could only be through the introduction into the race of some agency from without, which, coming into contact with it, should purify and ennoble it. Hence, in the dream which Nebuchadnezzar saw, that was represented as a stone cut out of the mountain without hands; and in the vision of Daniel it is referred to in these words: "I saw in the night visions, and, behold, one like the Son of man came with the clouds of heaven, and came to the Ancient of days, and they brought him near before him; and there was given him dominion, and glory, and a kingdom, that all people, nations, and languages should serve him: his dominion is an everlasting dominion, which shall not pass away, and his kingdom that which shall not be destroyed." And in the parable before us, the same thing is illustrated by the hiding of the leaven in the meal. Left to itself, human nature, bad to begin with, constantly deteriorates. If, therefore, the Lord Jesus Christ had been only a man, and the product of his age, he could have done nothing to

---

[1] Ibid. vii.

stop that process. Rather, following out the law which I have specified, he would have fallen below the age by which his was preceded. But he was different from other men, — even the God-man, — and so, as the leaven operated on the meal because of that active principle in it that was different from the meal, Christ, through that living power in himself which was different from all other men, wrought on the mass of mankind for its transformation and assimilation to himself. "By the mystery of his holy incarnation, by his cross and passion, by his precious death and burial, by his glorious resurrection and ascension, and by the coming of the Holy Ghost," he introduced a new element into humanity, which has been working for its renovation ever since. His divine teaching, his spotless example, his atoning death, his resurrection life, and his ascension gifts received for men, and shed forth upon men, — all combine to make the good news concerning him a regenerating power in the world; and it is the first preaching of this good news that is here spoken of as the "hiding" of the leaven in the meal.

How truly it was "hidden," must be evident not only from the silence of contemporary historians regarding it, but also from the statements made by the Christian apostles themselves concerning the beginnings of their work. Look at those few Galilean fishermen and peasants, in that upper room, surrounding a teacher who, within a few hours, was to be dragged from their fellowship, and nailed to a cross. Hear him saying unto them, "I appoint unto you a kingdom, as my Father hath appointed unto me, that ye may eat and drink at my table, and sit on thrones, judging the twelve tribes of Israel;"[1] and you may see in them, especially as, a few weeks

[1] Luke xxii. 29.

later, they were clothed with the might of the Holy Spirit, the first particles of the new leaven. Poor, despised, contemptible they were, to human view; and thus they may very fitly be spoken of as hidden in the mass, which, through their instrumentality, was to be permeated and transformed.

II. But the parable of the leaven suggests, in the second place, that the introduction of Christ and his kingdom into the world works a change upon the world. The leaven assimilates the particles of the meal to itself. So Christ, coming into contact with humanity, imparts to it his own nature. When he touched the leper, he was not defiled, but he communicated his own purity to the diseased man: so, when he took human nature on him, he was not thereby contaminated, but he conveyed healing to the race. This is seen in a very striking way in the history of individuals. Paul, Augustine, Luther, Bunyan, Newton, and many other names, at once leap to our memories as illustrations. But it is perhaps more impressively illustrated in the case of places. Look, for a crucial instance, at ancient Greece. Perhaps the highest culture ever reached without Christianity was seen in that classic land. There were the most mellifluous language, the loftiest eloquence, the noblest art, the acutest philosophy, the most spirit-stirring poetry; but what was the condition of the people morally? Read Mr. Lecky's "History of Morals," and he will tell you that it was a mass of reeking rottenness. All this went on until a man of Tarsus made his appearance, preaching the incarnation and the cross, and pointing his hearers to "the Lamb of God, that taketh away the sin of the world;" and then even in Corinth, the very capital of the world's iniquity, a check was given to the prevailing corruption, so that, after naming some of the worst sorts of sinners, Paul could write to the converts in that city, "Such were some of you; but ye are washed, but ye are sanctified, in the name of the Lord Jesus, and by the Spirit of our God."[1] Nor is that a solitary instance. It has always been so; it is so to-day. It has wrought a similar change in Madagascar, in Fiji, and in many of the islands of the Pacific, and nearer home in some of the streets and lanes of our own city. Indeed, all the corrective agents that are successfully at work upon the moral condition of humanity, whether at home or abroad, may be traced up to Christ and Christianity; and wherever the gospel is fairly, honestly, earnestly, and prayerfully tried, it is successful as "the power of God," in "turning men from darkness to light, and from the power of Satan unto God."

But this change, real and assimilating in its nature, is gradual in its progress. The leaven works on the particles of the mass next it, and by transmuting them makes them also leaven, which in its turn operates on that with which it comes into contact. The change is wrought in detail, and on particle by particle. So Christianity regenerates the individual, and through him the family, and, through the aggregate of such families, society at large. It is not volcanic in its character, working through shocks like those of an earthquake; but rather gradual, constant, pervasive, like the operation of the leaven. We have seen already how it commenced in the adhesion of John and Andrew to Christ; and if we transfer our starting-point to the day of Pentecost, we have the same fact illustrated. Beginning at Jerusalem, it found its earliest converts among the

[1] 1 Cor. vi. 11.

chosen people; but very soon, led in a way which they knew not, its disciples went to work among the Gentiles. After that it was taken from one centre of influence to another, and left to operate in each. Paul "hid" it in quiet places in Philippi, Thessalonica, Corinth, Athens, Rome; and such was its vitality, that, within a century or two after his martyrdom, Tertullian could write to the Roman emperor, with perhaps a dash of rhetorical exaggeration, but yet with substantial truth, "We are but of yesterday, and we have filled every thing that is yours, — your cities, islands, free towns, castles, council-halls, the very camps, all classes of men, the palace, the senate, and the forum. We have left you nothing but your temples. We can outnumber your armies. There are more Christians in a single province than men in all your legions." It is unhappily true, that in the course of centuries Christianity became corrupt, and lost much of its aggressive and assimilating force; but with the era of the Reformation it regained its power through the recovery of its purity, and with occasional times of apparent retrocession it has been in the main steadily advancing ever since. But probably the greatest progress which it has ever made in the history of the world has been seen during the present century. Almost within the period of two generations, the Bible has been translated into two hundred different languages; missionaries have gone to the East and to the West, to the North and to the South, and have, in many instances, already created a new civilization by their efforts. Every month is bringing fresh reports of their success, and almost every year is opening up new fields for their entrance. The Wall of China has not been able to exclude this leaven from that marvellous empire. Not twenty years have elapsed since Japan was open to receive it; and now the island of Corea has been entered, and we may look for new proofs of its power in that land which has been so long hermetically sealed from the outside world. With the exception of probably not more than one or two countries, all nations are now open to its missionaries. We could send its preachers almost anywhere, if we had but the men to send, and the money to sustain them. Shall we not, then, push on, and see the fulfilment of the prediction, "The mountain of the Lord's house shall be established in the top of the mountains, and all nations shall flow unto it"?

For — and this is the last thought in the parable — the change wrought by the introduction of Christianity into the world is to be universal. The leaven continued to operate on the meal until the whole was leavened; and so the kingdoms of the world are to become the kingdom of Christ. Many attempts to set up a universal monarchy by force have been made, but they have all been disastrous failures. Nebuchadnezzar, Cyrus, Alexander, Cæsar, Napoleon, each in his turn was ambitious to subdue the world. But they all lacked that which was needful for success, for force alone will not suffice for such an achievement. The cross, and not the sword, is here the conquering influence. The might, not of one who slays, but of One who was slain, is here the potent spell. Love, not violence, is the real leaven; and universal empire is to be His, over whose cradle the heavenly host sang the prophetic anthem, "Glory to God in the highest, peace on earth, and good-will to men." To the mere superficial observer, indeed, who thinks of the vast disproportion now existing between the population of even nominally Christian lands, and that of those whose inhabitants are Buddhists, Mohammedans, and heathens, such an expectation may seem little better than a "devout imagination." But when he takes a wider sweep, and goes more deeply into the matter, he may see reason to alter his opinion. Astronomers calculate the orbit and period of a planet, by taking observations of it at different and distant intervals; and from the comparison of these, they can predict with perfect accuracy both the course it will follow and the times which it will keep. Now, if we will take a forecast of the future history of the kingdom of Christ on similar principles, from the past, we shall be led to regard the universal diffusion of the gospel as among the most certain of future things. Let your first observation be made in the days of Paul, your second in the time of Constantine, your third in the age of the Reformers, your fourth in the generation of the Wesleys and the Whitefields, and your fifth at the present hour, and you will see reason to conclude that if the churches of Christ will but rise to their responsibility, and seize their opportunity, we are not so very far as some may suppose from the universal triumph of the gospel. For the greatest rapidity in its progress may be expected at the last, since every new convert becomes a new leavening agent; and so the advancement must be in a more accelerated ratio than that either of arithmetical or of geometrical progression.

Shortly before I came first to this country, I clipped a paragraph from an English newspaper, which told that a grain of wheat that had been picked up by an admirer of royalty, as it fell five years before from the hand of the Prince of Wales, had, by being sown, and its product sown again year after year, brought forth within that period as much as could, in the sixth year, be drilled into sixteen acres of land. Who can calculate how much land might be sown with its increase now? And so, if we would only catch as eagerly and sow as diligently the seed that has fallen from the hands of Christ, we might soon be able, with the fruit thereof, to cover the whole earth.

The sum of the matter, then, as brought before us in these parables, is this: Insignificant as the beginnings of Christianity were, the hope of the world lies in its diffusion; and that result will certainly be finally attained. It will change the character of the people among whom it is proclaimed, and by whom it is accepted; and it will go on in its regenerating course, until "men shall be blessed in Christ, and all nations shall call him blessed." But this diffusion of the gospel over the world is to be brought about by the agency of those who have already received it; and to us in this age, and in this land, God has given the high privilege of laboring in this beneficent enterprise. Shall we accept this privilege, or decline it? And, if we decline it, have we ourselves been leavened? These are the questions which I desire to leave with you to-night.

V

THE HIDDEN TREASURE, AND THE PEARL OF GREAT PRICE
Matthew 13:44-46

THE parables are two, but the subject illustrated by both is the same. There is indeed one point of difference between them, which will come up as we proceed; but in the main they both deal with the intrinsic preciousness of the kingdom of heaven, and the willinghood with which the individual man, when his eyes have been opened to perceive that preciousness, sacrifices every thing that is inconsistent with his possession thereof.

The incident described in the former of the two may well enough have been a literal fact. In those ancient days, there was little trade in which men could embark; no banks in which they could lodge their money, and no safe-deposit vaults on whose security they could depend. It was natural, therefore, that they should seek to preserve their savings by hiding them in some secret place; and so they very commonly buried them in the earth. It often happened, however, that, when a man had thus concealed his treasure, the secret of the place into which he had put it died with himself, so that it remained concealed until some lucky discoverer stumbled unexpectedly upon it. For the times were unsettled; and a sudden invasion of enemies might lead many to hide their riches in the ground, and flee for their lives, in the hope — alas! too often disappointed — that they would soon return and recover them. Thus it was, as Guthrie [1] has quaintly put it, that "the earth became a bank in which was accumulated, during the course of ages, a vast amount of unclaimed deposits." On such a "treasure," the man described in the parable accidentally came, when he was, perhaps, engaged in some common and ordinary pursuit. Then, having satisfied himself of its value, he obliterated all traces of his discovery; and, without making any one aware of his motive, he sold all that he had, in order that he might buy the field wherein he had made his "find."

In the second of the parables, we see a travelling merchant pursuing his regular business as a dealer in pearls, which he bought and sold for purposes of gain. He was no mere jewel-fancier hunting for rare and valuable gems which he might put into his collection, but a merchant whose trade was in pearls; and, finding one of surpassing value, he went and sold all that he had, and bought it, congratulating himself the while that he had made a splendid investment.

Thus each of these men discovered that which he accounted of supreme value, and took means to obtain it for himself. The one came upon it, as it were, by accident; and the other found it as he was prosecuting that which he had made the business of his life. Therein they differed from each other; but so soon as the discovery was made, each took earnest measures to make the good thing which he had found his own, and therein they were alike. Now, the Saviour says that the kingdom of heaven is like them both. In what precisely, then, does the resemblance consist? The question is

[1] The Parables of Christ, by Thomas Guthrie, D.D., p. 152.

important: and we may perhaps give the best answer to it by seeking to show, first, what the parables do not teach; and, second, what the truths are which they were specially intended to illustrate.

The treasure, and the pearl of great price, both represent salvation through Jesus Christ, which, rightly estimated, is "more to be desired than gold, yea, much fine gold." It brings to us what money cannot buy; namely, forgiveness of sins, and regeneration of character. It imparts to us what riches cannot secure; namely, happiness of heart. It is, in itself, a possession which moth cannot corrupt, and no thief can steal. It is an abiding joy, valuable not only to him who has it, but also, in a very important sense, to all with whom he comes into contact. It is, in a word, the chief good, the "one thing needful," the great end to which all earthly goods, even at their best, are but as means, and must be utterly and entirely subordinated.

So far all is clear. But no analogy will hold at every point, and we shall make the wildest work in our exposition, even of the Saviour's parables, if we attempt to run the parallel through in every particular. Let us carefully note, therefore, what those things in these parables are, which must not be pressed into spiritual significance.

Observe, then, in the first place, that they do not teach that the blessing of salvation through Christ is confined to any one particular enclosure. This treasure could not have been found anywhere else than in that special field, and so many have attempted to limit the possibility of obtaining salvation to one particular place. It has been alleged, for example, that the field here is the church; and from that assertion the inference has been drawn, that men can find salvation only in the church. Now, I do not undervalue the organization of the visible Church. It is Christ's own ordinance, and as such we ought to give it all the importance which he has attached to it. It is, indeed, indispensable for the edification of its own members, for the maintenance of gospel ordinances, and for the diffusion of the gospel at home and abroad. All efforts for the attainment of these ends, which are put forth outside of the church, and independently of it, are in their nature sporadic and ephemeral, lacking that element of permanence which Christ declared that his Church should possess, when he said that "the gates of Hades should not prevail against it." For all these objects, therefore, I magnify the church. But to say *that* is one thing, and to limit salvation to connection with the church is quite another. Yet that is done by those who associate regeneration with baptism, and affirm that he who partakes of the Lord's Supper is *ipso facto* Christianized. But the truth, as many passages of Scripture attest, is just the reverse. A man becomes connected with the church through his union to Christ: he does not become united to Christ through his connection with the church. Christ is the door; through him, men enter into the church. They pass, as already saved, into its courts; and, therefore, it will not do to say that salvation is to be found alone within its pale.

Others have affirmed that the field here represents the Bible, and they have alleged that it is only by digging diligently into its depths that men can discover the priceless treasure of salvation. Now, I can not, I dare not, speak disparagingly of that Book, the several parts of which were given through "holy men of

old," who "spake as they were moved by the Holy
Ghost." It is in itself a treasure "better than gold or
silver," and multitudes have found Christ and his salvation through the study of its pages. But still it is not
true that salvation is possible only for those who have
that book in their possession. Many were saved, through
him, before at least the New-Testament portion of it
was reduced to writing at all; and multitudes still are
saved to whom faith has come by hearing rather than
by reading. We cannot, therefore, accept the view of
those who would identify even the Sacred Scriptures
with the field which contained the hidden treasure.
The truth is, that salvation always comes through faith
in Jesus Christ; and wherever one is confronted with
him, and has his eyes opened to the perception of his
"unsearchable riches," that to him is what the field was
to the man who found the treasure in it. It may be the
reading of the Scriptures; or the hearing of a faithful
discourse in the sanctuary; or the perusal of a book
which he has taken up for quite another purpose than
to find salvation in it; or a conversation with a fellow-
man in some casual interview; or the shock of some
terrible calamity under which

> "The light of sense
> Went out, but with a flash that has revealed
> The invisible world."

But, in whatsoever connection it is that a man first
discovers Christ, and has a glimpse of his salvation, *that*
to him is the field of the former of these parables, and
the coming on the pearl of great price of the latter. A
glorious opportunity with infinite possibilities of spiritual blessing through Christ in it, — *that*, anywhere, is the
coming on the treasure in the field, or the meeting of

the man who has the priceless pearl; and the determination, at any sacrifice, to embrace that opportunity and improve it, is the selling of all he has to buy it.

Now, when we have got to this apprehension of the case, it is easy to see, in the second place, that these parables are not to be construed as teaching that salvation is a thing which a man can buy. "It cannot be gotten for gold." That is now one of the simplest commonplaces of the pulpit. But it was not so always. We cannot forget Tetzel and his drum, though Luther so effectually silenced the one, and made a hole in the top of the other. There was a time when indulgences were sold for money, and men could buy what Chaucer called "pardons come from Rome all hot." But it is not needful now that I should expose the hollowness of all such pretensions; for there is little danger, I should hope, of any one of you supposing that you can buy salvation as you would a jewel or a piece of land. More insidious by far is the temptation to imagine that we can deserve it by our deeds. But that also is a delusion. For even a perfect deed has no merit in it to atone for sin; and, besides, salvation, being not a condition of security only, but also and mainly a character, cannot be obtained in any such way. It is not a commodity outside of the man, which he can transfer to himself ready-made by purchase: it is a nature within him, and that can be imparted and fostered only by God. But how can we purchase that, or any thing else, from him? What can we offer to him, that is not already mortgaged to him? Hence, if we are ever to be saved, it must be by grace; and, whatever else the purchase of the field and the pearl may signify, it cannot mean that it is possible for us to buy from God, the regeneration of our souls.

But still again, thirdly, we must not suppose that the parable of the finding of the hidden treasure counsels concealment in the matter of our salvation, or teaches that the discovery of it in Christ is a thing which any one needs hide. When this man first saw the treasure, he covered it up again, lest any one should discover the value of the field, and outbid him in its purchase; and then, having made all his preparations, he went and bought the land. In all this he acted like a shrewd and unscrupulous man of the world, and a great deal of unnecessary discussion has been carried on over his conduct. But it is not in this part of his procedure that the point of the parable is to be found; and, in employing his eagerness to get possession of the field, for the purpose of illustrating the earnestness with which the true convert gives up every thing that is inconsistent with his possession of salvation, we are not to suppose that our Lord meant to express approval of his concealment of his discovery from him to whom, of right, the property belonged. According to the Jewish law, all such "treasure trove" rightfully belonged to the man on whose land it was found; and so the clear duty of the finder was to give to the owner notice of that which he had discovered. Without any hesitation, therefore, I condemn that part of his conduct, even as I condemn the dishonesty of the unjust steward, and the stolidness of the unjust judge. The analogy of the parable, however, does not turn on that, but rather on the joyful readiness with which he gave up every thing in order to get possession of that which he knew to be worth far more than all he had. And, therefore, we must not imagine that there is any deep spiritual meaning in his hiding of the treasure again, after he had first discovered it: least of all must we suppose that it enjoins, or even recommends, the convert to conceal his joy in his finding of salvation through Jesus Christ. Men hide that of which they are ashamed, but why should we be ashamed of Jesus and his salvation? Reason good has he to be ashamed of us, but surely we need never hang our heads for him. Men hide that which they are afraid of losing, or of having stolen from them. But who can deprive us of that which is within us? Our fellow-men can obtain the same blessing without taking from us the least degree of its enjoyment. Why, then, should we conceal it from them? Moreover, no man has any exclusive property in salvation. Who can bottle up the sunshine, or seek to keep that from his neighbor? Equally vain it is for any one to think that he can keep salvation all to himself. Indeed, if any such ideas enter his mind, it becomes a question whether he has himself been saved at all. For even as, when Jesus of old came to a village, it is written that "he could not be hid," so, when his salvation comes into a heart, it connot be buried or concealed there. No, it will make the eye sparkle with an unwonted brightness. It will irradiate the countenance with a light divine, "that never was on sea or shore." It will pervade the conversation with a new and gracious seasoning. It will transfigure the conduct with a glory akin to that of the Master, when the white lustre of his deity shone through the fleshly veil of his humanity on the brow of Hermon. Hide this treasure! One may as well seek to confine the irrepressible force of steam, as to prevent that new life which Christ puts within the heart, from making itself seen or felt wherever the man is. Evermore, like Peter, he will have to say, "we cannot but speak;" and, as in the case of Paul, there will be a "necessity" on him which will impel him to give it expression. If it can be hidden, it has not come from Christ, and is not genuine. If it be from him, it will reveal itself at the cost of any sacrifice, and in spite of any obstacle.

So much for the negative side of my subject. Now let us turn to the consideration of the positive, and see if we can bring out what these parables were really meant to teach.

And here, in the first place, we may observe that they illustrate the different ways in which men come to the discovery of the greatness of the salvation that is in Christ Jesus. We can see a clear distinction between this man, who, when he was not looking for any thing of the kind, came upon the treasure in the field, and the merchant whose business it was to seek for goodly pearls, and who, having found in the course of his search a certain pearl of great price, took means to possess himself of that. The former is an instance verifying the prophet's words, "I am found of them that sought me not:" the latter is an illustration of the truth of the promise, "those that seek me earnestly shall find me;" and always, in the history of the Church, there have been cases in abundance of both kinds. The woman of Samaria who went out on her ordinary errand to the well, and found Christ and his salvation there, is an example of the one: Nicodemus, who came as a genuine truth-seeker to Jesus, by night, is a specimen of the other. Zacchæus, who went out from curiosity to see the prophet of Nazareth, belonged to the former class; and the Ethiopian treasurer, who was studying the prophecies of Isaiah when Philip came to give him instruction in their meaning, must be numbered with the latter. Paul on his way to Damascus, breathing out threatenings and slaughter against the disciples of the

Lord, but confronted by the Christ with the question, "Why persecutest thou me?" must be enrolled in the former; and the noble Bereans, who searched the Scriptures daily, find their place in the latter. The careless sinner, engrossed in worldly business or earthly pleasure, until all at once, he knows not how, his eyes are opened "to see the invisible," is represented by the one: the anxious inquirer, earnestly seeking for something that shall raise him above himself, and resting not until he finds that in Christ, is represented by the other.

Now, this presentation of the case suggests two or three practical applications which find their fitting place just here. It is fraught, in the first place, with encouragement to the genuine seeker. If God is thus so good sometimes to those who are not seeking, much more will he keep his word to those who are. So let me urge them to persevere with earnest diligence and ardent prayer. In the very eagerness of your search, you have already begun to find. Your sincerity is the prophecy of your success. Yea, who knows but you may find the goodly pearl now, as I assure you that Jesus is here willing and waiting to be gracious unto you? Hearken to these words of his own: "Wherefore do ye spend money for that which is not bread, and your labor for that which satisfieth not? Hearken diligently unto me, and eat ye that which is good, and let your soul delight itself in fatness. Incline your ear, and come unto me; hear, and your soul shall live."[1]

But to those who have not been seeking, there is here also a lesson of importance. There may be some such with us in this place now. They may have come hither, perhaps, with no definite purpose. They may be here only to pass an hour or two in a day that is always a

[1] Isa. lv. 2.

weariness to them. Possibly they may have come simply to oblige a friend, or to gratify some curiosity about the preacher. The last thing they were dreaming of was their salvation. And, lo! here in this description of themselves, this telling them of "all things that ever they did," this setting before them of the sublime realities of salvation as of infinitely greater moment than all the best things of earth, they feel themselves confronted with Christ, and have their eyes opened, as they cannot doubt by God's own Spirit, to the transcendent importance of their eternal interests. O friends! this, this is the field in which you have come upon your "trove." I rede you, therefore, to beware how you deal with your opportunity, and I beseech you not to let it pass without securing the treasure. See that, like Paul, you apprehend that for which you are now apprehended of him.

But think again, not every man comes unexpectedly upon such a "find" as this man discovered. Not every careless sinner is thus casually confronted by Christ. Therefore be not tempted — you whose hearts have not yet been moved — to go on as you have been doing, in the vague expectation that something like the history of the Samaritan woman will be repeated in your case. You have no right to expect any thing of the kind. The promise is only to the seeker: therefore give up your carelessness, and begin your search.

Passing now to another point, I remark, in the second place, that these parables may fairly teach us that salvation is a matter of individual appropriation. This man in the field was not content merely with seeing the treasure, and the merchant was not satisfied simply with looking on the pearl: neither of them rested until he had made the prize his own. And, in like manner, salvation is not a blessing to me until I have accepted it *on Christ's terms*. We are not saved in the gross; but the Lord Jesus deals with us each alone, and each must decide for himself what he will do in the premises. My appropriation of his grace will not avail for you, neither will yours avail for me. Each here must answer for himself. Only that which I make my own can be to me a treasure; and Scripture everywhere insists on the necessity of this appropriation of Christ, in order to salvation. It is indeed the truth that underlies all its symbolic references to Christ. Thus, Jesus is the bread of life: but he is of no more avail to me, without my faith in him, than bread is unless I eat it. He is the water of life; but He is of no more value to me without my acceptance of him by faith, than water is unless I drink it. He is the light of the world; but he will do me no more good, without my believing reception of him into my heart, than the light will unless I open my shutters to admit it into my room. He is only *a* Saviour, or at most *the* Saviour, until I believe in him: when I believe in him, he becomes *my* Saviour. This appropriation, therefore, it is that is here symbolized by purchase. We make Christ our own by believing in him, and giving up every thing that is inconsistent with our possession of him, as really as this merchant made the pearl his own by buying it. This is vital, essential, indispensable. If the anchor do not reach the bottom, it might as well never have been dropped, and there is in such a case practically no bottom. If the drowning man will not seize the rope, it might as well never have been thrown to him, and there is for him practically no rope. In like manner, if we will not believe in Jesus, and give him the place which he demands as Lord and Sovereign of our hearts and lives, there might as well for us have been no Saviour; for he is *not* our Saviour. O sinner! will you not make the Saviour yours now, by resigning yourself, your all, to him, and accepting him as your only Saviour and Sovereign?

But finally here, these parables teach us that the perception of the value of salvation in Christ makes a man happy to part with every thing that is inconsistent with its possession. The merchant made a good investment when he bought the pearl, even at such a price. He was getting more than he gave. And the finder of the treasure had no sadness in his heart when he sold all that he had to buy the field. Herein, indeed, — in this "for joy thereof," of which multitudes lose sight, which perhaps the vast majority of readers never see, — is the gem of the parable of the hidden treasure; and, if I might, I would fain set it sparkling and prominent in the ring of my discourse. This man did not regret the selling of all that he had for the purchase of the field. He did not go round whimpering about the sacrifice he was making, or the self-denial he was practising. He gave much, but he got far more; and the joy of the getting swallowed up and into itself the pain of the giving. Now, in this it is, that he truly resembles the genuine Christian convert. You remember how the young ruler "went away sorrowful," wedded to his possessions; and here we have the true explanation of his making "the great refusal." He had no adequate conception of the value of Christ and his salvation. He saw not the infinite unsearchableness of the riches that are hidden in Christ. If he had, there would have been no hesitation in his heart, but "*for joy thereof*" he would have parted with every thing that stood in the way of his making them his own. Do not imagine that in saying this I am in any way exaggerating. Look at

Paul. We have seen how he, like this man, came upon his treasure "in the field." Now hear how he appreciated it. Men standing outside of him, and seeing only what he gave up, might call him a fool; but in sober truth, even when tried by a purely commercial standard, he was a wise and far-seeing spiritual merchant. Thus he speaks: "What things were gain to me, those I counted loss for Christ. Yea, doubtless, and I count all things but loss for the excellency of the knowledge of Christ Jesus my Lord." Here is no regretful look upon the past, no grudging of what he had given up, no chafing under what men would call self-denial; but rather a rejoicing over the super-excellency of the knowledge of Christ. We see the same thing at a later day in Augustine, when describing the crisis of his conversion, and how easy he found it, through this joy, to give up all those pleasures of sin which he had long dreaded to be obliged to renounce, which had long held him fast bound in the chains of evil custom, and which if he renounced, it had seemed to him that life would not be worth the living, he exclaims, "How sweet did it at once become to me, to want the sweetness of those toys! and what I feared to be parted from was now a joy to part with. For thou didst cast them forth from me, thou true and highest sweetness. Thou castedst them forth, and, for them, enteredst in thyself, sweeter than all pleasures."[1]

Thus, my brethren, that which to the eye of the worldling, looking from without, seems in the Christian to be self-denial and self-sacrifice, is, in the experience of the Christian himself, supreme satisfaction with the Lord Jesus. His old companions pity him because, to their thinking, he has had to give up so much; but he

[1] Trench on the Parables, pp. 124, 125..

is inwardly rejoicing that he has gained so much more. The man who is wedded to the world considers that the Christian life is a poor, humdrum affair, and pities the victim, who, as he phrases it, has to say of this and that form of worldly pleasure, "I cannot go into it." But the Christian himself has no longer any joy in such things, by reason of the joy that excelleth which he has in Christ. He thinks not of sacrifice in regard to them, for he has ceased to relish them. With him, it is not "I cannot go," but, rather, "*I have no desire to go.*" These things are nothing to him now, because Christ and his salvation are so much more than these ever were. It is no sacrifice to the matron mother, with her baby in her arms, to give up the doll that charmed her as a little girl; and in the same way, it is no sacrifice to the Christian to part with the myriad *shams* of happiness which the world pursues, since God in Christ has put the *divine reality* within his heart. Spare your pity, then, ye votaries of the world. The Christian has "meat to eat that ye know not of;" for, in the serene altitude of his fellowship with God, he does not miss the paltry pleasures of which you make so much.

And if there be any here who are saying within their hearts, "I would become a Christian, but there is so much that I must give up," may God open their eyes to the perception of the real treasure that is in Christ; and then, when they have made the sacrifice, they, too, will admit that the compensations of discipleship are infinitely greater than all that they have abjured. I cannot prove that to them by demonstration. It can be known only by experience; but from our own trial of it, there are multitudes of us who affirm that it has been so. I ask them, therefore, to have such faith in us as to make the sacrifice on our showing. May God even now reveal to you the riches of his grace in Christ, and move you at this moment to make the great acceptance, that, like the good Ethiopian, you, too, may go on your way rejoicing; and it will not be long until you come back exclaiming, "The half had not been told us. Now we believe, not because of your saying, but because we have heard him ourselves, and know that this is indeed the Saviour of the world."

VI

THE UNMERCIFUL SERVANT
Matthew 18:23-35

THE key to the interpretation of this parable hangs upon the door through which we enter on its perusal. The Lord had been speaking on the duty of dealing tenderly with "the little ones" of his kingdom, and was led thereby to treat of the manner in which his disciples should conduct themselves towards those who had trespassed against them. His injunction was to this effect: "If thy brother shall trespass against thee, go and tell him his fault between thee and him alone: if he shall hear thee, thou hast gained thy brother. But if he will not hear thee, then take with thee one or two more, that in the mouth of two or three witnesses every word may be established. And if he shall neglect to hear them, tell it unto the church; but if he neglect to hear the church, let him be unto thee as a heathen man and a publican."[1] Thereby, as is quite plain, he laid the responsibility for seeking a reconciliation primarily upon him who had received the wrong. The initiative was to be taken by him; and it was only after all proper exertions had been made by him in vain, that he was at liberty to treat the wrong-doer as "a heathen man and a publican."

[1] Matt. xviii. 15-17.

THE UNMERCIFUL SERVANT

This, you will observe, is precisely the opposite of the "code" of the world upon the subject. Commonly men in such circumstances wait until the offender comes to them with a confession and an apology; and even then they consider it to be a matter of simple option on their part, whether or not they will forgive him. If they do, they take credit to themselves for magnanimity; but if they do not, they think that no one has a right to blame them. But the course which Christ has enjoined is entirely different. He does not command the injured party to treat the whole matter with indifference, and take no notice whatever of the wrong that has been done to him. That would be comparatively easy, and many who do that flatter themselves that they are forgiving those who have trespassed against them. But the Lord's law is that he against whom the trespass has been committed should take measures to bring the evil-doer to a right sense of his guilt, and should freely pardon him on the expression of his penitence. If, however, kindly, wise, and repeated efforts have failed to bring him to repentance, then the offender is to be left to himself; while yet the person offended is to dismiss all malice and revenge from his heart, and to hold himself ready to recognize the very earliest indications of penitence which may be given by the other.

The law thus laid down cuts deep, and the enforcement of it made a profound impression on the heart of Peter, — so profound, indeed, that for once, unlike himself, he did not impulsively and immediately speak out about it, but allowed the Lord to go on for a season uninterrupted with his discourse. But though the Saviour, as he proceeded, was touching on some most important matters, and was, indeed, announcing what I may call the *magna charta* of social worship,[1] it would almost seem that Peter had not heard him. Probably he had been harboring resentment against some one of the twelve; for, if the harmonizers are right, there had just been a dispute among them as to which should be the greatest. It is not unlikely, therefore, that something had been said by one or more of them which had so wronged Peter, that he felt very hardly toward them, and therefore he could not get that exhortation of the Master out of his head. It had, indeed, most emphatically condemned him; and perhaps like the lawyer who, willing to justify himself, said, "Who is my neighbor?" Peter here was seeking for some salve to his conscience when he asked, "Lord, how oft shall my brother sin against me, and I forgive him? Till seven times?" But, alas! that question only indicated how far he had been from really comprehending the words of the Lord. For it was not a question of "how often" at all. Rather it was a matter of character which was to be manifested whensoever the occasion arose. Therefore, when Christ replied, "I say not, until seven times, but until seventy times seven," — that is (for the answer gives a definite for an indefinite number), there can be no limit of times, — he added this parable, whereby he shows that the forgiving spirit ought always to be in the heart of the forgiven man. To carry out the Saviour's law, therefore, there is no need to say "how often;" but all that is necessary is to keep constantly before us the fact that God has blotted out our transgressions, and will not remember our sins.

In the story itself, there is not much that needs verbal explication. A king calls all his servants to

[1] Matt. xviii. 20.

account; not for a final reckoning, but rather, as it would appear, at some unexpected time, that he might take note of their fidelity, and discover how the various departments of his kingdom stood. One of these servants, probably a satrap or viceroy over some distant dependency, was brought to him, — mark the expression "was brought," as perhaps indicating his reluctance to come, — who proved to be owing ten thousand talents. This, however reckoned, was an enormous sum; amounting, if an Attic talent be taken as the unit, to ten millions of our dollars. How he had come to be thus involved, we are not told. But he had nothing to pay; and, according to the law and custom of the times, the king commanded him to be sold, and his wife and children, that so far at least payment should be made and the defaulter punished. But at the urgent entreaty of the hapless debtor, who passionately cried, "Have patience with me, and I will pay thee all," — though how that was to be accomplished does not appear, — the ruler was better to him than he asked, "and loosed him, and forgave him the debt." "What a load was lifted from the man's heart thereby!" we are apt to say, "and how ready he will be to show kindness to others!" Yes, he might have been, if he had really felt it to be a load; but it seems, both from his expression "I will pay thee all," and his after-conduct, that he had not felt it to be very much of a burden, and so there was little gratitude in his soul. He had escaped from that which he feared, and his thoughts were more about his own good fortune than about his lord's magnanimity. "Himself" was the idol of his heart; and so, on "going out" from his lord's presence (ah! he would not have attempted it before his master's face), and finding a man who owed him a mere

beggarly item of a hundred pence, or about fifteen of
our dollars, he laid hands on him, and took him by the
throat, saying, "Pay me that thou owest." This man
was his fellow-servant, and besought him in precisely
the same words as he had himself used to his master.
He was owing only one hundred pence, whereas his own
debt had been thousands of talents. Still, there was no
compassion in his heart for him, and he sent him
remorselessly to prison. Such, conduct, very naturally,
made his other fellow-servants indignant, and they
immediately reported it to their lord; who at once
revoked his clemency, and delivered the heartless
wretch to the tormentors, saying, "O thou wicked servant, I forgave thee all that debt because thou desiredst
me: shouldst not thou also have had compassion on thy
fellow-servant, even as I had pity on thee?" "So likewise," adds the Lord, "shall my heavenly Father do
also unto you, if ye from your hearts forgive not every
one his brother their trespasses." This does not mean
that God revokes the forgiveness which he has once
bestowed, for his "gifts and calling" are "without
repentance," and we must not attempt to force the parallel here into the teaching of any thing like that; but
it is a symbolical way of saying that he who will not
forgive another has not really himself been yet forgiven. All controversies, therefore, over the bearing
of this parable on the doctrine of the perseverance of
the saints, are entirely irrelevant. That matter is not
in any manner brought up here; but the whole drift
and purpose of the parable is to show that he who
cherishes an unforgiving spirit has never been a saint
at all, and has never really accepted pardon for himself. As Edersheim has said, "The recall of the king's
original forgiveness of the great debtor can only be

intended to bring out the utter incompatibility of such harshness toward a brother, on the part of one who has been consciously forgiven by God."[1] Or, as Arnot expresses it, "If you get pardon from God, you will give it to a brother: if you withhold it from your brother, you thereby make it manifest that you have not gotten it from God."[2] This is the great thought of the parable; but as a whole the story is so rich in its evangelical suggestiveness, that I shall endeavor to bring out before you the leading truths which it specially emphasizes, and at the same time so to arrange and illustrate these, as to give its true climactic force to the conclusion which it was designed to establish.

I. Observe, then, in the first place, as clearly implied in this parable, *that we are all God's debtors.* Debt, in the New Testament, is a common figure for sin. That, however, does not imply that the obligation under which we lie as guilty before God is of a pecuniary sort, and such as can be cancelled by the payment of money. Duty is a moral thing, not a commercial. The neglect to discharge it, or the commission of that which is inconsistent with it, constitutes a moral offence for which silver and gold have no equivalent. Money and duty belong to different departments. If I may use an arithmetical formula, they never can be reduced to a common denominator. The law of God never can be satisfied with a pecuniary fine; and no one can purchase exemption from its obligation, or make atonement for its violation, by the offering of money.

But though, in its literal sense, as denoting money owed by one to another, the word "debt" cannot be

---

[1] Life and Times of Jesus the Messiah, vol. ii. p. 294.
[2] Parables, p. 193.

taken as identical with sin; yet when used figuratively, as signifying an obligation which one has failed to meet, it may well illustrate what the Scriptures mean by iniquity. For, what is sin? It is either a failure to come up to the standard of God's law, or a transgression of its commands; and he who has committed it is a debtor in the sense of owing satisfaction to that moral code which he has dishonored. Now, in this sense, we are all God's debtors; for "we have left undone those things which we ought to have done, and we have done those things which we ought not to have done." So much, I suppose, we should all be ready to acknowledge. But do we really mean what we say, when we make such a confession? Have we any "bill of particulars" in our minds at the moment? or do we use the words as a mere form, out of which all significance has long since departed? The question is important; for low views of sin, and false notions as to the nature of their own guilt, lie largely at the root of men's indifference to the salvation which God has provided. It is an easy thing to say, "I am a sinner," but it is another thing to feel all that the acknowledgment implies; and it is to be feared, that many who use the language of general confession would yet be found emphatically denying to their fellow-men that they had committed the sins of which their words before God seem to be the acknowledgment. Alas! it is too true; and the sarcasm of those who speak of the hypocrisy of such confessions is not without warrant in the prayers of many unctuous professors of penitence. Let us be honest with ourselves, therefore, that we may be honest with God. Let us compare our character and conduct with the requirements of God's law. Let us measure ourselves, not by the standards of conventionalism and custom, but by these words: "Thou shalt love the Lord thy God with all thy heart, with all thy soul, with all thy mind, and with all thy strength, and thy neighbor as thyself;" and let us see how far short we have come of their fulfilment. Let us analyze our conduct in the laboratory of the closet, and with the tests of Holy Scripture. Then our confession, instead of being a form, will become a reality; and the vague generalities which mean so little on our lips will give place to acknowledgments of particular sins, accompanied with shame and confusion of face for their commission. It would be a much healthier sign of the state of our consciences, if, instead of simply crying for mercy as "miserable sinners," each of us should specify the particular sins which he has committed; and for lack of that it is, that so many among us feel so little real sorrow for guilt, even when we seem to be asking for forgiveness. When, therefore, I draw from this parable the inference that we are all God's debtors, let each of us confess the sins of which he is consciously guilty; and then our acknowledgment, while it is the same for all, will be specifically distinct for each, and will be at least sincere.

II. Observe, in the second place, as clearly implied in this parable, that *none of us has any thing wherewith to pay his debt to God*. Here, again, we come upon a very prevalent error among men. When God calls us to a reckoning, by any solemn providence, such as affliction, bereavement, the loss of worldly possessions, or the like, and confronts us with himself, most of us, I believe, would be willing to acknowledge our guilt; but comparatively few, I fear, would admit that they could do nothing to make amends therefor. This servant said to his king, "Have patience with me, and I will pay thee all;" though where he imagined he was to get such a sum of money, is more than I can understand. But it is just the same with the sinner and his God. The moment his guilt is brought home to him, he is impelled to do something or to promise something, in the way of wiping out that guilt. Commonly the very last thing which he will admit is that he can do nothing to make atonement for it. He *will* go about to establish his own righteousness. He *will* try to make himself better. He *will* promise future obedience, as if that could be a satisfaction for the sins of the past. It is thus with him as it is too often with business men in a time of embarrassment; for, no matter how involved his affairs may be, the very last thing that a merchant will admit is that he is hopelessly insolvent. Hugh Miller, in his autobiography, thus describes what he learned by his experience as a clerk in the branch bank of Linlithgow: "I found I could predict every bankruptcy in the district; but I usually fell short from ten to eighteen months of the period in which the event actually took place. I could pretty nearly determine the time when the difficulties and entanglements which I saw, *ought* to have produced their proper effects, and landed in failure; but I missed taking into account the desperate efforts which men of energetic temperament make in such circumstances, and which, to the signal injury of their friends and the loss of their creditors, succeed usually in staving off the catastrophe for a season."[1] So the sinner, in his attempts to work out his own redemption, sinks only the deeper into the mire. Nor is this to be wondered at: for the law demands perfection; and, as his nature is depraved, every new effort which

[1] My Schools and Schoolmasters, pp. 494, 495.

he puts forth, being tainted with that inherent pollution, is only the addition of a new item to his guilt. We are, therefore, not only God's debtors, but we have, and we can have, no assets; so that we are hopelessly insolvent. We are not only guilty, but helplessly guilty. Let that be clearly understood and cordially accepted by you all; for many stumble at this stumbling-stone. So long as you seek to establish your own righteousness, you are but like a criminal on the tread-wheel, and every step descends with you as soon as you attempt to raise yourself upon it; or like a man who seeks to build a house upon a quicksand, in which every stone disappears as soon as it is laid. The simple truth is just as Toplady has sung it: —

> "Not the labor of my hands
> Can fulfil thy law's demands;
> Could my zeal no respite know,
> Could my tears forever flow,
> All for sin could not atone:
> Thou must save, and thou alone."

For none of us has any thing wherewith to pay God's debt.

III. This leads me to the third thing implied in the parable; namely, that *God is willing to forgive us all our debt*. It is, indeed, the very purpose of revelation to make that fact known to men; and in its proclamation David and Paul, Isaiah and John, Jeremiah and Peter, are in full accord. Take the following passages in proof of our assertion: "With the Lord there is mercy; and with him is plenteous redemption, and he shall redeem Israel from all his iniquities." "Come now and let us reason together, saith the Lord: though your sins be as scarlet, they shall be white as snow; though they be red like crimson, they shall be as wool." "Let the wicked forsake his way, and the unrighteous man his thoughts; and let him return unto the Lord, and he will have mercy upon him, and to our God, for he will abundantly pardon." "I will cleanse them from all their iniquity whereby they have sinned against me, and I will pardon all their iniquities whereby they have sinned and whereby they have transgressed against me." "If we confess our sins, he is faithful and just to forgive us our sins, and to cleanse us from all unrighteousness."[1] And if the presence of that word "just" in this quotation from John should provoke the question, how he can be just, and yet freely pardon the iniquity of the sinner, the answer is given by Paul: "Christ Jesus, whom God hath set forth to be a propitiation through faith in his blood for the remission of sins that are past, through the forbearance of God, to declare, I say, at this time his righteousness, that he might be just and the justifier of him which believeth in Jesus."[2] Or, again, "He hath made him to be sin for us, who knew no sin, that we might be made the righteousness of God in him;" so that "God was in Christ reconciling the world unto himself, not imputing their trespasses unto them." "In him we have redemption through his blood, even the forgiveness of sins."[2] But what need I more? Surely I have quoted enough to prove that God is willing frankly to forgive us all our debt. He asks no merit. He will accept no price. He will not sell pardon, either for our alms, or our fastings, or our penances, or our tears; for thus has his servant declared: "Not by works of righteousness

---

[1] Ps. cxxx. 7, 8; Isa. i. 18; Jer. xxxiii. 8; 1 John i. 9.
[2] Rom. iii. 25, 26; 2 Cor. v. 21; Col. i. 14.

which we have done, but according to his mercy he saves us by the washing of regeneration and the renewing of the Holy Ghost."[1] This is the very central truth of the gospel, that, indeed, which makes it a gospel, a message of good news to men. Let every sinner hear it, and rejoice. God is willing frankly to forgive us our debt.

IV. But now, observe in the fourth place, as implied in this parable, that *the reception of this forgiveness by us involves in it the obligation to forgive those of our fellow-men who have trespassed against ourselves.* The servant before us, after having received his lord's favor, went and demanded in the most peremptory manner the payment of a small debt which a fellow-servant owed him; and because he did not obtain that, he cast his poor debtor into prison. This drew upon him the condemnation of his lord, who revoked his kindness, and delivered him to the tormentors. Now, as we have already said, Christ thus teaches in a symbolical way, that we who have freely received God's pardon should also freely forgive those who have offended or injured us; and that, if we do not thus pardon those who have trespassed against us, we have not yet really accepted God's forgiveness.

But to prevent mistake, let us clearly understand how far this obligation extends. It does not imply that we are to take no notice whatever of the wrong that has been done to us, saying, "What does it matter to me? I can afford to let such a one do or say any thing he pleases." That would be saving ourselves, perhaps, a great amount of trouble; but it would not be the "gaining" of our brother, and it would not be forgiveness.

[1] Tit. iii. 5.

Nay, rather, it would be selfish indifference alike to our brother and his guilt. That which is forgiven is a trespass; and, while there is to be in our hearts the disposition to forgive it, we must also seek to bring our brother to the admission that it was a trespass, and to the expression of his sorrow for its commission. As Arnot[1] says, "Parallel with forgiveness there must be faithfulness. Faithfulness to the evil-doer himself and to the community comes in here to modify, not the nature, but the outward form, of forgiving." We must read the parable in the light of the plain and explicit commands concerning the dealing with an offending brother, as these are given in verses 15–17 of this same chapter. The obligation, thus interpreted, amounts to this: that we should dismiss from our hearts all hatred, malice, and uncharitableness toward those who have wronged us; that we should ourselves take the initiative, and open a door toward reconciliation, by using means to bring the offender to the acknowledgment of his guilt, and the acceptance of forgiveness; and that, when he thus confesses his sin and expresses his penitence, we should be ready to meet him with our frank and full pardon. But if, after we have faithfully and lovingly endeavored to set his wrong-doing before him, he continues obstinate and irreconcilable, this parable does not teach, and neither the word of God nor the spirit of the gospel requires, that we should be toward him precisely as if he had never injured us, and as if he were the most amiable person in the world; for then comes in the precept, "let him be to thee as a heathen man and a publican." "There is," as Arnot says, "no virtue in simply permitting a man to wrong you as often as he chooses, forgiving him and doing nothing more."[1] Forgiveness can

---

[1] The Parables of Our Lord, p. 198.

be exercised only where the wrong is acknowledged and repented of. The noble-minded prisoner who had done no wrong would not accept a pardon, because that would have been an admission of his guilt. But the same thing holds with one who has done wrong. The acceptance of forgiveness implies an acknowledgment of guilt; and if forgiveness in the right sense of the word is to be given by us, or accepted by the man who has trespassed against us, we must first bring him to a true perception and acknowledgment of guilt. To do nothing about it, is not to forgive, and is neither just to ourselves, nor kind to the wrong-doer. Willingness to be reconciled, together with the use of all proper means for the effecting of a reconciliation, and the dismissal from our souls of every thing like vindictive feeling, even when a reconciliation is found to be impossible, — these are the things which are especially enforced in this striking parable.

But how comes it that the obligation to cherish this forgiving spirit is connected with our reception of God's mercy? To that I reply, that all who really accept God's pardon are at the same time renewed into his image by the power of the Holy Spirit; and so, resembling him in character, they seek to do unto others as he has done to them. Gratitude to him will take the form of forgiving those who have sinned against themselves. Thus, altogether irrespective of any outward precept, the suggestions of the Spirit within them would impel them to forgive those who trespass against them. But there is no lack of outward precept in this case. Thus Paul, in writing to the Ephesians, says, "Be ye kind one toward another, tender-hearted, forgiving one another, even as God for Christ's sake hath forgiven you."[1]

[1] Eph. iv. 32.

And again, in his letter to the Colossians, we have these words: "Forbearing one another, and forgiving one another, if any man have a quarrel against any; even as Christ forgave you, so also do ye."[1] In like manner the example of Christ — which is the rule for every Christian — teaches the same thing; for in the very agony of his passion, at the very time when they were nailing him to the cross, there came from his heart to his lips that loving intercession, " Father, forgive them, for they know not what they do." And in the prayer which he gave to his followers, both as a pattern and a form, we have this petition: "Forgive us our debts as we forgive our debtors;" a petition which implies that our forgiveness of others is to be, not the ground on which we ask our own pardon, but the evidence that we are cherishing a God-like spirit towards those who have offended us. Yet it is a solemn thought, never to be forgotten by us, that every time we offer that prayer, we do virtually ask God to deal with us as we are dealing with others; and so, in the mouth of a revengeful or vindictive person, it is an imprecation of evil on his own head. "Conceive," says Augustus Hare, "an unforgiving man, with heart full of wrath against his neighbor, with a memory which treasures up the little wrongs and insults and provocations he fancies himself to have received from that neighbor, — conceive such a man praying to God Most High to forgive him his debts as he forgives his debtors. What, in the mouth of such a man, do these words mean? They mean — But, that you may fully understand their meaning, I will turn them into a prayer, which we will call the prayer of the unforgiving man: 'O God, I have sinned against thee many times from my youth up till now. I have been

[1] Col. iii. 13.

often forgetful of thy goodness; I have not daily thanked thee for thy mercies; I have neglected thy service. I have broken thy laws. I have done many things utterly wrong against thee. All this I know; and besides this, doubtless I have committed many secret sins, which in my blindness I have failed to notice. Such is my guiltiness, O Lord, in thy sight. Deal with me, I beseech thee, even as I deal with my neighbor. He hath not offended me one-tenth, one-hundredth part, as much as I have offended thee; but he has offended me very grievously, and I cannot forgive him. He has been very ungrateful to me, though not a tenth, not a hundredth part, as ungrateful as I have been to thee: yet I cannot overlook such base ingratitude. Deal with me, O Lord, I beseech thee, as I deal with him. I remember and treasure up every little trifle which shows how ill he has behaved to me. Deal with me, I beseech thee, O Lord, as I deal with him.' Can any thing be more shocking and horrible than such a prayer? Is not the very sound of it enough to make one's blood run cold? Yet this is just the prayer which the unforgiving man offers up, every time he repeats the Lord's Prayer. For he prays to God to forgive him in the same manner in which he forgives his neighbor. But he does not forgive his neighbor, and so he prays to God not to forgive him. God grant that his prayer may not be heard, for he is praying for a curse upon his own head!"[1]

I cannot conclude without pausing for a few moments to give emphasis to three facts which are all suggested by this parable, and which give tremendous force to the lesson which it teaches.

The first is, that our sins against God are vastly

[1] Alton Sermons, pp. 467, 468.

greater than our neighbor's trespasses against us. The servant's debt to his lord was ten thousand talents, but his fellow-servant's debt to him was a hundred pence: so the injuries which others have done or can do to us are small and paltry in comparison with the enormity of our offences against God. If, therefore, he forgives the greater, we may forgive the less.

The second is, that God himself is not a sinner, and is not induced by the consciousness of any guilt of his own to show mercy to the transgressor; but we are continually needing not only the forbearance of God, but also the long-suffering of our fellow-men. If, therefore, He who never offended any one, and does not need any forgiveness, so frankly forgives us, how much more ought we, who so frequently trespass, both against him and our neighbors, to forgive those who trespass against ourselves?

> "Forget not, thou hast often sinned,
> And sinful still must be:
> Deal gently with the erring one,
> As thy God has dealt with thee."

The third is, that implacability on our part is an evidence that we are as yet unforgiven by God. "If any man have not the spirit of Christ, he is none of his." The tree repeats itself in the framework of every leaf; and if in our lives there be revenge and unforgivingness, these things demonstrate that we have no living connection with the true vine. An unforgiving Christian is a contradiction in terms. "So likewise shall my heavenly Father do also unto you, if ye from the heart forgive not every one his brother their trespasses." Mark these words, "my heavenly Father." There are those among us who are constantly affirming that it would be inconsistent with God's fatherhood, if he should leave any unforgiven. But it is not so that the eternal Son has revealed to us the fatherhood of God. Nay, rather, just because the heavenly Father is love, he must be everlastingly opposed to a spirit so unlike his own as that of the implacable and unforgiving man. Here, indeed, to me, is the appalling lesson of the parable: that God the *Father*, who is now so willing to forgive us all, must and shall leave unforgiven all who cherish and manifest this unforgiving temper. "Take care how you offend me, for I never forgive," said one man to another, in the hearing of John Wesley. "Then," said the man of God, "I hope you never sin; for, with what measure ye mete, it shall be measured to you again." God grant that we may all so gratefully accept his forgiveness, as to be thereby impelled to seek forgiveness from the brethren whom we have wronged, and to grant forgiveness to those who have wronged ourselves!

VII
THE LABORERS IN THE VINEYARD
Matthew 20:1-16

THIS parable is perhaps harder to interpret than any other which the Saviour uttered. It will serve no good purpose to enter upon the controversies which have been carried on concerning it by commentators; yet it is important that we should define wherein the difficulties connected with its exposition lie, inasmuch as a clear apprehension of *that* may help us to the right solution of *them*.

Now, in the first place, we cannot disguise it from ourselves, that the story, on the face of it, is one which is exceedingly improbable. We all feel *that* as we read it, and only our reverence for our Lord prevents us from giving expression to that conviction. There is, indeed, nothing surprising in a householder going in the morning to the market-place to hire laborers to work in his vineyard. That was common enough in the times in which our Saviour lived. We can conceive, also, of circumstances which necessitated the employment of as many hands as possible, and which impelled him to go out at later hours in the day to send other laborers into the vineyard; though when it came to five o'clock in the afternoon, and only one working hour remained, we do feel it to be rather strange that he should engage others for such a brief time. But it is still more unusual to find an employer giving as much remuneration to those who wrought for one hour, as he did to those who wrought for nine or twelve. Josephus indeed tells us that the high priest Annas gave the workmen employed in repairing or adorning the temple a whole day's pay, even though they labored only for a single hour; but the very fact of his mentioning such a circumstance marks it as unprecedented. It was not the custom in those ancient days. It is not the custom now. None of you who are employers of labor would ever think of doing such a thing, as a rule; and the principles of political economy would condemn you, and insure your business failure, if you attempted to carry out such a plan. This householder, therefore, was no common character. He was what would now be called "peculiar." He was different from others, — eccentric, if you choose; had his own way of doing things, and did not care how other people regarded him; was not actuated by ordinary motives, and managed his vineyard on principles which were radically opposite to those in vogue among men. But when we come to think it out, we shall discover that he must be such an one, if he would truly represent God in his dealings with men generally. Is it not written, "My thoughts are not your thoughts, neither are your ways my ways, saith the Lord. For as the heavens are higher than the earth, so are my ways higher than your ways, and my thoughts than your thoughts"? If, therefore, this householder had been in all respects like every other householder, and his actions precisely the same as those of householders in general among men, he would have been no proper representative of the Head of the kingdom of heaven, and his doings would have borne no resemblance to the administration of that kingdom which is "not of this world." Hence we need not be disturbed about the unnaturalness or improbability of the story as a story. Speaking after the manner and standard of men, the gospel itself is unnatural and improbable; and only a householder who cared more for the culture of *men*, than for the production of *grapes*, could rightly represent Him who measures service not by its visible result, but by the spirit in which it is rendered.

A second and even more serious difficulty is in the fact that the act of this householder seems to be unjust. We have all a kind of sympathy with the grumblers who say, "These last have wrought but one hour, and thou hast made them equal unto us which have borne the burden and heat of the day." So common is this sympathy, that expositors have tried to remove the difficulty out of which it arises, by sundry suggestions of their own. Some, for example, have said that the householder's act was grounded in the fact that the late comers had done as much in one hour as the early ones had performed in twelve; but there is no word of that in the parable, and if that had been the explanation, it would have been easy for the householder to vindicate himself by saying, "You have no right to complain, for, judging [as a modern employer would say] 'by the piece,' they have earned as much as you." But instead of that, he simply falls back upon his right to do what he chose with his own. Others have supposed, that, while the late comers were paid with a brass denarius, the others were rewarded with a silver one or with a gold one; and so they tell us that there is one heaven for all, yet varying for each in glory and exaltation, according to his work on earth. But true as that is, for many portions of the Word of God attest it, yet it cannot surely be the truth taught here; for there is no hint of it in the parable, and it would have been easy for the householder to have justified himself if it had been really as this would represent. Nay, if the twelve-hour laborers had got a gold denarius, we may be sure there would have been no murmuring on their lips. We have to admit, therefore, the inequality of the treatment given to these laborers; and we must find the explanation of it in something else than the quantity of their work, — even in that which ordinary earthly employers take no thought of, namely, the spirit of the workers.

A third difficulty arises from the evident impossibility of finding spiritual analogues for each of the particulars in the parable. We can see that God is the householder, and Christ the steward, and the vineyard the Church. But when we go down into details, and ask who those are who were hired in the morning, and who those are who were sent to work at nine, twelve, three, and five o'clock respectively; or how it comes that there should be murmurers in the ranks of those who have really labored in the Church; or what the penny represents, — we are involved in uttermost perplexity, and cannot give a categorical answer to any one of such inquiries.

Now, these very difficulties prove that the interpretation of the parable is not to be sought in any such direction; and indicate that the grumbling workers are to be taken rather as the impersonations of an evil principle, that is found existing sometimes even in Christian hearts, than as actual and distinct entities in the Christian Church. They correspond in that particular, precisely, with the elder brother in the parable of the prodigal son; and we are to look for that which they represent, in a spirit that lurks sometimes even in the hearts of believing men, rather than in individuals who can be separately and distinctly identified in the church.

There is a good deal of elder-brotherliness, even in men of Christian character; and there is much of this hireling disposition, even in those who must still be reckoned genuine disciples. But wherever it is, it vitiates the character and service to such a degree, that those who have it, though they may be first as regards the duration and magnitude of the work which they have done, are yet last in the Divine appreciation of that work.

The parable, therefore, is the exposure of a spirit, rather than the portrait of an individual or the description of a class. It is a story with a purpose, rather than an affair of real life; and that purpose is the condemnation of the hireling disposition which would seek to deal with God on the principle of so much for so much, and would graduate reward in the manner of proportion as we would work a sum in the rule of three.

This conclusion as to the drift of the parable, which we have arrived at from the consideration of the nature of the difficulties which beset its interpretation, is thoroughly confirmed when we look at the occasion which called it forth. Glancing back to the concluding section of the preceding chapter, which ought not to have been thus arbitrarily separated from what so closely belongs to it, we find that the rich young man had just been tested by the Lord, through the searching command, "If thou wilt be perfect, go and sell that thou hast, and give to the poor, and thou shalt have treasure in heaven; and come, follow me." Unable to stand such an ordeal, he had gone "away sorrowful, for he had great possessions;" and the incident had led the Saviour to remark how hard it was for a rich man to enter into the kingdom of heaven. But Peter, speaking first, and perhaps also giving expression to thoughts which were as really present in the minds of his fellow-disciples as in his own, drew a self-righteous contrast between them and the youth who had just retired, saying, "Behold, we have forsaken all, and followed thee: what shall we have therefore?" The ardent apostle was a good man, but the spirit which those words evinced was not a good spirit. It was as if he had said to his Lord, "Thou didst promise to that wealthy young man, that if he gave up every thing, and followed thee, *he* should have treasure in heaven. But we have done just what thou didst ask him to do: now what shall *we* have for that?" Knowing the true love which was in Peter's heart for him, in spite of this apparently bargaining inquiry, the Lord answered with great tenderness, "Verily I say unto you, that ye which have followed me, in the regeneration when the Son of man shall sit on the throne of his glory, ye also shall sit upon twelve thrones, judging the twelve tribes of Israel. And every one that hath forsaken houses or brethren or sisters, or father or mother, or wife or children or lands, for my name's sake, shall receive an hundred-fold, and shall inherit everlasting life;" that is to say, "For you there shall be special honor; and for all who do as you have done, there shall be abundant compensation and everlasting life at last." But the Saviour does not stop there. To have done that, would have been to have left unreproved the disposition which showed itself in Peter's words. So he continued thus: "But many that are first shall be last, and the last shall be first;" as if he had said, "But take care of working in a mere hireling spirit, and for the sake of what you are to get: for if you do so, great as your service may seem to be, that will make it small in the sight of God; and so, while to outward view you are among the first, ye shall be ultimately among the last, for many that are first shall be last, and the last first." This phrase is repeated by the Lord at the end of the parable, with the addition of the words, "for many be called, but few are chosen." But the reference is not here to eternal election, for the word "chosen" is in this place employed much as we use the term "choice:" "many are called, but few are choice." The contrast thus is not between the elect and the non-elect, so called, but between two classes of real Christians, — the many average and commonplace believers who have still a large measure of the hireling spirit in them, and the few first-rate Christians who serve "all for love, and nothing for reward." Observe, Christ had said to the young man, "If thou wilt be *perfect;*" and the "*chosen*" here answers to the "perfect" there. Those are the princely and right royal disciples, who labor for love; and in the end, though their service on earth may seem to be as small as the pouring of a vase of ointment on the Saviour's head, or the casting of two mites into the treasury, they shall be first; while such as gave noble offerings, or did great achievements, if they did so in a spirit of pride or ostentation, or with the hope of gaining something thereby, will be last.

This is the thought which the Saviour has, as I may say, dramatized in the parable of these vineyard laborers. For, see, those who were sent first into the enclosure to work made a special agreement with the householder. Mark the statement: "when he had agreed with the laborers for a penny a day." In the market-place they made a definite demand. There was the common colloquy in such a case. "What is the rate of wages this morning?" — "We will go for so much." — "I will give you only so much." — "Nay, we must have the sum we named, we cannot go for less,"

THE LABORERS IN THE VINEYARD 111

and so forth. It was a bargain, so much for so much. But it was not so with those who went at the third, sixth, ninth, and eleventh hours. *They* left their treatment entirely in the hands of the householder. They trusted in his generosity, and did not require any agreement. It was enough for them that he had said, "Whatsoever is right I will give you." *They* left it to himself; but the others would have a specified sum. *They* did their work in faith; but the others, like Peter, pressed the question, "What shall we have therefore?" And this difference in the dispositions of the workers accounts entirely for the difference in their treatment by the householder. For, when the late comers presented themselves, they were paid with a denarius — probably to their own surprise, since from another parable we learn that the rewards of the "choice" disciples will be astonishing to themselves. But they had trusted him, and he would be better to them than they expected. When, however, the early laborers appeared, they thought that they were hardly used because they got only a denarius. "The others had received that: surely he was not going to put them on a level with those who had known neither the burden nor the heat of the day. If they who had been only an hour in the vineyard received a penny, manifestly those who had been there toiling for twelve hours should have twelve." — "But no," the householder replies: "you would have an agreement in the morning, and now you must be content with it in the evening. A bargain is a bargain. Since you held me to it before you began to work, I must hold you to it after you have ceased. My treatment of the others is nothing to you. I deal with my laborers as I find them. To the hireling I will show myself a hirer; but to the trustful and confiding one who thinks less of reward for his work than of joy in the work, and leaves himself entirely in my hands, I will prove myself more than worthy of his confidence. Take, therefore, what is yours, and leave me to dispose of what is mine." Thus interpreted, the parable is a striking confirmation of the Psalmist's words: " With the merciful thou wilt show thyself merciful; with an upright man thou wilt show thyself upright; with the pure thou wilt show thyself pure; and with the froward thou wilt show thyself froward." [1] The parable is the representation of the bargaining spirit, run to seed; in contrast with the trustful spirit, lovingly rewarded. The bargainers get only that which they stipulated for: the confiding ones get far more than they would have thought of asking. The bargainers are filled with dissatisfaction at the generosity with which the others were treated: the confiding ones are sent away with an exulting joy that they have been treated so well. The conduct of the first laborers represents what the spirit which Peter manifested would ultimately come to, if it were to obtain the upper hand: that of the others represents the outcome of the spirit of love and trust in the choice, first-rate, or, if you will, "perfect" Christians. The hireling spirit is selfish, unamiable, elder-brotherly, surly. The trustful spirit is humble, contented, happy, choice, and is itself a reward which is the forerunner of a great deal more.

Such, as it seems to me, is the main lesson of this difficult parable. And if this be a correct view of the matter, we need not perplex ourselves with the question who those are that are represented by the laborers who began at nine, twelve, three, and five o'clock re-

[1] Ps. xviii. 25, 26.

spectively. It makes little difference whether we understand the Jews to be the first, and the Gentiles to be the others, or whether we take the first to mean the apostles themselves, and the others to be those who should come into the kingdom at subsequent dates down through every after age. The pivot of the lesson is not in any particular interpretation of that sort. Nay, as one has admirably said, "The nature of the work in the vineyard, and its exhausting toil; the unwearied compassion of the lord of the vineyard, going out hour after hour to invite the unemployed, — these and all other details are but the feathers of the arrow, helping it to fly straight to its mark: but the point is, that those who were first hired were last paid and least paid; and this because the first hired entered on their work in a bargaining spirit, and merely for the sake of winning a calculated and stipulated remuneration; whereas the late hired laborers did their work in faith, not knowing what they were to get, but sure that they would not get less than they deserved."[1]

This, then, being the central thought of the parable, we are in a position, having obtained possession of that, to take note of two things which might otherwise elude our observation or produce a false impression on our minds. The first is the peculiarity of the expression, "*many* that are first shall be last, and the last shall be first." The parable teaches a change of place between the first and the last, yet not a change that shall be universal. All the first shall not be last, and all the last shall not be first. No, only many; and that for a reason other than their being either first or last. They shall not be last simply because they were first, nor first

[1] The Parables as recorded by Matthew, by Marcus Dods, D.D., p. 156.

simply because they were last. But, first in the magnitude and extent of their work, they shall be last because of the spirit in which it was performed; and last in the objective character of the thing done, they shall be first because of the subjective disposition of which their doing of it was the manifestation. Yet there will be first who shall remain first; and last, who shall remain last. If the doers of great and splendid deeds did them in a loving and trustful spirit, these, being first, shall continue first; and if the doers of little and inconspicuous matters did them in a hireling spirit, these, being last, shall remain last: for the Lord of the vineyard looks throughout at the spirit rather than the work.

Again, this view of the parable will keep us from so far mistaking its teaching as to suppose that it approves or recommends late coming into the vineyard. The third, sixth, ninth, and eleventh hours here do not refer to different seasons of the same individual life, — as if he who had declined to come in youth should come at middle age; and he who had refused in middle age should come in life's afternoon; and he who had refused all through life should come in the decrepitude of old age, or at the very approach of death. So far as appears, none of those who were engaged at the the later hours were in the market-place at the earlier. The persons spoken to were different each time; and those called at the eleventh hour, when asked, "Why stand ye here all the day idle?" could truthfully reply, "Because no one hath hired us." It is a truth, that, no matter how late in life a sinner comes to Jesus, he will be accepted; but that is not the truth taught here, and no one ought to presume on such a perversion of the parable as that which makes it mean that if he refuse to obey God's call in the morning, or at the third, sixth, or ninth hour, he may have an opportunity of obeying it at the eleventh, and may then come off as well as those who have been Christians all their lives. No, no! each of these companies of laborers obeyed *the first* summons which they received, and you will be like them only if you do the same. The hours here are not the different seasons of the same one life, but rather the centuries of an era; and the teaching of that part of the story may be, that we who live far down the ages, if we will but work for God in the apostolic spirit, in self-denial and self-sacrifice, from love and not from hire, shall receive an apostolic reward. The great ones of the Church were not exclusively among those called into it in the early stages of its history, and long service in the nineteenth century shall have an equal honor with martyrdom in the first. Or, more generally still, the meaning is, that it is not the time at which the service is rendered, or the length and magnitude of the service itself, that will determine the reward, but the spirit of the laborer. Stephen and James, cut off in the beginning of their activity, before they had well entered the vineyard, shall not lose on that account, but shall be side by side with Paul, who toiled on through forty years of suffering for Christ; and with John, who lingered in Ephesus till he reached an age of more than a hundred years. The hireling spirit in any man, or in any age, will get simply and only its hire; but the trustful disposition will always receive "far more exceeding abundantly" above its expectation.

The sum of the matter, then, is, that the motive gives its character to the work; and as men cannot see the motive, but must judge only from the work, it follows that there will be at the last a "reversal of human judgments," since God estimates all by that which is invisible to men, but which is naked and open to his sight. Many of those whom men have placed first shall then be found among the last; and many of those whom men have been wont to place among the lowest and the last, shall then be put among the highest and the first. That is the thought which Canon Mozley has elaborated and enforced in his great sermon on " The Reversal of Human Judgments," contained in his most suggestive volume of University Discourses. I call it a great sermon, not because it is strong either in rhetoric or illustration ; but because of the grasp with which it holds the reader of it to this one thought, and compels him, no matter in what department of God's vineyard he may be laboring, to analyze his own work and at the same time to examine his own heart, making the motive the test of the life. An English critic says of the book as a whole, that there are some sermons in it, "the reading of which would be enough to change the whole character and life of a man ; " and that to which I refer is one of these. Indeed, for my own part, I am inclined to put it among the foremost of the sermons known to me, that have been published in this century; for it clearly shows that very efficient work may be done, even in God's vineyard, by a man in whom there may be very little of the motive of true love to God inspiring the service. The church is composed, indeed, of those who have confessed Christ; but it is a society, existing for certain purposes, and, as such, it has its machinery for the carrying out of these purposes, like any other society that has been formed in the world. Now, the keeping of any part of that machinery in motion is in itself no more a spiritual work, than the carrying-on of any other machinery; and if it is not done with a spiritual motive, then, even though it be done for the church, it is not spiritual work such as God can value and reward. Thus, in a missionary society, the great object is spiritual; but it has to be sustained and carried on like any other business society; its books have to be kept like those of any commercial firm, and he who keeps them is not in that doing a spiritual work, any more than a bookkeeper in a mercantile house is doing a spiritual work. The mercantile bookkeeper may make his work spiritual by doing it as unto the Lord; but the missionary bookkeeper will make his secular if he does it simply for his wages, and as work. So, again, in the office of the ministry, there is much in common with ordinary departments of life. It gratifies literary tastes; it affords opportunities for study; it has associated with it a certain honor and esteem in the eyes of others; it furnishes occasions for the thrill that every real orator feels in the delivery of a message to his fellow-men, and the like. Now, if a man is in the ministry simply for these kinds of enjoyment, there is no more spirituality in his work, than there is in that of the *littérateur*, or the political orator. Theirs may be spiritual, indeed, if they are doing it out of love to God; but his must be merely secular if he does it only from such motives as have place in ordinary literature or eloquence. You see, then, how it comes, that in the estimation of men one may stand very high, may be, indeed, reputed among the first of vineyard laborers, and yet be placed among the lowest and the last by God. But I cannot put this thought with any thing like the force of Mozley; and, therefore, I conclude my discourse with a paragraph from him which may whet your appetite to such a degree that you will not rest until you have read the whole sermon: "The truth is, wherever there is action, effort, aim at certain objects and ends; wherever the flame of human energy mounts up, — all this may gather either round a centre of pure and unselfish desire, or round a centre of egotism; and no superiority in the subject of the work can prevent the lapse into the inferior motive. In the most different objects, this may be the same: it is a quality of the individual. Whatever he does, if there is a degeneracy in the temper of his mind, it all collects and gathers, by a false direction which it receives from the false centre of attraction, *round himself*. The subject or cause which a man takes up makes no difference. The religious leader can feel alike with the political, and as strongly, this lower source of inspiration; can be accompanied by this idolized representation of self, this mirror in which he sees himself growing and expanding in life's area. Are the keen relish for success, the spirit which kindles at human praise and the gusts of triumph, the feelings which accompany action upon a theatre, guaranteed no place in a man, by his having religious zeal? These are parts of human nature; and it is not zeal, but something else, which purifies human nature. So far as religion only supplies a man of keen earthly susceptibilities, and desire of a place in the world, with a subject, or an arena, so far that man stands on the same ground with a politician who is stimulated by this aim. They are the same identical type of men in different spheres. There is a conventional difference between them, but there is one moral heading. Both may be doing valuable work, important service, in a public sense; but if you do not think the politician a spiritual man because he is a useful man, no more must you think the active man in a religious sphere to be so. *Spirituality belongs to the motive.*"[1]

Now, that will help us to understand how it may come, that one may have a high reputation among men for religious work, and yet be among the last when God pronounces the verdict; for he sees, what men cannot see, the motive from which the whole activity has sprung, and tests it all by that. It is a solemn thought, and may well send us to examine ourselves. What are we in God's vineyard, — hirelings, or trusting, humble laborers, working for the love of Christ? They that work for reward do not get as much as they want: they that work for love get far more than they expect. And the moment we ask of Christ, "What shall we have therefore?" we vitiate the quality of our service. It is the same paradox which we have in the words, " He that findeth his life shall lose it, but he that loseth his life for my sake shall find it." He that seeketh happiness for its own sake shall never get it; but unto him that serveth God for love, happiness shall be added, and shall be itself a rich reward.

Beautiful exceedingly in this connection is the story, — mythical, no doubt, in form, but probably true in substance, — that is told concerning Thomas Aquinas. Worshipping one day in the chapel in which he was accustomed to perform his devotions, it is said that the Saviour thus addressed him: " Thomas, thou hast written much and well concerning me. What reward shall I give thee for thy work?" Whereupon he answered, " *Nihil nisi te, Domine,*" — " Nothing but thyself, O Lord!" And in very deed he is himself the best of all his gifts. He is himself the " exceeding great re-

[1] Mozley's University Sermons, pp. 80, 81.

ward" of all his people. Let the spirit of the Angelic Doctor, as enshrined in this simple story, fill our hearts, and there will be no room within us for the hireling's selfishness.

VIII
THE TWO SONS
Matthew 21:28-32

THE meaning of this parable is determined for us by the occasion which called it forth. Questioned by the chief priests and elders of the people, as to the nature and source of the authority which he claimed, our Lord replied by promising to give them a definite answer when they should tell him whether the baptism of John was from heaven or of men. This placed them between the horns of a dilemma: for they knew that if they should say it was of men, they would provoke the antagonism of the people, who held John as a prophet; and that, if they should say it was from heaven, Jesus would be ready with the retort, "Why then did ye not believe him?" They endeavored, therefore, to evade both alternatives by alleging that they could not tell whence it was; and this reply of theirs, which was an evident subterfuge, evoked the parable which forms our theme at this time.

Putting before them a hypothetical case, he questioned them as to the conduct of the parties whom he described in it; and then, turning their answer upon themselves, he virtually condemned them out of their own mouths. The story in some of its features is not unlike that which we had before us in our last discourse. Here, too, we have the proprietor of a vineyard. But it was not so large, and he was not so wealthy, as in the former instance. He was a small freeholder, not able and not requiring to hire laborers, but dependent entirely on the services of his sons. Accordingly, coming upon one of these in the morning, he said to him, "Son, go work to-day in my vineyard;" but was met with the rude and undutiful reply, "I go not." This answer must have deeply wounded the father's heart; but he said nothing, and, on coming to his other son, he repeated the command to him; who replied with seeming alacrity, "I go, sir," or, as it is simply in the original, "I, sir," — as if the youth had said, "You may thoroughly depend on me." But, alas! his eagerness was only in appearance; for he never looked near the vineyard, and went his way after his own enjoyment. Meanwhile, however, the other son, struck, perhaps, with the effect which his disobedience had produced on his parent, thought better of it, and went into the vineyard, and did the work which he had been requested to perform. Now, asks the Saviour at his priestly questioners, "which of these two did the will of his father?" And, apparently without any perception of the reference of the story to themselves, they replied, "The first;" wherupon he rejoined, "Verily I say unto you, that the publicans and the harlots go into the kingdom of God before you: for John came unto you in the way of righteousness," — that is, preaching righteousness, — "and ye believed him not, but the publicans and the harlots believed him; and ye, when ye had seen it, repented not afterward, that ye might believe him."

Now, this direct utterance points the moral of the parable, and furnishes the key to its interpretation. The father is God; the vineyard is the church. The sons are two classes of men to whom the command to labor in the church comes from God: the first is the type of openly abandoned and regardless sinners, who on receiving the command of God defiantly refuse obedience, but afterward, on sober second thought, repent and become earnest in working the work of God; the second is the representative of the hypocrites who in smooth and polite phrase make promises which they never intend to keep, and who, never changing their mind, take no further thought either of God or of his service.

In the primary intention of our Lord, the particular sons to whom the father gave his command were the Jews, to whom "at sundry times and in divers manners" he had spoken through the prophets, and who in the Saviour's own day had the entire Old Testament in their hands. But the great majority among them disregarded his words. Some openly set them at defiance: others, professing in their language a high regard for them, utterly ignored them in their conduct. Such was, in the main, the state of things among them when John the Baptist came preaching repentance and the coming of the kingdom of heaven: and the result of his labors was, that many of the flagrantly immoral were awakened, and became subjects of the kingdom; while few of the Pharisees, chief priests, or elders were brought to repentance through his appeals. The former were like the first son, who did not stubbornly continue in his disobedience, but after a season returned to his filial devotion and duty: the latter were like the second son, who said, and did not, and persisted in their inconsistency.

But while the special inference drawn from this parable by the Lord pointed its application to those whom he was at the moment addressing, there are beneath his words great general principles of permanent importance, which ought to be seriously pondered by every hearer of the gospel. They clearly delineate two classes of characters, which are to be met with in all generations, and of which the publicans and harlots on the one hand, and the Pharisees and chief priests on the other, were only individual specimens. But as parables of this sort, which set before us only one aspect of important truth, are exceedingly apt to be perverted by being interpreted as if they illustrated the whole truth, it may help to preserve us from error, if we distinctly define the limits within which its explanation must be kept.

Observe, then, in the first place, that the Lord does not express approval, and did not intend to approve, of the conduct of the first son, *in every respect*. When the father's command was given to him, he answered in the bluntest and most unqualified way, "I will not." There was no hypocrisy about him. He perhaps plumed himself on being an honest, outspoken fellow, who always said what he thought, and who hated to seem to be what he was not. Still, with all his frankness, he was disobedient; and we cannot suppose that the Saviour sanctioned that. This son is approved, not because he said "I will not," but because he repented of having said that, and proved the sincerity of his penitence by doing that which he had at first refused to do. Therefore, let no man suppose that it was in any way creditable to this son, that he said, "I will not." I am the more particular in insisting upon this, which may seem to some of you a mere truism, because there are many, even in our own times, who appear to think that the very open frankness of their iniquity is a virtue. From their mode of speech you might imagine that they believe they will be forgiven for being sinners, simply because they have never pretended to be saints. Just as sometimes, after a man has insulted you in the most blatant manner, he will speak as if he thought he was making a merit of his rudeness by saying, "I never go beating about the bush, I always say right out what I mean; I am none of your fawning flatterers, and if I have any thing against another I tell it to him straight;" so you will occasionally meet with one who appears to think that his sin ceases to be sin, because it is committed openly and without any profession of religion. "As for me," he says, "I make no pretence. What I seem to be, I am. Nobody can condemn me for being a hypocrite." And so, because he is not a hypocrite, he tries to make himself believe that he is not a sinner at all. Now, mark the fallacy that lies at the root of this delusion. The man supposes that it is only the making of an affirmative answer to God's commands, that involves the obligation to serve God. But is it really so? Am I not bound to honor Jehovah, and obey his commands, whether I make a promise to that effect or not? Does not the very making of such a promise spring out of the obligation that is felt prior to the making of it? God has a claim upon my service as my Creator, my Father, my Redeemer through Jesus Christ; and the very first question that faces me as a moral agent is this: "Will you acknowledge that claim, and serve Jehovah, or will you not?" If I will not, then my repudiation of it is not the less sinful because it is expressed openly, bluntly, and defiantly. Is a man any the less God's enemy because he is outspoken in his declaration of that fact? I grant, indeed, that, as between such a one and the hypocrite, the hypocrite is the more guilty of the two; but the greater guilt of hypocrisy must not blind the eyes of the abandoned man to the real and awful wickedness of his open iniquity.

Let it be noted, in the second place, that our Saviour does not approve of this son's conduct *as a whole*, as if it were the only good and proper way of meeting God's command, or as if there would be no danger in our trying to do all through exactly as he did. This man first disobeyed, then repented, and then obeyed. But because that is the only course which is here contrasted with that of the hypocrite, it does not follow that there is not a third which is better than either. It was well that this son repented; but it would have been better that he had never refused, but had gone right off to the vineyard, and joyfully commenced his work. It is needful to put this very plainly, because many, especially among the young, seem to set the conduct of this son before them *in its entirety* as the pattern which they mean to imitate. They think that they, too, will refuse for a while, promising to themselves that by and by they will repent; and their views are strengthened by many senseless and utterly immoral sayings current among men, such as these: "Let him sow his wild oats, and he will sober down by and by;" "Youth must have its fling," and the like. But while we are warranted to cherish the hope regarding such careless and abandoned sinners, that they may yet repent, and while we are commanded to labor and to pray with the view of bringing them to repentance, it would be an awfully perilous thing for any one to say deliberately, "*I will do just as this son did. I will take my own pleasure for a while, and then, when I've had my satisfaction, I will repent and do as God requires.*" In the case of this youth, there was no forelook to later

repentance, when the answer was first given. He spoke
for the moment merely; and there was, therefore, the
greater hope that he would ultimately bethink himself,
and turn from his evil way. But in the other case
there is a deliberate counting on the future; a wilful
putting of the soul into present danger, and a com-
pounding for that by the promise to itself of future
repentance: and these, when taken together, amount to
a "*tempting*" of the Holy Spirit which is dangerously
near the sin against the Holy Ghost. I know of no
peril more deadly than that; and just because of the
commonness of the sayings to which I have referred,
I would all the more emphatically warn you, my young
friends, of its insidiousness. Have nothing to do with
"*wild oats*" in any shape. You cannot dissever the
present from the future; and in the moral world, as in
the natural, you shall reap what you sow, *with an increase*. If you sow to the flesh, you will reap corruption, which is flesh in its most loathsome condition; if
you sow the wind, you will reap the whirlwind, which is
the wind in its most destructive violence; yea, even
although, like the first of these two sons, you should
afterward repent, you may depend upon it that God
will make you, in one form or another, to "possess the
sins of your youth." In the sorrowful remembrance of
the wasted past; in the deep and saddening conviction
that many precious opportunities have been irrecover-
ably lost; or in the consequences, mental, moral, or
physical, which your early follies will leave upon you,
God will make you to possess the sins of your youth.
But you may never repent. You may never have the
opportunity to do so; or, if you have, you may not
have the disposition to improve it, for sin may have
weakened your resolution, and taken your will captive.

Therefore let me urge you to give prompt, **present,** sincere obedience to Jehovah's call.

But looking now at the other son, I ask you to observe, in the third place, that our Lord does not design to condemn the making of a promise to God, when that is done sincerely and performed earnestly. This second son was not blamed because he said promptly, and apparently also cheerfully, "*I go, sir,*" but because he did not mean what he said. His purpose was to get for the moment the approval of his father, and at the same time to take his own way and enjoy his own pleasure. He represents the hypocrite, who seeks by a fair profession to combine the services of God and mammon. But because he is condemned for his hypocrisy, we must not suppose that it is wrong to confess that we are God's servants, *provided we do that sincerely.* Has not the Lord Jesus in many passages spoken of the duty of confessing him before men? and does not Paul in a well-known passage declare that "if we shall confess with our mouths the Lord Jesus, and shall believe in our hearts that God hath raised him from the dead, we shall be saved"?[1] It cannot be, therefore, that any thing in this parable should discourage the making of such a confession. What is here condemned is the making of it insincerely, — the saying of one thing by the lips, and of another thing in the heart and by the life. We should see to it, when we confess Christ, that we are acting a truthful part; but if we really love him, it is our duty and our privilege to confess him, and we shall find that strength and fellowship and happiness come to us in the wake of our doing so.

[1] Rom. x. 9.

But now, turning from the limits within which our interpretation of this parable must be kept, let us proceed to the consideration of those truths which, within these limits, it may be fairly regarded as enforcing.

I. And here, first, I mention the nature of the demand which God makes on every one to whom the gospel comes. "Go work to-day in my vineyard." Mark how practical true religion is: "*Go, work*." The test of sincerity is not in words, but in deeds; not in knowledge, but in the acting-out of our knowledge; not in profession, but in practice. The question of the Saviour to his followers is not, "What *say* ye more than others?" but, "What *do* ye more than others?" and on another occasion he speaks after this fashion: "If ye know these things, happy are ye if ye do them." Words are valuable only in so far as they are the truthful expression of an inward spirit, which will prompt also to appropriate deeds; and we can prove that we love God, only by serving him. Speech may be deceptive; indeed, a noted diplomat once said that the chief purpose of language is to conceal thought: but the habitual bent of the life is always a genuine index of the character. By works, then, we make manifest that we are the children of God. Observe, however, the expression which I have used. Works are the manifestation of our love to God, not the means of procuring his love for us. We labor, not to get God to love us, but because we already love him; and we love him because he first loved us. Or, to put it in another way: works are the indications that we possess true spiritual life, not the means of our becoming alive. We labor because we live, and not that we may be made alive.

Mark, again, the peculiar nature of the work by which

our love and life are to be manifested. "Go, work *in my vineyard*." Matthew Henry has said here very quaintly, "By the sin of Adam we were turned out to work upon the common, and to eat the herb of the field; but by the grace of our Lord Jesus we are called again to work in the vineyard." This labor consists in working out our own salvation, and building up our own character, according to the plan furnished by the Apostle Peter when he says, "Add to your faith virtue, and to virtue knowledge, and to knowledge temperance, and to temperance patience, and to patience godliness, and to godliness brotherly kindness, and to brotherly kindness charity."[1] Or, in another view, this labor is the cultivation to the fullest extent of that cluster of grapes which is the proper fruit of the true vine, and which Paul has thus enumerated: "love, joy, peace, long-suffering, gentleness, goodness, faith, meekness, temperance."[2] Nor is this all; for it is also real vineyard work to labor for the extension of the vineyard itself, by the diffusion of the gospel among those who know it not. By such works of faith, and labors of love, and patience of hope, we are to show that we are indeed the sons of God.

Mark, again, the promptitude of the obedience which is here required: "Go work *to-day*." "Now is the accepted time." There are only two passages, so far as I remember, in all the Scriptures, that refer to "to-morrow;" and they are these: "Boast not thyself of to-morrow, for thou knowest not what a day may bring forth." "Be not anxious for the morrow, for the morrow shall have anxiety enough for the things of itself. Sufficient unto the day is the evil thereof." And, though the meaning of each is distinct from that

[1] 2 Pet. i. 5, 6, 7.   [2] Gal. v. 22, 23.

of the other, yet they both agree in emphasizing the importance of *to-day*. By the work of the present, more than by the promises which we make for the future, do we make manifest what we are as in the sight of God; and if, when he says "to-day," we reply "*to-morrow*," then we are as really guilty of disobeying him, as if we had used the words of this son in the parable, and flatly answered, "I will not." Beloved, let us be faithful with ourselves here, and see if we are not involved in this condemnation. Are there not many among us who would shrink from saying to the Lord, "I will not," while yet we are habitually postponing the performance of duty, and are daily increasing our arrears of service to him? Which of us will dare to say that yesterday, for example, he left nothing undone of all that God in his providence put before him to be performed on his behalf? Let us be on our guard, therefore, in this matter; for procrastination grows upon us the more we yield to it. Our work accumulates, and our time for doing it diminishes, all because we are not fully alive to the importance of to-day. "To-morrow," says the proverb, "is the day on which idle men work, and fools reform." Let us show our industry by beginning to work for God now, and our wisdom by reforming at once, for still the command runs, "Go work *to-day;*" and evermore, as we waver in our obedience thereto, the Holy Ghost repeats the warning, "*To-day, if ye will hear his voice, harden not your hearts.*"

Finally, here mark the tender nature of the appeal which God makes to every man in this command: "*Son, go work!*" *Son?* Yes; for God is our Father. He has a father's right to our affection and obedience, especially if we confess that he has redeemed us from sin and ruin by the blood of Christ. True, we read of his having introduced us into "the glorious liberty of the children of God." But there is here no contradiction, for the true-hearted son delights to do his father's will, and in his estimation that service is perfect freedom. He accounts no sacrifice too great to be made, and no toil too severe to be undergone, in his service; and all this does not cease to keep hold of him when he comes to the discovery that God is his Father. His first utterance thereupon, like that of his Lord, is, "Wist ye not that I must be about my Father's business?" And still, as men seek to beguile him from his purpose, his reply is, "I must work the works of him that sent me, while it is day: the night cometh, when no man can work." Sonship is not incompatible with service. It only transmutes that service into joy. The heir-apparent to the British crown has for his motto the words, *Ich dien*, "I serve;" and only as he acts up to that noble ideal, will he prove himself worthy of the throne which he is one day to fill. Nay, higher yet, it is written of the Son of God, that, "though he were a Son, yet learned he obedience by the things which he suffered." So far, therefore, from being incompatible with sonship, service is its most loving expression; and we shall prove ourselves enemies and aliens if we refuse to render it. This is an unerring test by which we may determine whether or not we are the children of God; and it is important that we apply it faithfully, for only as we stand that test, shall we enjoy the fulfilment of the precious promise, "They shall be mine, saith the Lord, in the day when I make up my jewels; and I will spare them, as a man spareth his own son that serveth him."

II. But a second thing brought out in this parable is the danger connected with the making of an insincere confession of God. To the chief priests and elders the Saviour said, "The publicans and harlots go into the kingdom before you." He did not allege that it was impossible for them to enter it, or that their conversion was an utterly hopeless thing; but he gave them to understand that the difficulties in their way were greater than those which had to be encountered by the openly abandoned. Now, it is important to define the nature of these difficulties. They were not, to use a convenient though somewhat cumbrous phraseology, *objective*, or lying outside of themselves; but *subjective*, in the state of their own hearts. Outside of the soul of any sinner, there are no obstacles in the way of his salvation. But the particular condition of each sinner's heart determines for him the particular difficulties with which he has to contend in entering the kingdom by submitting himself to Christ; and what the Saviour here means to say is, that such difficulties are greater in the case of one who has made an insincere confession of submission to God than in that of open and abandoned transgressors. The state of soul produced by that insincerity makes it harder for him to enter the kingdom than it is for the publicans and the harlots to repent of their iniquities. For he is satisfied with himself; while they, for the most part, are filled with loathing of themselves. He thinks that he has done well because he has said, "I go, sir:" they know they have done ill because they have said so flagrantly, "I go not." He has deluded himself with the belief that he has done all that is required, when he has simply promised that he will do it, as many a man cheats himself with the notion that he has paid his debt when he has only given his bill for the amount: they are conscious that they have not only done nothing in the way of serving God, but that they have also committed grievous wickedness against him. Thus it comes, that when appeals to repentance are made by some faithful preacher, such as John the Baptist, to both alike, he complacently puts them from him, as not meant for him, because he has promised to do as God commands; while they are stirred up to cry, "What must we do to be saved?" and they give themselves no rest until they have returned unto the Lord. Self-righteousness is thus a greater obstacle to one's entering the kingdom than sinful indulgence, and there is more hope of the conversion of a great sinner than there is of that of a great Pharisee; or, in other words, it is a harder matter to get rid of righteous self than of sinful self.

But over and above that feeling of self-complacency which is produced by insincerity, we must not forget to mention that there is also a hardening influence connected with it, which tends to make the heart less receptive of the truth. It blunts the conscience; it dims the moral perceptions; it weakens the will; it paralyzes the energies. Indeed, we may say that there is perhaps no habit more subversive of all the nobler principles of our nature than that of continually saying, "I go, sir," without going after all. Still, let us be thankful that the salvation of such as are guilty of this habitual insincerity is not an utter impossibility. They may yet enter the kingdom if they will repent; and if, in describing the character of this second son in the parable, I have held up a mirror in which any one of you has seen himself, let such an one realize at once the danger of his position, and cry earnestly unto the Lord in David's prayer, "Unite my heart, and I will run in the way of thy commandments. I will praise thee, O Lord, with my whole heart."

III. But in this parable it is very clear, in the third place, that the Saviour meant to encourage sinners, even of the vilest description, to repent, and believe the gospel. "The publicans and harlots enter the kingdom:" there is, therefore, salvation for the chief of sinners. No guilt is too great to be washed away by the blood of Christ. No heart is too bad to be renewed by the Holy Spirit. Listen to these words: "Come now, and let us reason together, saith the Lord. Though your sins be as scarlet, they shall be as white as snow: though they be red like crimson, they shall be as wool." "He is able to save to the uttermost all that come unto God by him, seeing he ever liveth to make intercession for them;" and to the penitent thief who hung by his side the Lord Jesus said, "To-day shalt thou be with me in paradise." Therefore let no sinner despair. But, on the other hand, let no sinner presume or imagine, that, because it is said here that the publicans and harlots went into the kingdom before the chief priests and elders, therefore open sinners may be saved without repentance. This first son repented of his disobedience; and so it is only when a sinner repents, that he is forgiven and accepted. Very close is the relation which God has established between a sinner's turning from sin and receiving pardon. Take that matchless promise in the first chapter of the prophecies of Isaiah, which I have but now repeated, and in what connection do you find it? Here is the context: "Wash you; make you clean; put away the evil of your doing from before mine eyes; cease to do evil; learn to do well; seek judgment; relieve the oppressed; judge the fatherless; plead for the widow. Come now, and let us reason together." In the same way we have elsewhere in Isaiah this injunction: "Let the wicked forsake his way, and the unrighteous man his thoughts; and let him return unto the Lord, and he will have mercy upon him, and to our God, for he will abundantly pardon." So, too, the apostles everywhere preached repentance in connection with the remission of sins. If, therefore, we would be faithful, we must declare that there is salvation for the guiltiest and the vilest, if they will repent, and return to God through Jesus Christ. Not that their repentance deserves the pardon, but that there can be no pardon without repentance. Jesus Christ will save no man *in* his sins; but he will save any penitent, no matter how openly immoral he may have been, *from* his sins. Anew, therefore, I repeat the glad refrain of Peter's pentecostal sermon, "Repent and be baptized, every one of you, in the name of Jesus Christ, for the remission of sins, and ye shall receive the gift of the Holy Ghost." And what is it to repent? Let Bishop Wilberforce make answer: "It is to take the first turn to the right."

IX

THE WICKED HUSBANDMEN
Matthew 21:33-44

THIS parable, following close on that which we considered in our last discourse, deals with the same general subject; but it carries it to a higher application, and gives it a wider scope. The parable of the two sons exposes the treatment given by the chief priests and elders to John the Baptist; this of the wicked husbandmen holds up to view the rejection of Jesus himself by the Jewish people as a whole, and utters a solemn warning of the consequences that would ensue therefrom. The story is at once very simple and very sad. A wealthy householder, before setting out for a long absence from home, marked off a large space of ground suitable for a vineyard, planted it with vines, enclosed it with a hedge or a wall to keep out animals and marauders, digged in it a wine-press, or more properly a wine-fat, into which the juice of the grapes might flow, and built in it a tower for the accommodation of the watchers and laborers generally.[1] He did every thing, in short, that was necessary to make it a well-appointed vineyard, sparing neither labor nor expense to furnish it with the best in each department of cultivation. Having done all this, he let it out to husbandmen on certain stipulated terms. They were to have the full

[1] See Edersheim's Life and Times of Jesus the Christ, vol. ii. p. 422.

management of the vineyard, and he was to have a rental of some sort for their use of his property. Among the Jews, as Edersheim [1] tells us, "there were three modes of dealing with land. According to one of these, the laborers employed received a certain portion of the fruits, say a third or a fourth of the produce. In such cases it seems, at least sometimes, to have been the practice, besides giving them a portion of the produce, to provide also the seed (if it was a field), and to pay wages to the laborers. The other two modes of letting land were, either that the tenant paid a money rent to the proprietor, or else that he agreed to give the owner a definite amount of produce, whether the harvest had been good or bad." He adds, "There can scarcely be a doubt that it is the latter kind of lease which is referred to in the parable, the lessees being bound to give the owner a certain amount of fruits in their season."

After making such an arrangement, the owner went into a far country, much as one here might go to Europe for a long residence there; and while there he sent accredited agents, here called his servants, that they might receive in his behalf the stipulated portion of fruits. But the husbandmen had no intention of giving him any thing; and they cruelly maltreated his messengers, beating one, stoning another, and killing another. One would have thought that this would have provoked the proprietor to retaliate; but he simply sent other messengers of higher rank and greater importance than the former. These, however, were only similarly abused; and then, as a last resource, the householder said, "They will reverence my son." So he sent "his one son, his well beloved," as Mark has it; but his

[1] See Edersheim's Life and Times of Jesus the Christ, vol. ii. p. 423.

appearance only stirred the laborers to greater fury, for they said one to another, "This is the heir; come, let us kill him, and let us seize on his inheritance." "The owner is away," — as if they had exclaimed, — "he will never come back; if we kill his heir, there will be no one to dispute our claim to the property: therefore let us slay him, and take possession." So "they caught him, and cast him out of the vineyard, and slew him."

So far the story. Now turning to his hearers, the Lord asked, "When the lord, therefore, of the vineyard cometh, what will he do unto those husbandmen?" And they, apparently unconscious that they were pronouncing their own doom, replied, "He will miserably destroy those wicked men, and will let out his vineyard unto other husbandmen, which shall render him the fruits in their seasons." To this answer the Lord Jesus responded by making application to himself and them of a well-known passage in the Book of Psalms, and uttering a warning regarding the danger and destruction of those who persistently and defiantly rejected him. But we shall leave the consideration of these until we have settled the meaning of the parable to which they are appended.

The householder very clearly here, like the father in the former parable, is God. But what is the vineyard? A common answer is that it represents the Jewish Church, and there is no doubt that in Isaiah's beautiful allegory "the vineyard of the Lord of hosts is the house of Israel." So, again, the vine of the eightieth Psalm is the Jewish Church which was brought out of Egypt and planted in the Holy Land. And we cannot forget that the Lord Jesus himself represents the union between himself and his Church under this figure: "I am the vine, ye are the branches." But it is clear to me, in spite of all these analogies, that in this parable the vineyard with its appurtenances and belongings does not stand for the people at all. It rather signifies the special advantages and opportunities which were given to the people as the chosen seed, and in virtue of God's covenant with them. It would be running the parable into the ground, and allowing fancy to guide where reason alone should rule, if we were to undertake to say what is meant especially by the hedge, and what by the wine-fat, and what by the tower. We prefer, therefore, to content ourselves with the general assertion that the vineyard, with all in it, represents the *theocratic privileges* enjoyed by the Jewish nation under the Mosaic institute, the blessings which were peculiar to them above all other peoples on the face of the earth, and which came to them as the children of God's covenant.

Now, for these blessings they had to give a certain return. Privilege entails responsibility. The more one receives, the more he must account for. They who had enjoyed so many more favors at the hand of God than other nations, ought to have been just so much better than other nations, and ought to have cheerfully rendered to him the service which he sought. Holy lives, loving service, cheerful and devoted loyalty to himself, — these were the fruits God sought as the return for the giving of the theocracy and its blessings to them. Now, this interpretation of the vineyard as denoting the covenant advantages of the Jews, or what the Lord in the forty-third verse calls "the kingdom of God," as enjoyed by the Israelites, leads to the identification of the husbandmen with the Jewish people as a whole. Some have tried to restrict the reference of the husbandmen to the rulers and teachers among the Jews; but it was not from them alone that the kingdom was taken. It was from the Jewish nation as such; and therefore the nation as a whole, and not merely any one class in it, must here be symbolized by the husbandmen. But if that be so, it becomes easy to explain who the servants that were sent to claim the fruits for the householder represent; for, in this view of the parable, they stand for the prophets who came in Jehovah's name, at different stages in the history of Israel, and of whom many were grievously entreated at the hands of the people. Nor is it difficult to discover what, in this aspect of the case, is suggested by the removal of the householder from the vicinity of the vineyard into a far country; for, while it is true that God is everywhere present, it is also true that Jehovah in the early history of the Hebrew tribes was more conspicuously with and among them than he was at any subsequent stage of their national career. As Trench has finely said, "At Sinai, when the theocratic constitution was founded, and in the miracles which accompanied the deliverance from Egypt and the bringing into Canaan, the Lord may be said to have openly manifested himself to Israel, but then to have withdrawn himself for a while, not speaking again to the people face to face, but waiting in patience to see what the law would effect, and what manner of works the people would bring forth."[1] Or, as Goebel has expressed it, "He withdrew into expectant passivity, leaving room for the spontaneous development of the nation on the soil of the theocracy and under the influence of its institutions."[2]

But the result, as indicated by their treatment of

---

[1] Notes on the Parables, p. 197.
[2] Goebel's Parables of Jesus, p. 342.

his commissioned servants, was that they ungratefully rebelled against him. In the days of Elijah, Jezebel cut off the prophets of the Lord, and Ahab subjected Micaiah to the foulest indignity. In the reign of Joash, the people conspired against Zechariah the son of Jehoiada, on whom the Spirit of God came; and they stoned him with stones. Jeremiah was cruelly abused by those to whom he went as the messenger of the Lord; and the tradition has always been, that Isaiah was sawn asunder by the order of Manasseh. Thus the account given in the parable of the treatment of the servants by the husbandmen was literally true of the reception given by the Jewish nation to the prophets: "they beat one, and stoned another, and killed another." Last of all came the Son of God in the person of Jesus Christ, and him they crucified. There is thus a clear reference to himself in this part of the parable; and thereby the Lord at once indicates his knowledge of the designs of his enemies, and uses means if possible to bring them to a better mind. The words were spoken just two days after the triumphal entry into Jerusalem, and on the Tuesday of the crucifixion week: so we may be sure that they went right to the hearts of those who were already conspiring to bring about his death; and that enables us to understand how it came, that when, according to Luke, Jesus himself declared what the householder would do, in these words: "He shall come and destroy these husbandmen, and shall give the vineyard to others," they cried out in dismay, "God forbid!" They got just then a momentary sight of him and of themselves; but, alas! they deliberately closed their eyes again, and went defiantly on in the course that led to ruin both national and individual.

Here, then, is the interpretation of the parable: **The**

householder is God; the vineyard is the theocratic privileges enjoyed by those who were the chosen people of God, and as such were placed by him under the law of Moses; the husbandmen are the Jews themselves · the removal of the householder into a far country is the withdrawal of God from such open manifestation of himself as he made on Sinai, into " expectant passivity," waiting for the result to develop itself freely in the choice of the people themselves; the servants sent were the prophets, who were often cruelly maltreated by those to whom they were commissioned; the son is the Lord Jesus himself, the crucifixion of whom was the climax of the nation's iniquity, for which the kingdom of God was taken from it, and given to the Gentiles.

Now, with this key in our hands we shall be the better able to unlock the meaning of the solemn utterances which the Lord Jesus added to this probing parable. They are three. The first is a quotation from the hundred and eighteenth Psalm, which he very evidently appropriates to himself. If you look back to the beginning of the chapter, you will find there the account of his entrance in triumph into the temple, and of the offence which the chief priests and scribes took at the song of the children on that memorable occasion. Read verse 15: "And when the chief priests and the scribes saw the wonderful things that he did, and the children crying in the temple, and saying, Hosanna to the Son of David, they were sore displeased, and said unto him, Hearest thou what these say? And Jesus saith unto them, Yea: have ye never read, Out of the mouth of babes and sucklings thou hast perfected praise?" Now, the remarkable thing is, that from the same Psalm out of which the children took their song, the Lord extracts these words of reproof; as if he would say to them, "The children's instinct was correct when they greeted me with their joyful hosannas as the Son of David. I may not look like the Messiah now, but recall the words of that same ode in which they found their salutation. Is it not written there, The stone which the builders rejected, the same is become the head of the corner: this is the Lord's doing, and it is marvellous in our eyes? You may reject me; I know, indeed, that it is in your hearts to crucify me; and when you have succeeded in doing that, you think that there is nothing more to fear from me. But have a care: it is not the first time in your history that the rejected stone has been made at last the most important in the building. The words of the psalm, indeed, have become proverbial, but all previous fulfilments of the proverb have been but the prophecies and forecast shadows of that most terrible illustration of it, which shall be furnished by your rejection of me; for the cross will be but the lever that lifts me to the headship of the kingdom; and then" — and this is the second of the sayings which he has appended to the parable — "the kingdom of God shall be taken from you, and given to a nation bringing forth the fruits thereof." You have had your probation of privilege, but it is rapidly coming to an end; and if you persist for but a few days longer in the course which you are now pursuing, your limit will be reached, and the advantages which you have forfeited will be transferred to others. "From him that hath not, shall be taken away even that he hath." Thus in this saying there were enfolded the dethronement of the Jews from their pre-eminence among the nations, the withdrawal from them of their exceptional privileges, the destruction of their much-loved Jerusalem, and the calling of the Gentiles, — all because they

THE WICKED HUSBANDMEN 145

knew not the day of their visitation, and killed him, whom in their inmost hearts they had been compelled to recognize as the heir and representative of the King of kings.

Then, having another illustration suggested to him by the figure of the *stone*, he goes on to his third utterance: "And whosoever shall fall on that stone shall be broken; but on whomsoever it shall fall, it shall grind him to powder." First, the stone is a passive thing, lying, as it were, on the way, but yet so formidable and dangerous, that even to stumble over it would prove injurious to the man that falls upon it. Then, as if the vision of Nebuchadnezzar had risen up before him, and he actually saw the stone cut from the mountain without hands, and bounding down with ever-accelerating speed into the valley below, he adds, " but on whomsoever it shall fall, it will grind him to powder." Here, therefore, are two different treatments of the Lord, with their respective consequences, foreshadowed to us. The first is that of those who merely for a season stumble over certain difficulties regarding him. They are not satisfied, it may be, concerning his deity; they are offended perhaps, as even Peter was once, at the idea of his dying upon a cross; or they cannot unravel all the mystery of his atonement: therefore they do not yet accept him. That is bad. That is hurtful. They fall over the stone, and are broken. Not only are they still unsaved by him, but their consciences become blunted; they learn the habit of procrastination; their wills are enfeebled, and their hearts are hardened. If they will not accept this stone as the foundation on which to rear their characters, their whole moral natures cannot but be injured. For we must build either on Christ or on self. To build on Christ is to be founded on a rock, and to have the stability of that rock imparted to the fabric which we raise; but to build on self is to be founded on the sand, and when the storm comes there will be a dread catastrophe, and corresponding injury. Yet such injury may not be absolutely irreparable if at least it occur in time; for those who have been thus hurt may be stirred up thereby to alter the whole plan of their lives, and begin anew by the acceptance of Christ as their only Saviour and Sovereign, and in that case, though they can never be quite as they might otherwise have been, they shall be saved eternally.

But if one persistently and defiantly rejects Christ, and justifies thereby the Jews in their treatment of him, he does not fall over the stone, but the stone falls upon him, and he is eternally destroyed. "*Ground to powder*," — what a terrible expression! describing utter, hopeless, remediless perdition. One of the greatest of living English preachers has in this connection a very striking passage which I cannot refrain from quoting. "I remember," says Dr. McLaren of Manchester, "away up in a lonely Highland valley, where beneath a tall black cliff, all weather-worn and cracked and seamed, there lies at the foot, resting on the greensward that creeps round its base, a huge rock that has fallen from the face of the cliff. A shepherd was passing beneath it; and suddenly, when the finger of God's will touched it, and rent it from its ancient bed in the everlasting rock, it came down, leaping and bounding from pinnacle to pinnacle, — and it fell; and the man that was beneath it is there now, ground to powder. Ah, my brethren!" he proceeds, "that is not my illustration; that is Christ's. Therefore I say to you, since all that stand against him shall become as 'the chaff of the summer threshing-floor,' and be swept utterly away, make him the foundation on which you build; and when the rain sweeps away every refuge of lies, you will be safe and serene, builded upon the Rock of ages."[1]

Here, my hearers, I might well conclude; but I tarry only to condense the teachings of this solemn parable into three portable and practical remarks.

The first is, that the greatest privilege a man can enjoy is to have the kingdom of God intrusted to him. The Jews were the most favored people of antiquity. They had the oracles of God committed to them. When others were in darkness, they enjoyed the light of revelation; but, instead of thanking Jehovah for these things, they only plumed themselves upon them, as if, simply because they had received them, they were better than their neighbors. We condemn them for that; but let us take heed that we are not therein uttering our own doom. For we are now where they were, — nay, our privileges are vastly more exalted than theirs. What they had merely in type and symbol, we have in reality. They had but the Old Testament, we enjoy also the New; while the blessings of Palestine were as nothing compared with those of America. The kingdom of God has not merely come nigh us, but it is in the midst of us. From our very earliest years we have known all about the old, old story of Jesus and his love; and Christ has been proclaimed to us in sermons, and sung to us in songs, and commended to us in books, on every hand. We are tempted to say, What could God have done more for any people than he has done for us? We have touched the high-water mark of privilege; and there is not a sinner in the land who may not hear, if he chooses, of the great salvation.

[1] McLaren's Sermons, first series, p. 13.

You have heard of it often; you are hearing of it now. Will you realize that in so doing you are enjoying the very highest favor that a sinful man can know? There is nothing better that even God can give you, unless you are willing to accept the Saviour; and then he will come in and sup with you, and you with him.

But now, if this be so, it follows in the second place, that the greatest sin a man can commit is to reject Christ. That is the sin of sins, the condemning sin; and every man to whom the gospel is preached must either commit that sin, or accept the Lord as his Saviour. He cannot be neutral. He may try to hold the matter in suspense, like Pilate who said, "What shall I then do with Jesus who is called Christ?" but he must either accept or reject at last. He can do no otherwise; and if he rejects, he sins against the greatest grace and the brightest light.

Then, finally, there follows this terrible inference: The darkest doom is that of those who are guilty of this greatest sin. It will be more tolerable for Sodom and Gomorrah in the day of judgment than for us, if we persistently reject Christ and his salvation. "On whomsoever" that stone "shall fall, it will grind him to powder." O beloved! will you ponder these words well, and, if you have not yet received Christ, open you hearts this very moment, and let him in?

X

THE ROYAL MARRIAGE FEAST

Matthew 22:1-14

THIS parable, like that of the wicked husbandmen, belongs to the Passion Week of our Lord, and deals with the same general subject which it illustrates. But as that was a development of the thought which underlay the story of the two sons, so this is, in many respects, an advance upon that of the wicked husbandmen. What in that was represented as a repudiation of responsibility, is in this portrayed as a despising of favor; the son of the householder, in that, is the king's son in this; while, in the episode of the wedding garment, the application of the principle beneath the parable is widened so as to include under it not only those who refuse the invitations of the gospel, or contemptuously ignore them, but also those who insult the giver of these invitations, even when they profess to be accepting them. The former parable stopped with the declaration that the vineyard would be given to other laborers; but this goes forward to the time when that prophecy should be fulfilled, and has a word of warning to those who should then come into the enjoyment of the privileges which the Jews had forfeited. We cannot read it, therefore, without feeling, that, as the crisis of the cross is drawing near, the Lord "reveals himself in ever-clearer light as the central person of the king-

dom," and sets before his hearers not only the greatness
of the privilege, but also the vastness of the peril, that
is involved in the possession of the gospel.

The parable may be described as a drama in three
acts. A king is about to give a splendid feast in
honor of the marriage of his son. Great preparations
had been made for the occasion. Long before the appointed day, invitations had been sent to those whose
presence at the banquet was desired, to notify them
of the time which had been fixed, so that they might
know to keep clear of all other engagements, and be
ready to celebrate the wedding with every demonstration of enthusiasm. Then, on the morning of the day
on which the festival was to be held, and in accordance
with a custom prevalent in the East, servants were
sent out to " call them that were bidden." But they
were met with a blunt refusal. Those who had been
invited " would not come." It was a disappointment to
the king: yet perhaps they had acted ignorantly and
thoughtlessly, so he gave them an opportunity for re-
consideration; and later in the day he sent other servants to them, to say in his name to them, " Behold, I
have prepared my dinner; my oxen and my fatlings are
killed, and all things are ready: come unto the marriage." But they made light of the whole affair, as if
it were a matter of no importance whatever. Some of
them went on with their business on the farm and in
the store, as usual; deeming it of more consequence by
far to make a little gain, than to accept the royal invitation. Others of them were actuated by such bitter
animosity to the monarch, that " they took the servants,
and entreated them spitefully, and slew them." This
conduct on the part of those whom he was seeking to
honor and bless was of such a nature that the king

could not pass it by with impunity; therefore "he sent his armies, and destroyed those murderers, and burned up their city." This is the first act of the drama; and the curtain falls upon a scene not unlike that which was witnessed when the troops of Titus stormed the walls of Jerusalem, and gave its gorgeous temple to the flames.

But the feast was not to be postponed because those first invited to it would not come to its enjoyment; and therefore, in the second act, we hear the king commanding his servants to go into the highways, and bid to the marriage "as many as they could find." Then we see the servants going forth, and gathering men of every class and condition, irrespective of former character or present rank, and asking them to the marriage. Next we behold the motley multitude trooping into the palace, and taking their places at the tables which had been prepared. This is the second act; and the curtain falls upon a festive hall, crowded with guests from the east and from the west, from the north and from the south, all apparently filled with gladness at the grand event they celebrate.

But once again the curtain rises. The scene is the same; but the king has come in to look upon the guests, and his entrance is the signal for the outburst of rapturous applause. When that has ceased, the royal eye scans the tables, and marks the appearance of each guest. For a time nothing but joy is seen upon his countenance; but by and by it assumes an aspect of sorrow, mingled with sternness and decision, for he sees one guest "who had not on a wedding garment." These garments he had himself provided: why should any one refuse to wear them? So he went to the person who had so insulted him, and said, "Friend, how camest thou in hither not having a wedding garment?" and he was speechless. Then said the king to the servants, "Bind him hand and foot, and take him away, and cast him into outer darkness; there shall be weeping, and gnashing of teeth." For it is one thing to be called to the feast, and another thing to accept the call in its true and proper significance. "Many are called, but few are chosen." Such is the story.

Now, in the interpretation it will be well to preserve the division into three parts which I have indicated. Of the first part, then, the central idea is the invitation of certain parties to a royal marriage-feast. The relation of the Jews to their God is, all through the Old Testament, spoken of under the figure of the marriage covenant: and in the marriage of the king's son here, we have hinted at the truth which is broadly stated by Paul when he speaks of the Church as the wife of the Lord Jesus; and by John, when he calls it "the bride, the Lamb's wife." But it will be observed, that, as the parable proceeds, the marriage idea drops almost entirely out of sight, and that of the feast alone remains; for the main design of the Lord was to teach certain truths under the similitude of a banquet. What, then, does this feast represent? Plainly, whatever it may be used here to symbolize, a feast suggests provision, excellent in quality, abundant in quantity, and varied in character, in the enjoyment of which a multitude of guests have great fellowship and happiness. Now, nothing will fit that description better than the spiritual banquet which is set before men in the blessings of the gospel. There we have presented to us, pardon of sin, favor with God, peace of conscience, the exceeding great and precious promises of the Scriptures, access to the throne of grace, the comforts of the

Holy Spirit, and the well-grounded assurance of eternal life in heaven. In the common participation of *these* things, believers have high and holy communion with each other and with God, which fills their souls with the purest and most exalted happiness; so that to them the ancient oracle has been fulfilled, and "in this mountain shall the Lord of hosts make unto all people a feast of fat things, a feast of wines on the lees, of fat things full of marrow, of wines on the lees well refined."[1]

This, then, being the feast, the interpretation of the other matters is not difficult. The king is God, and the son is the Lord Jesus Christ, whose marriage is his union to the Church, which he is ultimately to present to himself "without spot or wrinkle or any such thing." The first bidding to this feast was given to the Jews by the prophets, under the Old-Testament dispensation, in appeals of which those in the fifty-fifth chapter of Isaiah may be taken as a specimen. The servants sent forth on the feast-day, to call them that were bidden, are the preachers in the lifetime of our Lord upon the earth, and may be held as including John the Baptist, the Lord himself, and especially the twelve apostles and the seventy disciples, who, commissioned by the Saviour, went forth through the length and breadth of Palestine, telling their countrymen everywhere that the kingdom of God was come nigh them; and the result of *their* mission as a whole, though there were here and there individual exceptions, is only too truly described in the graphic words, "they would not come." The "other servants" sent out later in the day to say, "Behold, I have prepared my dinner; my oxen and my fatlings are killed, and all things are ready: come unto

Isa. xxv. 6.

the marriage," — are the preachers of the gospel after Pentecost, who were commissioned to proclaim salvation full and free to all who would believingly and penitently accept its blessings, but who still for a season restricted their labors to the Jews; and, though they met with signal successes in many places, yet the result of their work as a whole was that the Jewish nation as such rejected their overtures. Some did so in the most disdainful manner, not deeming them worth any attention whatsoever, because their minds were exclusively devoted to worldly affairs; but others were exasperated by the very offers, because the presentation of pardon involved in it a tacit accusation of sin, and they turned upon the preachers with persecuting fury, stoning Stephen, killing James with the sword, and haling others, women as well as men, to prison, — all of which may be found described in the early chapters of the book of the Acts of the Apostles. Nay, we need not confine ourselves to the early chapters; for all through that book we see that the Jews, to whom Paul everywhere made the first offer of the gospel, were always the most bitter, the most implacable, and the most pertinacious persecutors of the apostles and their assistants.

The destruction of those who had maltreated the servants, and the burning-up of their city, represent the rejection of the Jews, which culminated in the overthrow of Jerusalem, when the Roman armies, which were "the rod of God's anger," took away the place of the Jewish nation, and scattered the people over the world. Thus far, therefore, the parable of the marriage-feast runs parallel with that of the wicked husbandmen.

But now, in the mission of the servants to the highways, there is superadded the calling of the Gentiles. The wedding *must* be furnished with guests; and therefore, though the Jews despised the invitation, others were called in their room. As Paul said to his fellow-countrymen in the synagogue of the Pisidian Antioch, "It was necessary that the word of God should first have been spoken to you; but seeing ye put it from you, and judge yourselves unworthy of everlasting life, lo! we turn to the Gentiles;"[1] and they, or at least many of them, gladly received its message of mercy. This is the second part of the parable.

Yet a warning had to be given to them also, and this is furnished in the concluding section of the story. To understand it thoroughly, we must believe that the not unusual custom of providing the guests with the required wedding garment had been followed by the host, but that this man had refused to avail himself of the offer, and had defiantly and contemptuously pushed past the attendants, and taken his place at the table, altogether disregarding the commands of the monarch, and thinking perhaps that his own dress was too good to cover. As a recent writer has said,[2] "Similar audacity in entering a king's presence without putting on the robe sent by him for that purpose has been known to cost a prime minister his life. A traveller who was invited, with the ambassadors he accompanied, to the table of the Persian king, says, 'We were told by the officer, that we, according to their usage, must hang the splendid vests that were sent us from the king, over our dresses, and so appear in his presence. The ambassadors at first refused; but the officer urged it so ear-

[1] Acts xiii. 46.
[2] The Parables as recorded by Matthew, by Marcus Dods, D.D., pp. 224, 225.

nestly, alleging, as also did others, that the omission would greatly displease the king, since all other envoys observed such a custom, that at last they consented, and hanged, as we did, the splendid vests over their shoulders.'" Thus this rejection of the preferred garment by this man in the parable indicated a lack of sympathy with the giver of the feast, and a positive disaffection toward him, as really as the refusal of the invitation by the others had done; and so a punishment equally severe with that which had been meted out to them was visited on him, for he was excluded from the feast,—put out into the darkness of the night, to misery, unsheltered and unrelieved.

Now, what does this wedding garment represent? Many have been forward to answer that it symbolizes the robe of Christ's all-perfect righteousness; but my conviction is, that its significance goes deeper even than that. When Paul exhorts the Romans to "put on the Lord Jesus Christ," he is urging them to holiness of character, rather than to become partakers of the justifying righteousness of Christ; and in that injunction, as it seems to me, we have the interpreting clause of this wedding garment. The insisting upon the wearing of this festive dress is thus, as Goebel has expressively put it,[1] "nothing but the requirement, indispensably grounded in the ethical nature of the kingdom of God, that every one who would actually have part in its blessedness [should] acquire the corresponding moral character, and therefore obtain the moral righteousness that corresponds to the holy will, supreme in God's kingdom." In this view of the case, therefore, the refusing to wear that garment indicates "the want of a moral character and walk corresponding to God's holy

[1] Goebel on the Parables, p. 374.

will." The garment, therefore, is a character consistent with the acceptance — simple, sincere, and loyal — of the gospel of Christ. For there is no true acceptance of the gospel where there is no beginning of holiness, and no growth in likeness to God himself; according as Paul has said, "Know ye not that the unrighteous shall not inherit the kingdom of God? Be not deceived: neither fornicators, nor idolaters, nor adulterers, nor effeminate, nor thieves, nor covetous, nor drunkards, nor revilers, nor extortioners shall inherit the kingdom of God."[1] It is one thing to profess to accept the gospel: it is another thing to accept it in reality. It is one thing to *say* that you are a Christian, and another to *be* a Christian indeed. It is one thing to be called, and another thing to respond to that call whole-heartedly and in its entirety, so as to make manifest that we are "called, choice, and faithful."

Such is the simple yet solemn explanation of this important parable. Its one great lesson is, that the enjoyment of privilege does not insure the improvement of privilege; and its one terrible warning is, that the abuse of privilege will result in the condemnation of God's wrath. These principles are applied, first, to the case of the Jews, who for their continued resistance to God's invitations were rejected at last by God, and given over to destruction; and, second, to the Gentiles, who are thereby informed that despite the gathering of all classes into the kingdom which the Jews had forfeited, every one who has not a character in harmony with God's will be cast out into perdition. And the fact that only a single guest was thus discovered and treated gives awful emphasis to the truths that we have to do with God as individuals, and not as classes merely,

---

[1] 1 Cor. vi. 9, 10.

and that not even one, without the garment of holiness, will be able to conceal himself among the other members of the kingdom, from the all-searching eye of the eternal King.

But now, leaving the drapery of the parable, and its original application to the Jews and Gentiles, as such, let us consider very briefly the four different ways of treating God's invitations in the gospel which are here set before our view.

First, we have it complacently ignored by those who went their ways to their farms and to their merchandise. Now, on a superficial examination, one is apt to imagine that those who act in this fashion are less guilty than the remnant who despitefully entreated the servants and slew them, and that, consequently, they are not in such great danger as these others. But both of these ideas are mischievous and untrue. Look first at the matter of their guilt, and I am sure I am not wrong in affirming that we feel it a greater insult to be slighted than to be opposed. He who ignores me altogether does thereby say in effect that I am not worthy of his notice; and I feel that to be a greater contempt of me than if he sought to treat me with violence. But man is made in the image of God; and it is therefore probable that the insult to his grace is felt by him to be greater in the case of those who simply "make light of it," than in that of those who openly and defiantly reject it. Nay, is not something like that involved in the Saviour's words to the angel of the church at Laodicea: "I would thou wert cold or hot; so because thou art lukewarm, and neither cold nor hot, I will spew thee out of my mouth"?[1] He prefers an open enemy to one

---

[1] Rev. iii. 15, 16.

who treats him with indifference. Now, carry that principle out, and you come to the conclusion that to treat God's overtures in the gospel as not worth your notice is a more serious offence, in his eyes, than it is to attack him with open and avowed enmity. Yet how many are thus despising the gospel and the gospel's Lord! Jesus stands knocking at the door of their hearts, sometimes through conscience, and sometimes through trial, sometimes through the spoken words of his messengers, and sometimes through the still small voice of his Spirit; but they heed him not. They go on with their business, their pleasure, their sins, just as if he were not there. They use him in such a way as would be insulting to a fellow-man, and then solace themselves with the opiate that they have not rejected him, and so their guilt cannot be great. Friends, it is a delusion of the Devil thus to think. Awake, I beseech you, to the real nature of the case, and beware of doing dishonor thus to the King of kings!

But it is equally untrue that he who thus slights the message of God's grace is in smaller danger than others. He who neglects a warning, equally with him who opposes the messenger that gives the warning, leaves the purport of it unheeded, and becomes a victim to his folly. If I were in a boat on the river in the rapids, it would not be necessary, to insure my destruction, that I should enter into violent controversy with those who would urge me from the shore, to take heed and come to land: all I should have to do would be to shut my ears to their entreaty, and leave myself alone; the current would do the rest. Neglect of the gospel is thus just as perilous as the open rejection of it. Indeed, half the evils of our daily life in temporal things are caused by neglect; and countless are the souls who are lost for this same cause. Leave your farm for a little, then; let your merchandise alone for a season; settle first, and before all things else, what you will do with this invitation which God has given you to the gospel banquet: then, that accepted, your farm will become to you a section of God's vineyard, and your business will be a means of glorifying him.

But, in the second place, we have the gospel-offer violently rejected. The remnant despitefully entreated and slew the servants of the king. That is no longer common among us. There have been times when they who sought to preach the gospel did so at the risk of their lives; but those days, thank God, are gone, never, as we hope, to return again. Yet there is still a violent rejection of the gospel, common among certain classes. There are some who are open infidels, and decry every thing that is associated with the Church of Christ. They will not listen with patience to its ministers, and they take every opportunity of setting themselves up against their message. Oh that they would hear the voice which arrested the persecuting Saul on the way to Damascus! "It is hard for thee to kick against the goads." The goads are uninjured, but what of your feet the while? You cannot harm the gospel, but you can harm and you are harming your own souls. It may seem easy to oppose the messenger; but it is another thing to set yourselves up against Him by whom he is commissioned, and that is what you do in opposing the gospel invitation. Why will you thus break yourselves by rushing against the thick bosses of the Almighty's buckler? Bethink yourselves therefore, while ye may; accept the proffered favor now, lest at length ye be overtaken with swift destruction as the voice of the Almighty cries, "Behold, ye despisers, and wonder, and perish." Ah, what words are these: "He sent forth his armies, and destroyed those murderers, and burned up their city"! And if God spared not the ancient people of his love and choice when they rejected his own Son, take heed lest he also spare not thee.

We have here, thirdly, the inconsistency and insolence of the man who professed to accept the invitation, and yet failed to comply with the conditions on which alone true acceptance of it was possible. He pushed into the festive hall without having on a wedding garment. So there are to-day many who have nominally accepted Christ, while yet it is evident, from the absence of the holiness which he requires, that they are really rejecting him. This comes nearer home to many of us, perhaps, than either of the other cases which I have specified. For the Church of Christ has won for itself respectability, and importance in the world; and connection with it is, in itself, a sort of certificate of standing and reputation in the community: so that men may be tempted to join themselves with it for the temporal benefits which it may bring, and without giving any heed to the requirements which the Lord Jesus demands of its members. They may profess to accept his invitation, and even take their places at his table, without having the character which is a constant accompaniment of the sincere reception of his grace. As one [1] has thoughtfully said here, "conformity to God, ability to rejoice with God and in God, humble and devoted reverence, a real willingness to do honor to the King's Son, — these are the great attainments. But

[1] Dods on the Parables, as before, p. 228.

these constitute the wedding garment, without which we cannot remain in his presence, or abide his searching gaze. It will come to be a matter between each one of you singly and him; and it is the heart you bear towards him, that will determine your destiny. No mere appearance of accepting his invitation, no associating of yourself with those who love him, no outward entrance into his presence, no making use of the right language, is any thing to the purpose. What is wanted is a profound sympathy with God, a real delight in what is holy, a radical acceptance of his will. In other words, and as the most untutored conscience might see, what is wanted is a state of mind in you which God can delight in, and approve of, and hold fellowship with."

Now, the acceptance of the gospel invitation in that state of mind; the acceptance of it really, sincerely, whole-heartedly, — is the fourth way of dealing with it that is set before us in the parable; and that state of mind he will give to us, even as the king here provided the wedding garments. The invitation is to all, without limitation or restriction, bad or good, old or young, of whatever color or nation. All are called; but they only truly accept, who, in so doing, yield themselves up to God, to be as he wills, to do as he commands, to live as he ordains. For this feast is not a thing for an hour or two, but for a lifetime, nay, for an eternity; and we could not endure to be with God, if we were not also growing in likeness to God. Thus, from another side of the subject, the truth impressed upon us by the episode of the wedding garment is the same as Jesus unfolded to Nicodemus : " Except a man be born again, he cannot see the kingdom of God." You cannot have the forgiveness without the purity, the happiness without the holiness, the feast without the garment; but when you are ready to submit yourselves to the great law of the kingdom, which links privilege and character indissolubly together, then you may have both.

XI

THE TEN VIRGINS

Matthew 25:1-13

THE primary reference of this parable is to the second coming of Christ, and it was designed to enforce the lesson of constant watchfulness for that event. In the discourse which precedes this chapter, our Lord, while speaking most unqualifiedly of the certainty of his coming, and declaring that the time of it was known only to the Father, had repeatedly emphasized the statement that it should take the world by surprise, so that his own people ought to be always in readiness to meet him. That was the point to which his exhortations tended, and that also is the pivot on which the issues of the parable turn; for the unexpectedness of the appearance of the bridegroom revealed at once the difference between the two groups of virgins.

The story itself need not detain us long, for it is so perfect in its simplicity that nothing is required to aid us in its comprehension. Any attempt to tell it in other words would only produce a weak dilution of the original narrative, and all efforts at pointing out its beauties would be like holding up a taper to display the glory of the sun. It is so realistic in its details as to give an accurate description of an Eastern marriage-procession, and it may well enough have been founded on some actual history. But what can equal the group-

ing of the various figures; the startling suddenness of
the midnight cry; the haste of the surprised sleepers;
and the sadness of the disappointed ones, as they cry
with piercing earnestness, " Lord, Lord, open to us "?
Even as a work of art, this parable is faultless as its
author; and though there were no spiritual meaning
throbbing beneath it, we could not but be impressed
with its simple naturalness, its rapid movement, its tra-
gic pathos, and its silent close as the midnight gloom
folds in upon and hides the sadness of those who are
shut out. When, however, we go deeper into it, and
discover its spiritual significance, we find ourselves
concerned; and we have no time for admiring the
beauties of the parable, because of the pressing and personal importance of the truths which it suggests. It
shall be my aim now to set these before you as briefly
and pointedly as possible. I shall not attempt to give
a meaning to every minute detail of the story, but content myself with setting before you, in a few pertinent
remarks, what I judge to be the pith and marrow of its
instruction.

I. Let us observe, then, in the first place, that we have
here two characters contrasted. Of the ten virgins, five
were wise, and five were foolish. Now, that we may
define the difference between them, it is needful that
we have first a clear conception of the things in which
they were alike. Note, then, that they all had some
knowledge of, and regard for, the bridegroom, and desired to honor him by going forth to meet him as he led
home his bride. Note, further, that they all had lamps
which at the moment were burning. Note, once more,
that while the bridegroom tarried they all slumbered
and slept. Not until his coming was announced did

the difference between them develop itself. But then it was seen, that some of them had prudently provided for certain contingencies by taking with them a reserve supply of oil, while others had contented themselves with simply filling their lamps. Now, it is indispensable to a right understanding of the parable, that we settle plainly what is meant in the one case by the presence, and in the other by the absence, of this store of oil. Clearly, in all outward things the wise and the foolish virgins were alike. The difference between them was internal. But what, precisely, was it? The going out with a lamp is commonly understood to mean the making of a profession, while the absence of the reserve store of oil is supposed to signify the want of sincerity in that profession. The foolish virgins are thus held to represent hypocritical adherents of Christ, while the wise are taken to signify genuine disciples.

But this restriction of the oil in reserve, to sincerity, seems to me to narrow unduly the scope of the parable. For the foolish virgins had a real regard, such as it was, for the bridegroom: they had actually gone out so far to meet him, and they were dreadfully disappointed by their exclusion from the feast. They did not feign any of these things. There was a genuineness about them, so far as they went; only they did not go far enough. Hence I cannot restrict the reference of this part of the story to deliberate hypocrites. Indeed, I believe that the number of those who make a Christian profession by connecting themselves with the visible church, while yet they consciously design to impose upon its officebearers, is comparatively small; and therefore, if we confine the warning conveyed in the fate of the foolish virgins to them, I greatly fear that many whom it was designed to arouse may fail to perceive its reference to them, and may sleep on in security despite its call to watchfulness. I am disposed, therefore, to regard the foolish virgins as symbolizing those who have had some feelings of attachment to the Lord Jesus, and certain impulses Christ-ward to which they yielded at the time; but they were not constant. Their emotion was a real thing, and when they were acting upon it you could not call them hypocrites; but it was not the right thing. They were animated by impulse alone, not by principle or conviction. Their religion did not go down into the lowest depths of their nature, but was rather a thing of surface. It went down a little way, but it did not go the whole way; and therefore, when it was put to the proof, it failed. Thus I should identify the foolish virgins with those who in the parable of the sower are represented by the seed "which fell upon rocky ground where it had not much earth, and forthwith it sprung up because it had no deepness of earth; and when the sun was up it was scorched, and *because it had no root* it withered away;" and of whom our Lord himself thus gives the description, "He that received the seed into rocky places, the same is he that heareth the word, and anon with joy receiveth it; yet hath he not root in himself, but dureth for a while; for when tribulation or persecution ariseth because of the word, by and by he is offended."[1] Here, you observe, there was a real reception of the seed, and a real growth so far; and so, when a profession was made, you could not call it hypocritical. But it was not abiding. It wanted depth. It had no root; or, in the imagery of the parable before me, there was no reserve of oil from which to replenish the lamp.

So, again, you have the same phase of character

[1] Matt. xiii. 5, 6, 20, 21.

hinted at in the Lord's words as recorded by Luke:[1] "For which of you, intending to build a tower, sitteth not down first, and counteth the cost, whether he have not sufficient to finish it? lest haply, after he have laid the foundation, and is not able to finish it, all that behold it begin to mock him, saying, This man began to build, and was not able to finish. Or what king, going to make war against another king, sitteth not down first, and consulteth whether he be able with ten thousand to meet him that cometh against him with twenty thousand?" Now, that was precisely the case of these foolish virgins. They had not thought of the possibility of the bridegroom's delay. They had not sufficiently counted the cost; and so they had nothing in reserve on which they could fall back, and by which they could be sustained through a time of emergency.

But if that be so, you are ready to ask how it comes that this particular difference is set forth here by the having, or the not having, of oil in reserve. Now, the answer to that must be, that the shape of the analogy is determined by the character of the story, so that what in the parable of the sower is indicated by the having of no root, is here portrayed by the having of no oil. Yet it is interesting to note, that throughout the Scriptures oil is used to represent the Holy Spirit, and that in their union to the Holy Spirit, formed by their faith in Christ, and maintained by their constant study of his word, their habitual dependence on him in prayer, and their continuous obedience to his commands, believers are represented as having that unfailing supply of strength by which they are sustained in every duty and prepared for every emergency. As in Zechariah's vision[2] the two olive-trees stood, one on each side of

[1] Luke xiv. 28-32. [2] Zech. iv. 2-4, 11, 12.

the golden lamp, emptying into its bowls the oil out of themselves, and thus sustaining its never-failing light; so the Holy Spirit in the believer's heart gives him grace sufficient for him in every hour of need.

The separate vessel in which this oil was carried by the wise virgins must not so far mislead us as to induce us to believe that this oil is something outside of the believer. It is rather the reserve force of character in the Christian himself, which has been accumulated by him through his constant faith in Christ and obedience to him, whereby he has maintained unbroken his union to the Holy Ghost. His religion has a root in principle and conviction, which draws its sustenance from the Lord himself. It has been clearly understood, intelligently received, and deliberately maintained. It may have had little of the effervescence of emotional excitement about it at the first, but there was a deep determination in his soul. He has forecast the future, and, knowing his own weakness, he has sought ever to hold fast by the strength of the Omnipotent, so that he has been able to stand the strain of every storm. You see, then, wherein the difference between these two characters lies. It is not in sincerity so much as in constancy; not in leaf so much as in root; not in emotion so much as in principle; not in surface so much as in depth; not in the manifestation of character at the moment, so much as in the reserve force of character that can meet any contingency.

II. Now, this analysis of the difference between the two classes of characters here symbolized prepares the way for the second remark which is suggested by the parable; namely, that character is revealed by crisis. "At midnight there was a cry made, Behold, the bridegroom cometh: go ye out to meet him;" and this startled the virgins from their slumber. No blame is here attached to them for having fallen asleep. Both classes, wise and foolish alike, were folded in unconsciousness; but this apparently was necessary, in order that both alike should be taken unawares. Again, it is, for the purposes of exposition, immaterial whether the coming of the bridegroom be interpreted to mean his appearance at the end of all things, or, as some have preferred to understand it, his coming to begin a personal reign upon the earth: the principle involved is, that he will come unexpectedly, and that the suddenness of his appearance will be a test of character. These virgins were all taken by surprise; and that revealed at once which of them were prepared, and which of them were not prepared, to meet the bridegroom.

The great truth here taught, therefore, is that character is revealed by emergency. It is in moments of surprise that a man's true self comes out to view. He is the ablest general who can in an instant find some resource when an ambushed foe starts up before him. He is the most skilful mariner, who, in sudden extremity, can rise to the occasion, and bring his vessel and his crew safely into port. Nothing will more correctly reveal what is in a man, than the coming upon him of some crushing and unlooked-for crisis. Let it be temporal ruin by the failure of all his calculations, or the disappointment of all his hopes; let it be the entrance of the death-angel into his home, and the removal from it of his nearest and dearest earthly friend; let it be his own prostration by some serious illness which puts him face to face with his dissolution: and forthwith the extent of his resources is unfolded, and it is at once discovered both by others and by himself, whether he is animated by unfailing faith in the Lord Jesus Christ, and sustained by the grace of the Holy Spirit, or whether he has been deceiving himself, and all the while relying on some other support. It was a shrewd remark of Andrew Fuller, that a man has only as much religion as he can command in trial. Let us therefore look back upon the past, and analyze our experience at such testing times as those to which I have referred. We have all had them. We have all heard already, in some form or other, this midnight cry, "Behold, the Bridegroom cometh;" for, in every such surprise as those which I have described, Jesus was coming to us. How did we meet him then? Did our lamps go out? or were we able to trim them, and keep them burning brightly all through? Oh, if by any such event we discovered our utter resourcelessness, let us betake ourselves now to Christ, that he may thoroughly renew us by his Holy Spirit, and so prepare us for that last and solemnest crisis when over the graves of the slumbering dead the archangel shall cry out, "Behold, the Bridegroom cometh," and all shall arise to stand before his great white throne. In mercy these minor surprises have been sent to show ourselves to us before the last and greatest one. Let us see to it, therefore, that we learn true wisdom from them, and so forecast the future as to prepare for it by maintaining unbroken fellowship with the Holy Spirit.

III. But now, in the third place, let us observe, as suggested by this parable, that character is a personal thing, and cannot be given by one man to another, but must be acquired and manifested by each one for himself. In the moment of urgency, the foolish said unto the wise, "Give us of your oil, for our lamps are going out." But the wise answered, "Not so, lest there be not enough for us and you; but go ye rather to them that sell, and buy for yourselves." In the house of a well-known citizen of Boston, there is an exquisite group in marble, representing the wise and foolish virgins. The wise is kneeling, in the act of trimming her lamp; and the foolish, with a face full of the most pathetic entreaty, seems begging from her a share of the oil which she is pouring in to feed the flame; but her sister, with a look of inexpressible sadness, and her hand uplifted as if to guard her treasure, is as if she were saying, "*Not so.*" It is a touching rendering of the parable; and, as I looked at it, I was not surprised to be told that a famous New-England essayist had said, as he was gazing at it, "*She should have given her the oil.*" Who has not often sympathized with that feeling as he read the parable? We are apt to think that the five sisters were just a little stingy, and that what seems to be their selfishness was not at all in keeping with the benevolence which the gospel enjoins. But, not to insist upon the fact that it is impossible to construct an allegory which will hold in every particular, the answer made by the owner of the group to the man of genius is conclusive. "If," said he, "you and your neighbor have each signed a bill for a certain sum to fall due on a certain date, and you by dint of economy and perseverance have been able to lay by just enough to meet your own obligation, while your neighbor, wasting his hours on trifles, has made no provision for the day of settlement; and if, on the morning on which the bills fall due, he should come, beseeching you to give him some of your money to help him to pay his debt, — would you give it him?" That is a pecuniary illustration; and there is no evading the force of the argument, even when it is so put. But the parable treats of character; and that may be always labelled "*not transferable*," for its qualities cannot be given by one man to another, even if he were ever so willing to part with them. You cannot give me your patience to support me in the hour of my anguish. I cannot give you my courage to fortify you for the discharge of dangerous duty. There is much, indeed, that we can and ought to do for each other. We may pray for each other. We may direct the anxious one to Christ. We may sympathize with the sufferer in his time of trial. We may, through long years of intimate companionship, even do much to help to form the character of a friend. But we cannot give to another the qualities which we ourselves possess, but in which he is deficient; for these are not like oil or wine or money, which can be passed from hand to hand. They are a man's own untransferable possession, and that is the truth which is emphasized by the act of the wise virgins in refusing to share their oil with their foolish sisters. This is a matter far too little thought of by us all. We give so much to each other, and receive so much from each other, in common life, that we are apt to suppose that in moral things, as well as in secular, there may also be this mutual reciprocity. But it is not so. The severest passages in a man's life isolate him from his fellows, and he has to go through them by himself. Abraham received no strength from man when he went calmly up Moriah to offer Isaac in sacrifice. Jacob was "left alone" on that memorable night when there wrestled with him the mysterious angel till the breaking of the day; and times of peril and suffering, such as temporal calamity or personal affliction bring, must be met by each alone in the strength of that character which he has chosen to make and mould for himself in the past. When we come to die, we must meet the last enemy, not with the faith and courage of the friends who stand around our bed, but each for himself alone in his own character.

Now, if that be so, how perilous it is to leave off preparation for these testing times until they have come upon us! If we would meet them satisfactorily, we must fit ourselves for them in common things, and when no such emergency is upon us. Here, therefore, comes in with peculiar force the closing moral of the story: "Watch ye, therefore, for in such an hour as ye think not the Son of man cometh." He who is faithful in that which is least is faithful in that which is greatest; and he who has formed his character by faith in the Lord Jesus Christ, and obedience to him in the ordinary matters of daily life, is he also who can meet the solemnest experiences without a quiver, and is prepared for any sudden surprise. We all know how true that is in common life. When, in times of danger, some great leader comes suddenly to the front, and shows that he has the very qualities which the occasion needs, it will always be found that he has been preparing himself, — unconsciously, perhaps, but really, — for years, by the careful discipline of daily labor, for the work which is now so successfully performed by him. While others were asleep, he was at his toil; and by the study of many earnest months, perhaps also by the labor of many midnight hours, he has been laying up that reserve supply, on which at the moment of necessity he has been able to draw. Thus, though the revelation of his ability may have been sudden, the growth of it has been gradual; and because in times of quiet and safety he kept up the discipline of work, the crisis which swept others into oblivion only floated him into fame.

Now, the same thing holds in the spiritual department. If in our daily life we seek to form and maintain, by the help of the Holy Spirit and through faith in Christ, a holy character, then, when the testing hour comes, we shall be able to stand. But if we have been satisfying ourselves with a merely nominal Christianity, and have not endeavored to carry out in every respect the principles of the gospel, then the crisis of sudden temptation or unexpected trial will only reveal our weakness, and we shall be proved to be none of Christ's. The daily work of the blacksmith not only leaves, as its result, the articles which that day he has made, but adds also a certain deposit to the strength of his arm and the skill in his craft, which he has in store for the undertaking of something else. So, every time we perform a duty out of regard to Christ, the soul is made thereby so much the stronger for something else; and every time we overcome a temptation through faith in Christ, the soul is made so much the mightier for the resistance of the next assault. The daily life of the man who meets every duty as something to be done for Jesus, and bears every trial as something to be borne for Jesus, has its result not only in the doing of these duties, and the bearing of these trials, but also in the deposit of reserve force which is left thereby in his character for future emergencies.

Here, as it seems to me, therefore, is the full meaning of that store of oil which the wise virgins carried with them; and if that be so, it gives, as we have said, new point to the injunction with which the parable concludes: "Watch ye, therefore, for ye know neither the day nor the hour wherein the Son of man cometh." For, in a very important sense, the Son of man is coming to us every hour of every day.

Each new hour brings new duties and responsibilities from him to us. The last one we had laid some new obligation on us. It brought some work to be done, or some evil to be resisted, or some privilege to be improved. Have we risen to the occasion? If we have, then we have brought out of it some reserve force of character, on which afterwards we may draw; but if we have not, then we have come out of it weaker than we were before we entered it. Thus, whether we will confess it to ourselves or not, there is a constant process going on within us, either of invigoration or of deterioration; and, if we meet Christ continually as he comes to us in the common duties of a common day, we shall not be dismayed at last when he comes in state with the flaming outriders of his majesty. He is the same Christ, and our acquaintance with himself will keep us from being terrified by the accessories that are round about him.

The upshot of the matter, then, is, that each one of us is making for himself the character in which he is to meet all future emergencies; and, according as we make that, we shall be found at last with no oil wherewith to trim our lamps, or with a reserve supply, from which we may replenish them, and keep alive their light. For we cannot give to or receive from each other here. How important, therefore, it is, that we should make that character after the pattern and on the principles of Christ! Here is the plan: "Add to your faith virtue; and to virtue, knowledge; and to knowledge, temperance; and to temperance, patience; and to patience, godliness; and to godliness, brotherly kindness; and to brotherly kindness, charity."[1] Thus the faith is the first, and the love is the cope-stone; but the faith

[1] 2 Pet. i. 5-7.

itself must rest on Christ. Let us begin with that, and go on after this plan, seeking every day to serve the Lord ; and so, singularly enough, the longer our lamps shall burn, the larger also will our reserve of oil become, and in the end "an entrance shall be ministered to us abundantly into the everlasting kingdom of our Lord and Saviour Jesus Christ."

IV. But, as another truth suggested by this parable, I remark finally that lost opportunities cannot be recalled. When the door was shut, the foolish virgins could find no entrance into the feast, though they sought it with the most agonizing earnestness. Now, we shall greatly miss the practical value of this thought if we restrict it only to the opportunities to which death puts a period. No doubt that is the most solemn application of the analogy involved in the words, "and the door was shut." But every day is bringing opportunities, which, if we neglect them, can never return again. Others may come, but these will come never more. Thus, to illustrate from God's offers of grace, I proclaim to you now the gospel of forgiveness and regeneration on the condition of your repenting, and returning to the Lord. You may refuse it to-night; and it is possible that five years hence God may again bring you and me face to face, and I may repeat the offer which I have just made. It will look the same; but it is not the same as I am making now, for, though it will make the same demand on you, it will have in it five years less of happiness and usefulness than that which I make here to-night. You may go away rejecting it again; and ten years hence, it is not probable, but it is possible, God may again bring us together, and I may then again press on your acceptance God's overtures in the same words. It will look the same offer, and it will make the same demand; but it will not be the same offer, for it will contain in it ten years less of happiness and usefulness than that which I press upon you now. You know the story of the ancient sibyl who came to King Tarquin offering for sale nine books which she declared would be of great value to him in the government of Rome. She asked what seemed an exorbitant price, and he would not buy them. On that she retired, and burned three of the books: then she came back, and asked the same sum for the remaining six. He again refused; and she retired, and burned three more, only to come back, and ask the same price for the remaining three. Then, by the advice of his councillors, he secured them on her own terms. Now, beneath that old fable there is an important truth; for, the longer we refuse God's overtures, the less these overtures contain, while the demand upon us is still the same for the remainder. How many more of these books of privilege are you going to suffer to be destroyed? And what a motive there is in all this for immediate acceptance of God's offer of mercy!

But we see another application of this truth in the openings for service which God continually puts before us. We may have to-day an opportunity of doing good or of getting good. If we let that slip, the door that opened to it will be shut, and it never will be opened again. Other doors may open, but that one never more. Ah, how much more watchful and industrious we would be through life, if we more constantly remembered that! But then at last comes *death*, and shuts the door of all opportunity, putting an end to our probationary state. O friends, shall that door shut us in, or shut us out, from the marriage-feast? That is for us the question of questions; and if we would not be guilty of the folly of these short-sighted virgins, it becomes us to look well to our supply of oil. For it will be too late to go for it when it should be already in our lamps. And oh the agony of finding ourselves at length excluded from the heavenly feast so long as that feast lasts! Very powerfully has the English poet-laureate set the lesson of this parable to the music of his melodious verse, and his lines will form the most fitting close to our meditation on it.

> "Late, late, so late! and dark the night and chill;
> Late, late, so late! but we can enter still."
>   "Too late, too late! ye cannot enter now."
>
> "No light had we; for that we do repent;
> And learning that, the Bridegroom will relent."
>   "Too late, too late! ye cannot enter now."
>
> "No light! so late! and dark and chill the night!
> Oh, let us in, that we may find the light!"
>   "Oh, no! too late! ye cannot enter now."
>
> "Have we not heard the Bridegroom is so sweet?
> Oh, let us in, though late, to kiss his feet!"
>   "Too late, too late! ye cannot enter now."

May God grant that these terrible words shall never be addressed to any one of us! Amen.

XII

THE INTRUSTED TALENTS
Matthew 25:14-30

THE parable of the talents, which forms our subject for this evening, has in it so much in common with that of the pounds, which is given in the nineteenth chapter of Luke's Gospel, that the two are apt, by the merely superficial reader, to be considered as identical. But when we examine the circumstances in connection with which each was spoken, and the lessons which each was designed to teach, we find that they are quite distinct. That was uttered by the Lord as he was drawing nigh to Jerusalem, and before his triumphal entry into the Holy City: this, on the Mount of Olives, three days after his public procession to the Temple. That was addressed to the promiscuous multitude: this was meant more particularly for the twelve. In that, the same sum of one pound is given to each servant: in this, one receives five talents, another two, and another one. That illustrates different degrees of improvement of the same opportunity, with corresponding gradations of reward: this sets before us equal proportionate improvement of different opportunities, with equal proportionate reward. That was designed to correct the error of those who were looking for the immediate coming of the kingdom of God: this was intended, in conjunction with the story of the ten virgins, to teach that the right attitude of the disciple of Jesus, toward his second coming, is one of combined readiness and activity; while in both the episode of the unprofitable servant is meant to warn us all of the suggestive fact, that talents unused are as really wasted as if they had been flagrantly abused.

Thus distinct from the parable of the pounds, that of the talents is the needful complement to the story of the virgins. The Lord Jesus was as far as possible from being one-sided in his teachings; and when he insisted strongly on any particular quality, he took care always to guard his hearers from supposing that nothing else was needed. When he urged them to action, he supplemented his precept with something which reminded them of the importance of devotion; and when he spoke of the necessity of attending to inward character, he combined with that a strong enforcement of outward exertion. So we find, that immediately after the parable of the virgins, which taught the lesson of watchfulness, we have this of the talents, which emphasizes the duty of work He does not mean, however, that we should alternate vigilance with activity, but rather that the two should be combined, as in the case of the wall-builders of old, concerning whom Nehemiah writes: "The builders every one had his sword girded by his side, and so builded; and he that sounded the trumpet was by me."[1] Our watchfulness for Christ's coming is not to degenerate into idleness; but while we watch, we are to work, each in his allotted sphere, with the talents wherewith he has been intrusted.

How necessary that caution is, we may see illustrated in the case of the Thessalonians, who, misun-

[1] Neh. iv. 18.

derstanding Paul's references to the second advent of the Lord so much as to believe that it was just at hand, gave up their ordinary occupations, thereby causing great disorder, and reducing themselves to dependence on the charity of others for their daily food. Similar things have been witnessed also in times greatly nearer our own, among Adventists and others; and, therefore, we cannot but admire the prophetic foresight of the Lord, in that, when he himself refers to his second coming, he bids his followers not only watch in readiness for it, but work in earnestness toward it; or, as Trench has excellently put it, " While the virgins are represented as *waiting* for their Lord, we have here the servants *working* for him; there the inward life of the faithful was described, here his external activity. . . . That parable enforced the need of keeping the heart with all diligence; this, of giving all diligence also in our outward service if we would be found of Christ in peace at the day of his appearing."[1]

The story itself is true to the Oriental life of the period; for, when a wealthy man was leaving his home for a while, two courses were open to him for the arrangement of his affairs. Either he might make his confidential slaves his agents, committing to them the tilling of his land, and giving to them his money to be used by them in trade; or he might take advantage of the money-changing and money-lending system which had been introduced by the Phœnicians, and which was at the time in full operation throughout the Roman Empire. In the present case the lord adopted the former of these courses; and there was at least a tacit understanding, if no formal contract, that the servants would be rewarded for their fidelity.

[1] Notes on the Parables, p. 262.

This being the state of the case, the main lines of interpretation are not difficult to discover. The master is the Lord Jesus Christ. The servants are, in the first instance, the twelve to whom the parable was originally addressed; but, in a broader sense, the members of the visible Church. The talents are primarily, perhaps, the gifts received for his followers, and dispensed to them, by the ascended Christ; but we may view them in a more extended light as the opportunities of service which Christ has given to all who come into contact with his word. The going-away of the lord into a far country is the withdrawal of Christ as a visible presence from the earth; and the return of the lord, "after a long time," is the second coming of Christ, when the final reckoning of judgment shall be held. The trading of the servants with the talents is the faithful use made by his professed disciples, of the opportunities of service which Christ has given them; while the treatment of the servants by their master on his return sets before us the principles on which the awards of the Judge of all the earth shall ultimately be made.

I. Now, with these outlines before us, we may be able, under their guidance, to bring out some of the most suggestive features of the teaching of the parable. First of all, we have here an explanation of the diversity which exists between individuals in the matter of opportunity of service in the cause of the Redeemer. We all observe the fact that there is such a diversity. Some have received five talents, some two, and some only one; and at first, some dissatisfaction may be felt with what looks like inequality in the distribution. But here is the account of the matter: "to every man according to his several ability." The talents, therefore, do not denote the original endowments and qualities which men bring into the world with them, or the possessions into which they come by right of birth. No doubt, these also are gifts of God, which ought to be held and used by men as stewards of his "manifold bounties." But it is evident that the reference here is not to these. It is rather to those opportunities which have been given to men in consequence of their abilities and environment. In his bestowment of spiritual opportunities, Christ has regard both to the natural abilities and providential surroundings of each man; and as, in the sovereignty of God, there is diversity in the latter, so, in the gracious administration of Christ, there is similar diversity in the former. No man has more opportunities of service than he can avail himself of to the full, and every man has just as many as he can use with advantage. When this principle is clearly understood, it takes away all ground for pride in those who have received five talents, and all cause for discontent in those who have obtained but one. Jealousy has no place here. Each has precisely what is fitted to his ability and circumstances, — no more, no less. From him who has received more talents, the full improvement of all he has will be required; but he to whom fewer have been given will be held responsible only for those that have been conferred upon him. If Christ has given you only one talent, it is because he sees that at present you could not handle more. If he has given you five, it is because he sees that you are competent to deal even with them. As Trench has said, " The natural is the ground upon which the spiritual is superinduced; and grace does not dissolve the groundwork of the individual character, nor abolish all its peculiarities, nor bring all that are subject to it to a common standard. The natural gifts are as the vessel, which may be large, or may be small, and which receives according to its capacity, but which in each case is filled; so that we are not to think of him who had received the two talents as incompletely furnished, in comparison with him that had received the five, any more than we should affirm a small circle incomplete, as compared with a large."[1] Observe, each vessel is filled; and therefore there is no room for jealousy between different individuals, or for dissatisfaction with our several opportunities, for each is endowed up to the measure of ability to use that which he has received. The man with the one talent may not be able, will not be able, to fill so wide a sphere as he who has five; but he can fill *his own* sphere, and that is all that will be required at his hand.

Now, it is of great importance that we should remember this principle; for there are few things that so paralyze the energy of the soul as, on the one hand, pride because our sphere is so large, and, on the other, discontent because it is so limited. The practical result of both is uselessness, by reason of unfaithfulness. How important, therefore, that we should learn the lesson which this expression of the parable teaches, and which the poet has put into the following lines!—

> ' Be sober, then, be vigilant; forbear
> To seek or covet aught beyond thy sphere:
> Only be strong to labor, and allow
> Thy Master's will to appoint the where and how.
> Serve God; and winter's cold or summer's heat,
> The breezy mountain or the dusty street,
> Scene, season, circumstance, alike shall be
> His welcome messengers of joy to thee;
> His kingdom is within thee! Rise, and prove
> A present earnest of the bliss above."

[1] Notes on the Parables, pp. 267, 268.

II. But another suggestive thought in this parable is, that new opportunities come to us with our improvement of those which we already have. The first servant said, "I have gained five talents more;" and the second exclaimed, "I have gained two other talents besides them." By utilizing what we have, we get what we have not. By doing what we can, we attain ability to do that which was originally impossible to us. The world is familiar with this law in the matter of money-making. The foundations of colossal fortunes have been laid in the taking advantage at first of little opportunities. One of our religious weeklies lately had a series of brief articles entitled, "Willing to Shovel," which showed how men who ultimately became millionnaires began with the earning of a few cents by doing such work as cleaning the snow from the sidewalks, or sawing wood in the cellar. But the same thing holds in public life. Take such a career as that of either of our two martyr Presidents, and you will see how, when the one talent is utilized, it ultimately increases into ten. There is a difference between the boy on the tow-line of the canal, and the statesman in the Senate, or the President in the White House; and it was all the result of his using to the full opportunities just as they came.

But the principle holds true also in the spiritual department. A young man in a church begins to take an interest in Sunday-school work. This draws the attention of some of its members to him. He is asked by one of them to make an address at some social gathering. He does it so admirably, that, though he is only a grocer's apprentice, his pastor and some friends go home saying, "That youth is admirably fitted for the ministry of the gospel." The matter is put before him: he expresses his willingness to do any thing for which God may open the way. Arrangements are made for his education; he enters on the work of the pastorate: and, after years of service in smaller spheres, he finishes his life as the minister of one of the largest and most important churches in the metropolis of the land. That was the career of Alexander Raleigh, — one of the most eloquent preachers whom London has heard in the present generation. But there have been scores, I had almost said hundreds, like it, where even the one talent has become ten, and multitudes more where the two have become four. The true method of increasing our sphere is to fill to overflowing that in which we are. The horizon will widen as we climb the hill. Only, to secure that widening, we must keep walking up. This is the principle of Christ's administration of the kingdom of God; and wherever you go, you will find illustrious examples of its operation. Even now, therefore, it is true that "to him that hath, shall more be given;" and we have in this the foretaste and earnest of the awards of the judgment at the last. For, when he who has made the five talents ten lays down his work at the Master's feet, the response of the Lord is, "Thou hast been faithful over a few things: I will make thee ruler over many things; enter thou into the joy of thy Lord." So heaven shall give new opportunities of service to them who have made the most faithful use of those of earth. As much as the ten talents are superior to the five on earth, so much will the "many things" of heaven be superior to the "few things" of earth. So much, — nay, ineffably more. The reward of heaven is thus a wider sphere of service than earth could furnish, without the weariness which is here the consequence of labor, and with a fuller fellowship in that joy which Christ has in the doing of the Father's will. What the nature of the service shall be, we cannot tell, any more than we can rightly image to ourselves the intensity of the joy; but there is the principle, and it is all the more assured to us by the fact that we see it in operation here and now. The kingdom is one in heaven and on earth, and the law for both of these stages is the same. Faithful service widens opportunity. That is the seed-thought in this part of the parable. Will you act upon it now, that your life on earth may increase in usefulness, and your experience in heaven may be one of exalted, joyful, and laborious honor?

III. But now we come to the darker side of the picture, which tells us what must be the result of neglecting our opportunities; for it is time that we should look at the conduct and doom of the unprofitable servant.

Here let us observe, first, what is said concerning the man with the one talent. It is not alleged that he had wasted his Master's goods, like the unjust steward, or that he had spent the talent in riotous living, as the prodigal did his portion; but only that "he went and hid the talent in the earth." He simply did nothing with it. Now, that means that he "neglected" his opportunities. He did not lead a scandalously wicked life; yet he took no care to improve the openings for the service of God and his generation which were put before him, but passed them by as if he had never seen them. Not the doing of positive wrong, but the neglect to do that which God has given us the means of doing; not the commission of grievous sin, but the leaving undone of that which we have the ability and opportunity to do, is what here is charged, on his own confession, on this slothful servant. And, indeed, that is serious enough; for to do nothing at all, when we can do much, is the most heartless way, often, of doing wrong. Life, like money, ought to be made productive; and the interest to which it is to be put is that of earnest and laborious exertion in the service of Christ, not only for the upbuilding of our own characters, as the parable of the virgins enforced, but also for the benefit of our fellow-men, as that of the talents has specially emphasized. Life, like seed, is to be sown, not hoarded; and the field in which we are to sow it is human hearts, our own, and those of our neighbors. When we put the matter in this way, we see how easy it is for one to lose one's life by no positive iniquity, but simply by neglect; and so the warning that we should not allow our great and golden opportunities to slip by us unimproved becomes all-important. To this end, let us daily endeavor to make ourselves and the world better by laying ourselves out for the service of the Lord Jesus, and seeking to do every thing in his name. Even a heathen emperor was accustomed to say, "To-day I have lost a day," when, in the evening, he could not point to any thing which he had that day done for the welfare of his race; and, in the Christian sense of the word, that is a lost life, no matter how blameless otherwise it may seem to be, in which the man's own salvation has been neglected, and the service of "his generation by the will of God" ignored.

But the case of this wicked servant has some other features of special interest for us. Thus it is noticeable, that he was the man who had received the one talent. It is not said, indeed, that he hid it in the earth *because* it was only one; and I do not desire to impute motives to him. Neither do I wish to produce upon you the impression that only they who have very limited spheres are in danger of neglecting their opportunities; for that is far from being the case, and many of those who have received five talents are guilty of failing to improve them. But yet, it is true that many are content to do nothing because they cannot do "some great thing." They think that if they were only in other and better circumstances, they would exert themselves to purpose, for then it would be worth the while; but now, they say, "We have no influence. If we had only the abilities of such an one, or the wealth of such another, or the position of such a third, we might do something; but as it is, it is useless to attempt to do any thing," and they do nothing. Now, in answer to all such excuses, we have to say, first, as we have said before, that we are not accountable for what we have not, but only for what we have; and, second, that if a man neglects the work that is lying at his hands *now*, however lowly that may be, he would equally neglect the opportunities of a wider sphere if he were put into such a position. He who buried the one talent would have buried the five if he had received them; for, though the smallness of the trust may have aggravated him, the reason of its doing so, as, indeed, also of his failure to employ it, was in his character, and not in its littleness. "He that is faithful in that which is least is faithful also in much, and he that is unjust in the least is unjust also in much."

Again, it is exceedingly significant, that this servant alleges in excuse of his conduct, that he knew that his master was "an austere man, reaping where he had not sowed, and gathering where he had not strewed." And those who neglect God's service do so because they cherish wrong views of God himself. They are afraid of him as an exacting task-master, and therefore they try to do as little for him as possible; whereas, if they only loved him as the God and Father of our Lord Jesus Christ, who gave his Son that we might be redeemed, they would feel that no service which they could render would be adequate to express their gratitude. As Dr. Dods has said,[1] "All wrongness of conduct is at bottom based on a wrong view of God. Nothing so conduces to right action as right thoughts about God. If we think, with this servant, that God is hard, grudging to give and greedy to get, taking note of all shortcomings, but making no acknowledgment of sincere service, exacting the utmost farthing, and making no abatement or allowance; if we one way or other virtually come to think that God never really delights in our efforts after good, and that whatever we attempt in our life he will coldly weigh and scorn, — then manifestly we shall have no heart to labor for him."

Now, concerning this view of God's character, two things have to be said. In the first place, even if it were true, those who hold it are acting with egregious inconsistency when they let the opportunities of life pass unimproved; since, the more rigorous God is, the more sure he will be to take notice of and punish their unfaithfulness. That is the answer made by his lord to the insinuation of the servant here, and so out of his own mouth he was condemned. But, in the second place, it is not true that God is thus austere and hard. He "doth *not* exact day labor, light denied." He does *not* require from any one an account of that which he has *not* received or cannot use. Neither does he

[1] The Parables of our Lord, p. 261.

deal with men after the fashion of a tyrant. He is a loving Father, if only they will let him love them. His law is such that in the keeping of it they may find their highest good; and his gospel is all love together, — love in its source, love in its manifestation, love in its effects: so that it is a libel alike on his character and revelation to call him "austere." But if men so think of him, they cannot but neglect their opportunities; for so to think of him, is to become a slave crouching in blind terror before him, and altogether set against his service, instead of a son delighting in his affection. *Here is the heart of the whole matter.* So long as a man has this estimate of God, he will imagine that his sphere is smaller than it ought to be, and his life will become aimless and indefinite, without any concentration of purpose or any energy of activity. But if, through faith in Jesus Christ, we accept God as our Father, who has forgiven our sins at the cost of the great sacrifice on Calvary, and who is following us continually with his love, we shall be led to offer him the homage of our hearts; and our lives, catching the fervor of our spirits, will sphere themselves into unity and completeness, and find their chosen orbit in rotating around him as their centre of attraction. We will say, like Paul, "The love of Christ constraineth us; because we thus judge, that if one died for all, then these all died; and that he died for all, that we who live should not henceforth live unto ourselves, but unto him who died for us and rose again."[1] Wondrous paradox, yet suggestive truth! the *fear* of God as an "austere" One makes us heedless of his service; but the *love* of God as our Father and our Friend, through Christ, inspires us with devotion to himself, and impels us to become his earnest servants. Let

[1] 2 Cor. v. 14, 15.

us, therefore, seek this "spirit of adoption," and shut our ears to all such misrepresentations of Jehovah as this servant made. There be many in these days, young men, who would caricature God to you, and endeavor to persuade you that he is "an infinite tyrant," only that they may set you against him, and prevail upon you to repudiate your allegiance unto him. *But believe them not.* His name and nature is Love. His gospel is a revelation of mercy. His reign is one of justice, and in the cross of his Son all these attributes are seen in blended harmony, working together for the salvation of men. "Gracious is the Lord, and righteous; yea, our God is merciful." "God so loved the world, that he gave his only begotten Son, that whosoever believeth in him should not perish, but have everlasting life." Keep these truths before your minds. Lay them up in the memories of your hearts; and the more you realize their meaning, the less likely will you be to yield to the enticements of those who would gild sin with a plating of respectability by representing it as a revolt for liberty against the tyranny of God. Ah! there are no more hapless slaves than those who are thus "lords of themselves, that heritage of woe;" and that is perfect freedom which lovingly accepts the service of God.

IV. But we must look now, for a moment or two, at the sentence pronounced on this unprofitable servant. "Take the talent from him;" that is, let his opportunities forever cease. Here is a clear end of probation. "And give it to him who hath ten talents;" that is, the opportunities forfeited by him will be added to those gained by the faithful. How that is to be done, we cannot tell; and yet we have, even in this life, a clear analogy to what is here implied, in the fact that the duties which have been neglected by a servant who is dismissed are turned over to be performed by one who has been already proved to be trustworthy, to the increase at once of his honor and emolument. "Capacity is extirpated by disuse,"[1] while its diligent exercise enlarges and ennobles it. That is the law here; and, so far as we may judge from this parable, it will be the law at the final judgment, and will determine the ultimate destiny of each. But this is not all. "Cast ye the unprofitable servant into outer darkness: there shall be weeping, and gnashing of teeth." Who among us can contemplate such a doom without emotion? — "darkness," where no ray of God's countenance ever penetrates; "darkness" unrelieved, unmitigated, and eternal; "outer darkness," away from the abode of God and of the holy; "outer darkness," made more miserable by the wailing of those who now unavailingly upbraid themselves for their folly and their selfishness. And this is to be the end of burying our talent by neglecting our opportunities. Oh, let us be warned in time! for the warning here is given in love, in order that we may be kept from continuing in that course which must have this dreadful result. Never but once, during his abode on the earth, did our Lord blast any created thing; and that was when he came to the fig-tree, looking for fruit, and found thereon "nothing but leaves." He did not blight it into perpetual barrenness because it produced wild fruit, or because it bore poisonous figs, but because he found on it "nothing but leaves;" and so the curse of an eternal withering shall fall at last upon the soul which has done nothing with its opportunities upon the earth.

[1] Horace Bushnell.

> "Ah! who shall thus the Master meet,
> And before his awful judgment-seat
> Lay down for golden sheaves
> Nothing but leaves?"

Let us not, I beseech you, be found at last in this great condemnation. And, that we may guard against it, let us begin now to cry, like Paul, "Lord, what wilt thou have me to do?" that like him also we may fill our lives brimful with that ministry of love and self-sacrifice which shall be crowned at last with the Divine commendation, "Well done, good and faithful servant: thou hast been faithful over a few things, I will make thee ruler over many things; enter thou into the joy of thy Lord."

XIII

THE GROWTH OF THE SEED
Mark 4:26-29

THIS parable is recorded by Mark alone. It is the only one that is thus peculiar to him. He gives, in all, but four of the Lord's parables. Of these, two are to be found also both in Matthew and Luke, and one in Matthew. This alone has a place only in his narrative. For that reason, some have attempted to show that we have in this also only a modification of some other parable, such as that of the tares; but my conviction is, that all who study it with candor and attention will agree with Neander[1] when he says that it "bears the undeniable stamp of originality, both in its matter and form."

It is distinct from all the others; and yet its very position here indicates that it is to be regarded as supplementary to that of the sower, and was designed to complete the history of the growth of the good seed which fell on the good ground. As you will remember, the object of the parable of the sower, so-called, was to illustrate the truth that the fate of the seed after it has been sown depends on the nature of the soil. You cannot have forgotten, also, that it gives a minute account of what happened in the cases of that which fell by the wayside, of that which fell on a thin layer

---
[1] Life of Christ, Bohn's translation, p. 346.

THE GROWTH OF THE SEED 197

of earth just above a rock, and of that which fell among thorns. But no such details are furnished concerning that which fell on good ground. We are simply told that "it brought forth fruit, some an hundred-fold, some sixty-fold, and some thirty-fold." Thus the only points to which attention is directed by it are, that, in the good ground, the seed was productive, though not all equally productive. But no incidents, like the devouring by birds of that which fell by the wayside, or the rapid springing-up and after withering of that which fell on rocky soil, or the being choked by the overgrowth of other things, as was the case with that which fell among thorns, are specified in regard to the germination of the seed on the fourth kind of soil. Here, however, in this parable which Mark alone has preserved, the full story of the growth of the seed on the good ground, so far as man can see it, or has any thing to do with it, is told. That which the parable of the sower merely summarizes, this one minutely describes. It may, therefore, be regarded as a kind of appendix to the parable of the sower, supplementing what, as to the good ground, had been left vague and indistinct therein.

But we shall come at the particular teaching of this beautiful allegory, if we enumerate with care these following things; namely, the facts which it presupposes, the truths which it illustrates, and the lessons which it enforces.

I. Let us attend, first, to the facts which it presupposes. It is implied very clearly, then, that the seed used is good seed. The germinating principle exists not in wholesome grain alone. The tares spring up, and bring forth fruit, as well as the wheat; the berry of the deadly nightshade, as well as the acorn of the oak; the seed of the poisonous hemlock, as well as the shoot of the vine. Even so an evil word spoken, or a dark suggestion insinuated, or a false doctrine inculcated, will produce fruits after its own kind, as surely as the truth will reproduce itself, and bring forth results of righteousness and peace. But in this case, the sower used good seed, even that which is described by Christ in his comprehensive interpretation of the first of his parables, " The seed is the word of God."

It is implied, again, in the allegory before us, that this good seed was sown. " So is the kingdom of God, as if a man should cast seed into the ground." Weeds propagate themselves. They produce their seeds, and the winds of heaven may scatter them abroad, or the fowls of the air may carry them hither and thither; or the happy schoolboy, laughing the while at the fancy that he can tell the hour thereby, may blow them with his breath: and wherever they fall, if there be soil, they grow. But grain must be cultivated. It will not thus sow itself. The law regarding all the cereals is, that they must be sown and gathered in by men. Now, is not the analogy here most suggestive? Is it not true also in the spiritual department, that weeds sow themselves? There needs no labor to fill the heart of a child with disobedience, selfishness, or impurity. All you have to do is to leave him alone. The moral atmosphere around him is laden with germs of iniquity; and there is, alas! within him only too kindly a soil for the reception of such things, so that they are sure to spring up there in luxuriant abundance. And what is true of a single soul is equally so of a neighborhood, a nation, and the human race as a whole. It is in vain here that we trust to nature alone. We can reclaim waste places only by reducing them to cultivation, and sowing in them seed that shall by and by wave with harvests of precious grain; and we can secure the elevation of the depraved in our city streets, the evangelization of our nation, and the conversion of the world, only by diffusing the gospel of the grace of God. "For whosoever shall call on the name of the Lord shall be saved. How then shall they call on him in whom they have not believed? and how shall they believe in him of whom they have not heard? and how shall they hear without a preacher? and how shall they preach except they be sent?"[1]

Once more, it is implied in this parable, that the seed fell on good ground, into which it found an entrance. As I have already hinted, the difference between this allegory and that of the sower is, that, in the case before us, the seed has all fallen into good ground, whereas, in the other, that could be said of only one portion. That which alighted on the wayside never got into the soil at all; that which fell among thorns got into uncongenial and pre-occupied soil, and that which fell upon the rocky ground had no deepness of earth. But here not only was the good seed sown, but it fell into favorable soil; and so it grew without interruption. You have heard of the wheat that was found in the case of an Egyptian mummy. For many centuries it had lain there without growing, for it had not there those circumstances which are indispensable to growth. But when it was taken, and put into the soil where it could have the influences of the earth and heat and light and moisture, it very soon sprung up, and brought forth many-fold. Now, in the same way, the word of God will not grow in a heart unless it be by that heart

[1] Rom. x. 13-15.

received. So long as it is outside of the heart, it takes no root in the man. It must be held, not by the cold mummy grasp of a dead hand, but by the warm, earnest embrace of a living and believing heart; and then it will spring up. To no purpose, therefore, do we look for the fruit of truth in the soul, until it is believed. We may hear it, we may examine it, we may reason about it, we may even enjoy the excitement of controversy about it; but until we believe it, we keep it still outside of us, and it cannot grow in us. This is why so many constant worshippers in our sanctuaries show no spiritual improvement from their sabbath privileges. They enjoy the accessories of the service; they are pleased with the intellect or eloquence of the preacher: but they do not believe the truth that is presented to them; and so " the word preached doth not profit them, not being mixed with faith in the hearing of it." There can be no spiritual growth unless the word is believingly received into the heart. What a man believes in, that he grows to be. If he believe in selfishness, he will become selfish; if he believe in pleasure, he will become a pleasure-seeker; and if he believe in Christ, he will become Christ-like. The root of growth is faith. The seed will not spring up unless it finds a congenial soil.

II. But, passing now to the consideration of the truths directly illustrated by this parable, it is pertinent to observe that it confines our attention to what goes on in the development of the seed between the time of its being sown and its being harvested; and it tells us that all that lies between these two limits takes place according to laws, the operation of which is inscrutable to men, but the existence of which reveals itself in the uniform sequence of certain stages which are reached in the gradual evolution of the grain from its initial condition to maturity. Or, to put it in a more compact form, this parable treats simply and only of the growth of the seed, and sets before us these three things regarding it: namely, the mystery of the mode, the gradualness of the progress, and the definite and regular stages through which that progress passes.

There is, first, the mystery of the mode. "It springeth up, he knoweth not how." No man can explain the growth of a grain of wheat. He may talk learnedly of many things connected with it, and may give them long, hard, and almost unpronounceable names; but in the end, all his discourse leads virtually up to this: that God hath so fitted the seed to the soil, and the soil to the seed, that, when a corn of wheat falls into the earth, it springeth up. The husbandman can do many things to the soil. He can plough and harrow it; he can enrich it with the addition of fertilizing substances; he can prepare it for the reception of the seed. He can also choose the quality of the seed; and, after it has sprung up, he can remove obstructions to its growth that may have appeared in the shape of weeds. But *he* cannot make the seed to grow. It is not in his power to command at the right time the heat of the sun or the moisture of the clouds. He cannot order the process of germination. God has kept that in his own hands; and the farmer very wisely leaves it with him, "and sleeps and rises, night and day," letting God work for him.

Now, it is not otherwise in spiritual matters. The sower of truth cannot make it grow in the human heart, nor can he explain how it germinates there. He can only say that God hath so constituted the soul, that, when truth is received by it, it cannot lie dormant there, but must spring up and produce its appropriate effects. He may choose the kind of seed he shall employ. He may vary his methods of instruction to suit the varied capacities of those whom he seeks at different times to teach; and as the truth is springing up, he may be instrumental in removing error from association with it. But he *cannot make it grow:* the power to do that belongs to the Spirit of God alone. No man can command those spiritual influences which he has kept in his own hand. He worketh where, when, and how he pleaseth. We may pray for his baptism, but we cannot command it; and it was only impious presumption which induced the leaders of the Salvation Army, a year or two ago in England, to put down in the programme of one of their protracted meetings, for a certain day, at a certain hour, " Descent of the Holy Ghost."

Neither can we call at will those providential dispensations, which, in the culture of the heart, correspond to the changes of the weather in the growth of the crops. We cannot bring upon each other affliction or health, adversity or prosperity, sorrow or joy, bereavement or blessing, by the agency of which the growth of a holy character is so furthered in some men, and by the absence of which it is so hindered in others. All these things are out of our power. They are beyond our control. They come, we know not how. They are arranged by God according to his wisdom; and as the pious husbandman, when he has sown his seed, leaves all the rest with God, so, after we have scattered the good seed of the Word, we ought to look up in faith and prayer to the Lord of the harvest, and wait patiently for the result. As the Apostle James has

THE GROWTH OF THE SEED 203

said, "Behold, the husbandman waiteth for the precious fruit of the earth, and hath long patience for it, until he receive the early and the latter rain. Be ye also patient; stablish your hearts, for the coming of the Lord draweth nigh."[1] Neither ought we to allow the mystery which shrouds the mode of the Divine operations to keep us from availing ourselves of their benefits. Men do not wait to understand every thing about meteorology before they take advantage of the winds to propel their ships, and we ought not to let the unfathomableness of the mystery of the mode of the working of God's Spirit in the human heart keep us from availing ourselves of his gracious agency. It is a problem not yet solved, how the light and heat of the sun are maintained; but we do not on that account refuse to accept these blessings, and utilize them. Let the same common-sense characterize our proceedings in spiritual things; and the man who proclaims the truth will leave God to take care of its growth, while he who hears it and receives it will humbly and gratefully rejoice in its peace.

But emphasis is put in this parable, also, on the gradualness of the growth of the seed. The processes of nature are for the most part gradual; so much so, indeed, that at any one point you can scarcely detect that there is a difference from that which immediately preceded. Thus, if one were to lie down day by day beside a field of growing grain, he would not be able to mark distinctly the progress made in any one particular hour. I question, indeed, if in such circumstances he would be able to tell when precisely the blade began to pass into the ear, or when the first yellow tinge began to make its appearance, and the ear began

[1] Jas. v. 7, 8.

to fill. The fact that there has been progress is apparent, but the growth itself has been so gradual as to be almost imperceptible. There are times, indeed, when there seems to be a great start taken. These are the fine "growing days" of which the farmer speaks, when, after refreshing rain, there comes genial warmth, and one thinks he can almost see the stalks pushing themselves up. But, generally speaking, the growth from day to day is all but imperceptible.

Now, it is so also with the growth of a holy character in a man, from the up-springing of the good seed of the word in his heart. There are times, indeed, when it appears as if a great start were taken, and it develops more rapidly than at others. Such, for example, are seasons of trial and affliction, when, after the tears of genuine repentance, there comes the warmth of deep, fervent love to Christ. Oh, these are "growing days" indeed, and those who have passed through them can bear testimony to this fact. But commonly the growth from day to day is all but imperceptible, like that of the child at your feet who seems no bigger to-day than he was yesterday, and will appear no bigger to-morrow than he is to-day. "The path of the just is as the shining light, that shineth more and more unto the perfect day." There is progress, but it is not always easy to trace it from one day to another. By little and little, even as one color shades into another, a man becomes aggravated in sin; and by little and little, even as the tide advances on the shore, one becomes eminent in holiness. That is not a plant which springs up in a man like the prophet's gourd in a single night. One does not vault into it by a single bound, but he grows into it through faith and prayer and obedience and patience; yet, though the daily advances may be hardly discernible, the great out-standing stages are well defined.

This brings me to the third thing emphasized in this parable; namely, that, in the up-springing of the good seed into Christian character, there are distinct stages of development, — "first the blade, then the ear, then the full corn in the ear." In growth, there are easily recognizable landmarks, like the landing-places in a stair, which are perfectly distinguishable from what goes before and from what follows. Thus, in the fruit-tree we have the bud, the blossom, and the fruit; and in human life we have infancy, childhood, youth, and manhood. We may not be able to discover just when the one of these passes into the other, but we can recognize each when we see it. Just so, in the Christian character, we have different stages indicated by different marks. One who has had any large experience in dealing with the disciples of Christ will ordinarily have no great difficulty in deciding whether a man be a recent convert, or a Christian of some standing, or a venerable and (as the old-fashioned phrase used to be) "well-exercised" believer. In the first you will commonly find zeal predominant; in the second, a certain censoriousness which is the shadow of knowledge; and in the third, humility and love. In the first you will have a dash of intolerance; in the second, a little cynicism; and in the third, a broad and wide-embracing charity. Courage comes ordinarily before knowledge, and knowledge before patience; while love comes to its maturity only in the ripened saint. Every one who has attended to the training of his own children knows that there are certain faults, or tendencies, or crudenesses, which seem to belong to particular ages. Those special ages, indeed, have brought with them some great acquirements that are valuable; but along with these there appear, almost with the certainty of a law, certain characteristics which often give a parent trouble. With his first-born, he is especially at a loss. But as other children come into the home, he has grown accustomed to the phenomena; for now the eldest has left all such things behind, and therefore he "winks at" them in the younger ones, and waits patiently until they, too, have outgrown them. Now, it is just similar in the Christian life. The new convert, when we meet such a one for the first time, is apt to be a little trying to us. He is all fire, and sometimes he scorches us with his flame. The older Christian, too, who is in the stage of the bud, or the unripe fruit, is apt to be troublesome with his acrid humors; but these are just the qualities attendant on the degree of growth at which he has arrived. Rightly looked at, they are the evidences of a new period of development; and the best thing we can do with them is to let them alone, and wait in patient love until our friends have grown out of them. We need not look for the ear before the blade, nor for the full ripened ear when it is time only for the appearance of the ear. But we are to be satisfied when we have the evidence of growth in the presence of such things as indicate that a new stage has been reached.

III. Now, if this be, as I believe it is, the true interpretation of this parable, we are in a position to get from it the lessons for our own practical life, which it so suggestively teaches. And among these, I place first the important truth, that all who are in any way engaged in sowing the good seed of the word of God should accompany their work with prayer. The sowing is our part: the making of the seed to grow is God's. Remember what Paul has said: "I have planted, Apollos watered; but God gave the increase. So then neither is he that planteth any thing, neither he that watereth, but God that giveth the increase."[1] This may teach us humility, but it will also lead us to entire dependence upon God. Whether, therefore, we be parents, or teachers, or preachers, let us accompany our sowing with prayer, that God may keep us from laboring in vain, and crown our efforts with an abundant harvest.

But, as a second lesson from this parable, I urge that we should not look for ripeness before it is due. Growth takes time, and it follows its own laws. We ought not, therefore, to look for certain qualities of character too soon, or out of their due and proper course. You cannot have the ear before the blade, nor the ripe harvest just when the ear appears. You must not expect the boy to be as sedate and solid as the man, neither should you look in the young convert for those qualities of character which can come only as the results of long experience. Many parents do great injury to their children, by expecting certain excellences in them too soon. I always pity the first-born of a family, or an only child, just on that account; for his seniors are not willing to let him be long enough a child, and almost always forget the proverb that "you cannot have an old head on young shoulders." But I fear that similar injury is sometimes inflicted, in a similar way, on young Christians. Sufficient allowance is not always made by those of riper experience, for the crudeness and immaturity which are inseparable from that stage of development at which they have arrived.

[1] 1 Cor. iii. 6, 7.

Burns once complainingly said to his brother Gilbert, "Man, you're no' for young folk;" meaning, thereby, that he did not sufficiently understand and make allowance for the peculiarities of youth. And, similarly, there are many Christians to whom it may be said that they are not for young Christians. We must not insist upon it, that they should be in every respect like those who have been long in Christ. But we ought to moderate our expectations, and be content to wait for the growth which requires time for its development. And this rule must work both ways, so that the young Christian is not to judge the older harshly because of his apparent lack of effervescing emotion. Let us be charitable toward each other. The young convert must not expect that the aged believer is to be like him, any more than the aged believer is to insist that the young convert must in all respects resemble him. The blade will be the ripened ear by and by. It is on the way thereto. Give it time, and God will give it ripeness.

Finally, let all Christian workers look forward with hopefulness to the coming harvest; for there is nothing in which we can engage that will yield a richer increase than the sowing of the good seed of the word of God. The Lord is not stinted in his blessings. We sow in single grains, we reap full ears; we sow in handfuls, we reap in bosomfuls; we sow in days and years, we reap eternity. There is joy in sowing, there is a deeper joy in seeing the seed springing up; but the richest joy of all is that of harvest-home. It is a gladsome thing to preach the word of life, even though sometimes one may preach it in tears; there is a yet more inspiriting joy in seeing that word take root in human hearts, and bring forth the fruit of holy living: but the most thrilling joy of all is that of the heavenly ingathering, when the servants of the Lord shall come to him with rejoicing, "bringing their sheaves with them." My hearer, shall that bliss be yours?

Of one thing we may be sure: a harvest of some sort there will be, for we all are sowing now; and, if we are sowing the wind, we shall reap at length the whirlwind. Either, therefore, our ingathering shall be of blessing, or it shall be like that described in such terrible language by the prophet: "Because thou hast forgotten the God of thy salvation, and hast not been mindful of the rock of thy strength, therefore shalt thou plant pleasant places, and shalt set it with strange slips. In the day shalt thou make thy plant to grow, and in the morning shalt thou make thy seed to flourish; but the harvest shall be a heap in the day of grief and of desperate sorrow."[1] There are but the two alternatives. "Be not deceived: God is not mocked; for whatsoever a man soweth, that shall he also reap. He that soweth to the flesh shall of the flesh reap corruption; but he that soweth to the Spirit shall of the Spirit reap life everlasting."[2]

May God help us to lay these truths to heart.

[1] Isa. xvii. 9, 10.   [2] Gal. vi. 7, 8.

XIV

THE TWO DEBTORS
Luke 7:36-50

THE parable to which we have now come is so inseparable from the history in which it is embedded, that we can rightly interpret *it* only by entering fully into the details of *that*. But we need not regret this necessity, for the story is one of the most touching which even the word of God contains; and we shall all be the better for coming once again into contact with "the heart of Christ," as it is here revealed. The expositor's only anxiety is, lest, by his handling of that which is so exquisite, he should leave the mark of his defiling touch upon its loveliness, — lest, by his very effort to explain its meaning, he should weaken the force of that which is in itself so effective. Still, even with such risks before him, it is important that he should carry on his work; for here, too, there are subtle suggestions and profound lessons which yield themselves only to patient investigation.

The Lord had been invited to eat with one of the Pharisees, and had accepted the invitation. There is nothing in the narrative of Luke, — who alone records the incidents, — by which we are able to identify either the place in which this Pharisee resided, or the date at which this feast was given by him to Jesus. Neither can we recognize in the principal characters to whom we are here introduced, any one whom we meet with elsewhere in the Gospels. The Simon of this feast could not be the Simon of Bethany, and the woman of this anointing could not be Mary the sister of Lazarus. Only the most wilful and irrational determination to make a contradiction where there is really none could induce any one to persist in the assertion that the banquet here described is the same as that of which we have an account in the twelfth chapter of the Gospel by John.

Neither is there any — the least — warrant for the idea that the woman of this history was Mary Magdalene. She is one of the unnamed females in these inspired histories; and we are in full accord with Bishop Hall, when he writes thus regarding this matter:[1] —

"I hear no name of either the city or the woman: she was too well known in her time. How much better is it to be obscure than infamous! Herein I doubt not God meant to spare the reputation of a penitent convert. He who hates not the person, but the sin, cares only to mention the sin, not the person. It is justice to prosecute the vice: it is mercy to spare the offender. How injurious a presumption is it for any man to name her whom God would have concealed, and to cast this aspersion on those whom God hath noted for holiness!"

But now, how came Simon to invite Jesus to his house? He was a Pharisee, and as such belonged to that section of the Jews who were at this juncture beginning to show open antagonism to the Lord. All the Pharisees, however, were not equally bad. We cannot forget that Nicodemus was one of them; and this man, though he had not got so far as Nicodemus was when he recognized in Jesus a teacher sent from

[1] Contemplations, pp. 529, 530.

heaven, had yet a certain respect for him as a rabbi, or religious instructor. He was interested in him, and thought it possible that he might be a prophet; but he had not yet arrived at the conclusion that he was. There was, therefore, beneath this invitation of the Lord at this time to his house, a wish to scrutinize him more closely, and so to obtain the means of coming to some definite decision regarding him. Hence, while he was glad enough to receive him, he did not show him any great honor. In fact, he dispensed with even the usual courtesies offered by a host to his guest, and treated the Saviour with a patronizing air, which seemed to say that it was distinction enough for Jesus to be at his table, and that he had no right to expect any further civilities. He had heard him, and had thereby had his curiosity aroused to find out more about him; and so, as the best means of gratifying that, he asked him to dinner. But that was all. If there was any favor in the case, his view of the matter was, that it was he that conferred it by giving the invitation, and not Jesus by accepting it.

And how came the Lord to accept of such an invitation? Simply out of his great grace. He held himself aloof from no class of men. Now we find him the guest of Levi the publican, and again that of a Pharisee like Simon; but all the time he was the friend of sinners. It was part of his plan to accept hospitality wherever it was proffered to him, in order that he might thereby reach all classes and conditions of men. Therefore he did not decline the request of Simon, but went to his house, just, indeed, as he came to earth itself, "to seek and to save that which was lost."

But now the guests are in their places, not sitting cross-legged on the floor, like modern Orientals, nor seated on chairs, as with ourselves; but reclining, after the old Roman fashion, on couches, the head being toward the table, and the feet, unsandalled, stretched out behind, while the body rested on the left side and elbow. Around the walls of the room sit some of the inhabitants of the place, who have heard of the feast, and who have come in to see the banquet and to listen to the conversation. For on such occasions there is, even at this day, in Eastern society, much more latitude allowed than there is with us. Thus in one of the earliest, and still one of the best, of the books of Eastern travel, being the report of the party of which Andrew Bonar and Robert McCheyne were members, we find the following statement: "At dinner at the consul's house at Damietta, we were much interested in observing a custom of the country. In the room where we were received, besides the divan on which we sat, there were seats all round the walls. Many came in, and took their places on these side seats, uninvited and yet unchallenged. They spoke to those at table, on business, or the news of the day; and our host spoke freely to them." It is added, that they found the same custom in existence in Jerusalem. So, in the case before us, the seats at the sides of the room were occupied by spectators, who had come in to be present at, though not to be partakers of, the feast. Among these was a woman of the city, a poor waif, who had been living on the wages of iniquity, and who bore upon her countenance the signs of her depravity. In a small town, everybody knows all about everybody else; and so her appearance and reputation were familiar to all in the apartment. We may suppose, therefore, that her entrance caused some little flutter of sensation. But when, in a paroxysm of uncontrollable emotion, she stood "at the feet of Jesus," and "began to wash them with her tears, and did wipe them with the hairs of her head, and kissed his feet, and anointed them" with ointment taken from an alabaster vase, we may be sure that her actions took the whole party by surprise. Indeed, they were properly understood only by the Lord himself: and they were so, first, because it is only love that can interpret love; and, second, because Jesus alone was acquainted with the unrecorded history which lay between her sinful life and her so singular behavior at this banquet. It is only love that can interpret love; and therefore that which seems unusual and extravagant to on-lookers is, between lovers themselves, only the ordinary language of affection. So it came, that Judas said, regarding the offering of Mary, "To what purpose is this waste?" and so, in the every way similar instance of this woman, the unloving Simon viewed her conduct with displeasure. But Jesus knew better. His own love, which found its unusual expression in the cross, was at no loss to comprehend the meaning of this impassioned and devoted penitent.

Besides, as I have said, there was an unrecorded history lying behind this manifestation. For the two must have met before. This was not the first time she had seen the Lord. Already she had heard his words, and been brought to her true self by their gracious influence. Perhaps she had been in the crowd when, but a short while before, he had given that loving invitation, "Come unto me, all ye that labor and are heavy laden, and I will give you rest. Take my yoke upon you, and learn of me, for I am meek and lowly in heart; and ye shall find rest unto your souls. For my yoke is easy, and my burden is light," — words which we cannot read without the deepest emotion, but which, as they came from him, must have made their way straight to her heart. In any case, on some previous occasion, virtue had gone out of him to her, and had awakened new hope within her. She saw the possibility of being forgiven, even for her life of sin. She felt uprising within her the determination to become a pure and noble woman. Nay, she had the persuasion that she was already pardoned and accepted by God; and so, unmoved by all surrounding discouragements, conscious of nothing but that He was there to whom she owed her new-born blessedness, she eagerly threw herself upon his feet, and took this method of telling him "all that was in her heart." She came thus to him, not as a penitent seeking pardon, but as a sinner already forgiven; and so that which looked like extravagance to others was perfectly natural in her, and thoroughly acceptable to him. It was but "the return and repercussion" in her of that love which he had already shown to her. Her tears were, as Luther calls them, "heart-water;" they were the distillation of her gratitude. She had not come, indeed, to weep: she had come designing to use the ointment only. But her tears had, as it were, stolen a march upon her: they had come unbidden and unexpected, and had rather interfered with the fulfilment of her purpose. But in order that her original intention might be thoroughly carried out, she wiped them from his feet with her flowing tresses, and then poured over him the precious ointment, whose odor filled the house.

But Simon did not comprehend her in the least. He looked on in amazement, not unmingled with disgust. He knew the reputation of the woman; but he knew nothing whatever of the change which had been wrought upon her, and he was surprised at the manner in which

Jesus received her attentions. Nor let us judge him
too harshly; for there is something to be said for him,
after all. He had a regard for morality; he would not
have spoken to such a character as he conceived this
woman to be. But the misfortune was, that he judged
entirely by appearances. He condemned her before he
had possession of all the evidence. He knew that she
had been a sinner, but he did not know that she was now
a forgiven penitent. And, erring thus regarding the
woman, he erred also of necessity regarding Christ; for
he said within himself, " This man, if he were a prophet,
would have known what manner of woman this is that
toucheth him; for she is a sinner." He had desired to
convince himself whether Jesus was a prophet or not,
and now he had found it out! He argued it out within
himself after this fashion: "A prophet is a discerner of
spirits, and a holy man; now, if this man is a discerner
of spirits, he must know the unholiness of this woman,
and, as being himself holy, he would not let her touch
him as he now does; or if, knowing her character, he
allows her thus to approach him, he must be himself
unholy: and in either case he can be no prophet." But
he spoke no word. All this was merely the thought of
his heart. And he was shaken out of it by the excla-
mation of the Lord, who showed him that he was a
discerner of spirits after all, by answering the argument
which he had not himself ventured to utter. "Simon!"
exclaimed he, "I have somewhat to say unto thee."
And he said, "Master, say on." Then came the parable: "There was a certain creditor which had two debtors; the one owed five hundred pence, and the other
fifty. And when they had nothing to pay, he frankly
forgave them both. Tell me, therefore, which of them
will love him most." Simon answered either in a kind

of supercilious tone, as if he thought the question of no importance; or in a constrained manner, as if he felt that something was to be made out of his reply to his own disadvantage: "I suppose, that he to whom he forgave most." And Jesus said unto him, "Thou hast rightly judged."

Now, the history over which we have come has furnished the key to the interpretation. The creditor is Christ, the two debtors are Simon and the woman. The debts are different, perhaps, objectively, in the magnitude of the sins of each, but rather, perhaps, subjectively, in the depth of the conviction of each. Both alike, however, are hopelessly bankrupt; and to both alike frank forgiveness is offered. Now, presuming in both cases that the forgiveness is accepted, Simon was right in answering that he to whom he forgave most will love him most. It follows, therefore, that the love which this woman manifested in such an unusual way was the consequence of her acceptance of forgiveness for unusual sin. She had been a great sinner, but she was now a forgiven sinner; and the fact that she had been forgiven so much was the explanation of that demonstration of her affection which had so scandalized Simon.

But if the acceptance of pardon by her is the explanation of her warmth, where shall we find that of the coldness of Simon? Plainly, in this: that he had not accepted forgiveness, even for the fifty pence which he owed. That was the inference which the Lord designed his host to draw. But, as he seemed either unable or unwilling to draw it for himself, the Lord did it for him in an indirect but yet most forcible manner. Turning to the woman, he said to Simon, "Thou seest this woman. I entered into thine house, thou gavest me no water for my feet; but she hath washed my feet with tears, and wiped them with the hairs of her head. Thou gavest me no kiss; but this woman, since the time I came in, hath not ceased to kiss my feet. My head with oil thou didst not anoint, but this woman hath anointed my feet with ointment." What, then, — this is the suggested application, — is the inference from all this in the light of your answer to my question? Clearly, that she has been forgiven much, and that thou hast not been forgiven at all. Her love is the result of Her acceptance of forgiveness; and because she has been forgiven much, it is that she loves so much: but your indifference is an evidence that you have not yet accepted pardon, even for the smaller sins which you acknowledge you have committed. " Wherefore I say unto you, Her sins are forgiven." You can see that from her love; and they must have been "many" sins, "for she loveth much." " But to whom little is forgiven, the same loveth little."

Such is clearly the meaning of the parable in its application to Simon and the woman; and, thus understood, we perceive at once that all the controversy which has been waged over it, as to the ground of forgiveness, is irrelevant. For the woman's love was the result and evidence of her having been forgiven, not the reason why she was forgiven. And so, when the Lord adds, turning to the woman the while, " Thy sins are forgiven, go into peace," he is not giving her *then* pardon for the first time, but rather formally expressing with absolute certainty, that of which already she had had the inward assurance. We may illustrate this from the case of her who was afflicted with the issue of blood. You remember how she came behind the Lord, and touched him, saying within herself, "If I may but touch his clothes, I shall be whole;" and straightway she felt in her body that she was whole of her plague: that corresponds to the first coming of this woman to Jesus, when she knew in herself that she was forgiven. Afterward, when she who had been cured heard him asking, "Who touched me?" she came forward, and told him all that was in her heart: that corresponds to this woman's approach to Jesus here in the banquet-hall. Finally, when Jesus said to the woman whom he had already healed, "Daughter, thy faith hath made thee whole: go in peace, and be whole of thy plague," that corresponds to his expression here, "Thy sins are forgiven [or, more literally, "have been forgiven"] thee, go into peace." The forgiveness in the latter case, like the cure in the former, had been already given and received; but assurance was made doubly sure by the formal expression at the end of the interview. With a glad heart, therefore, this woman must have left the house of Simon. But the guests, seeing the plight in which their host was left, endeavored to shield him by raising a new issue; for they said, "Who is this that forgiveth sins also?" Their device, however, did not mar the graciousness of Christ; for he simply met it by reiterating to the woman the assurance that she was freely pardoned, and by sending her away "into the peace of God, which passeth all understanding."

Only one question now remains, and it is this: Does not the teaching of the Lord here encourage sinners to go to great lengths in iniquity, in order that at last, being forgiven much, they may love much? Now, as every one can see, that is but another form of the objection to the doctrines of grace, as such, which Paul thus enunciates, "What shall we say, then? Shall we continue in sin that grace may abound?" and we may meet it, as Paul meets it, by saying, "God forbid!" But we may show its untenableness in another way. The aggravated sinner may be nearer the kingdom than the self-righteous Pharisee. Christ told his hearers once that the publicans and harlots would go into it before them. That is because it is much harder to part with righteous self than it is to give up sinful self. Yet that would be no valid reason for a man's giving himself up to gross iniquity; and in like manner, when the Lord says, " to whom little is forgiven, the same loveth little," he gives no countenance to those who would sin much in order to be forgiven much. Indeed, there is an inconsistency in the very conception; for, how could one who sincerely desires forgiveness at all be willing to go further into sin?

But perhaps the true answer to the question is to be had in the idea at which I have already dimly hinted; this, namely, that the debts here are not regarded objectively in the magnitude of the sins, but subjectively in the conviction of the sinner. And the fact that an offering almost identical with that brought by this woman to Jesus was made also by Mary of Bethany seems to tell in favor of this view of the case. The great sinner and the great saint touch hands in the act of anointing the Lord.

> "Man's hasty lip would both reprove, —
> One for the stain of too much sin,
> One for the waste of too much love;
> But both availed His smile to win," —

because both offered sincerely. The one, in her new-born religious life, sees something of the enormity of her sinful career; the other, in her growth in holiness, has learned to discover the vileness of sin, of whatsoever sort: and so, sisters in the love of Jesus, they, as it were, meet with their vases of ointment in his presence, both pardoned and both forgiven. There are aggravated sinners who have no deep sense of sin, and there are great saints who regard themselves as the chief of sinners. The measure of one's gratitude for forgiveness is the conception which he has of his sin. He who makes light of sin will make light also of salvation. But he who has a profound conviction of the evil of sin as the abominable thing which God hates, will have an overwhelming sense of God's love in granting him forgiveness. The deeper our apprehension of the exceeding sinfulness of sin, the greater will be our love to Him who gives us deliverance from it. And where there is that sense of the hatefulness of sin, there will be no disposition to go deeper into it.

I conclude with one or two inferences from this whole subject.

1. Let sinners of every name and degree be encouraged by this narrative to go at once to Christ. He will in no wise cast them out. There are no more touching stories in the Gospels than those which tell how Jesus dealt with the most degraded class of sinners. Recall his conversation with the woman of Samaria, at the well of Sychar. Bring up before you once again that scene in the temple, when the scribes and Pharisees dragged in before him the woman who had been taken in the very act of sin. Then read anew this narrative which has been before us to-night, and say if the prophecy regarding him was not true, " A bruised reed shall he not break, the smoking flax shall he not quench." A bruised reed was not deemed worthy of the shepherd's trouble when he was piping in the field; and so he

flung it away, and got another. Smoking flax gives an offensive odor; and rather than be annoyed with it, the housewife will take it out of the lamp, and tread upon it. But it was otherwise with Jesus. That which others would cast away, he sought to retain, and turn to good account. That which others would give up as hopeless, he would not abandon. Though a man might seem to be as good-for-nothing as a bruised reed, he would receive him and restore him. Though a woman might be as repulsive as smoking flax, and the world would cast her out of society, and trample on her, he would deal gently with her, and fan the spark into a flame which would burn brightly for the illumination of others. Where men perceived no promise of success, and would have been tempted to give up the individual as hopeless, he would labor on until the reed which had given forth a note jangled and out of tune was restored to its original condition, and gave its own quota to the harmony of Jehovah's praise. Oh, what hope there is even for the most degraded sinner here! "This man receiveth sinners." They said it in reproach, but it is still his brightest glory. Whosoever thou art, then, and whatsoever be thy guilt, make application unto him, for he will in no wise cast thee out.

2. But, as a second inference from this whole subject, let us learn, that, if we would be successful in raising the fallen, and reclaiming the abandoned, we must be willing to "touch" them, and to be "touched" by them. In other words, we must come into warm, loving, personal contact with them. What an uplift Christ gave to the soul of this poor woman, when he, the pure and holy, let *her* thus approach him! And this was his way all through his ministry. When he would heal the leper, he did not stand afar off, and cry, "Keep at a

distance! keep at a distance, for thou art unclean." Nay, but he did a new thing in Israel. He touched the leper, yet was he not himself thereby defiled; for the purity within not only repelled the pollution, but communicated itself to the poor victim. And with the healing of his body, what a thrill would vibrate through the leper's soul, as he said, "Here is one, and he the noblest of them all, who is not afraid to touch me"! So in our measure, in dealing with the moral lepers of society, we must touch them if we would raise them. In that historic story which had so much to do with awakening the conscience of this country to the sin of slavery, you remember that Miss Ophelia could do nothing with the little colored incorrigible so long as she shrank from her touch as from a toad. Contact is needed if virtue is to go out of us. When the Lord wished to save the human race, he touched it by taking on him our nature, without our nature's pollution. So we must take the nature of the degraded, without its impurity, if we would help him. We must stoop to take him by the hand, or to let him grasp our hand, if we would lift him up. Those who are the greatest elevators of their fellows are not the haughty Simons who scowl upon the outcasts, but the loving disciples of Jesus, who go in among them, and try to understand them, and seek to show them tokens of affection. Society, ay, even the Christian Church itself, has been too long in learning this lesson: but we have fallen now on better times; and many a noble woman and many an earnest man has gone down into the sinks of iniquity, unappalled by dangers, and unrepelled by unpleasantness, and has brought back priceless souls which shall shine forever in the diadem of Christ. Let us imbibe their spirit, and follow their example. If Jesus touched and received sinners, what right have we to stand aloof from them? He was without sin; but we — God help us! — we are sinners in his sight, not greatly different from them. Why, then, should we be so pharisaical? Oh! as we read this narrative, let us learn the lesson of these simple lines, —

"Deal kindly with the erring,
Oh! do not thou forget,
However darkly stained by sin,
He is thy brother yet.

"Heir of the self-same heritage,
Child of the self-same God,
He hath but stumbled in the path
Thou hast in weakness trod.

"Deal kindly with the erring:
Thou yet mayst lead him back,
With holy words and tones of love,
From misery's erring track.

"Forget not thou hast often sinned,
And sinful yet must be:
Deal kindly with the erring one,
As God has dealt with thee."

Finally, if we wish to love God much, we must think much of what we owe to him. Low views of sin lead to a light estimate of the blessing of pardon, and a light estimate of the blessing of pardon will lead to but a little love of God. This cuts deep, my brethren. Your love to God will be but the other side of your hatred of sin; and there, as it seems to me, is the radical defect in much of the religious experience of the day. Men make light of their obligation to Christ because they have first made light of sin. Low views of the evil of sin are at the root of all heresies in doctrine and all unholiness in life. Get rid of all such minimizing ideas of sin, I beseech you; and to that end come near the cross, for nowhere does sin seem so vile as it does there. May God open your eyes to see it there; and then you will hate it with an utter hatred, and, being forgiven, will love Christ with an **exceeding love**.

XV

THE GOOD SAMARITAN

Luke 10:25-37

THE occasion which called forth this parable is as well known as the parable itself. One of the class of lawyers, who were not solicitors or barristers, as among us, but rather expounders of the books of Moses, came to Jesus with the inquiry, "Master, what shall I do to inherit eternal life?" We cannot tell what his motive was for proposing such a question. The Evangelist informs us that he was "tempting" Jesus; but the word so rendered simply means that he was putting him to the test, and it may be used either in a good or a bad sense. It is possible that this inquirer thought that he might succeed in embarrassing the Lord, either by reducing him to silence or by entrapping him into some inconsistency. But as the question which he put had reference to the most important subject which can engage the attention of any man, I am inclined to believe that he was sincere. The Lord replies to him, as he did to so many others, by putting a question in his turn. Through the understanding of that which they already knew, he sought to lead men up to the perception of that which they were inquiring after. So he said to this man, "What is written in the law? How readest thou?" In answer the lawyer gave a correct summary of the ten commands, according to the word of Moses in

Deuteronomy and Leviticus; whereupon, desiring thereby to bring him to a sense of his own sinfulness and helplessness, the Saviour said, "Thou hast answered right: this do, and thou shalt live." But he had not done that; and as the point of the Saviour's probe was coming a little too near to be quite comfortable, he sought to fence off all further thrusts by diverting the conversation into a discussion about the meaning of a word. So he asked, "Who is my neighbor?" and he got for answer this simple story, which, like the picture of a skilful artist, speaks for itself, finding its way at once "through the eye to the heart," and disdaining all elaborate exposition as absolutely unnecessary.

But two things must strike every attentive reader. The first is, that the parable was not so much an answer to the question formally put by the lawyer, as an exposure of the state of heart which the putting of that question revealed. The inquirer wanted a definition of the word "neighbor." The Lord answers by showing him true neighborliness in contrast with selfish indifference. He wished to know whom he was to consider as his neighbor: the Lord answers by showing him the actions of one who did not need to put any such question, and leaves him to draw the inference, that, wherever the true spirit of benevolence is present, it will not stand in the face of suffering, mocking it with the cry, "Who is my neighbor?" but will recognize the claim of every afflicted and down-trodden fellow-man to sympathy and succor. Thus the parable does not tell us in form who our neighbor is, but it shows us how true love works.

But the second peculiarity of this parable is, that it is not an allegory, each figure in which represents a spiritual analogue; but simply an illustrative example of the working of benevolence, as contrasted with that of selfishness. If we look at the parable of the sower, we find that Jesus gives the interpretation after this fashion, "This is he which received seed by the wayside;" "He that received the seed into stony places, the same is he," etc.; "He also that received seed among the thorns is he," etc.; "But he that received seed into the good ground is he," etc. Each kind of ground thus represented or signified a different sort of hearer of the Word. But you could not so interpret the parable of the good Samaritan. You could not say the traveller is so and so, the thieves are such and such, the priest is this class, and the Levite that, and the good Samaritan a third, while the inn is meant to symbolize one thing, and the two pence another. That would lead us into unending absurdity. The interpretation is given by our Lord, when, pointing to the good Samaritan, he said, "Go, and do thou likewise." Therefore the story is an idealized example of true benevolence in contrast with utter selfishness. It may have been actual fact. There is nothing of improbability about it. The road from Jerusalem to Jericho was dangerous from its being infested with robbers; priests and Levites were likely enough to be often on it, as Jericho was a priestly city; and a Samaritan might be there on business. So that there is no inherent impossibility, or even improbability, in the supposition that it was an actual occurrence. We incline, however, to the view that it was purely imaginative, but the product of that highest sort of imagination which gets at the deepest truth through fiction. In any case, it is not an allegory, but an illustration, designed to show us what we must avoid, as well as what we must cultivate, if we would truly and fully love our neighbor as ourselves.

First we see a traveller set upon by robbers, who

strip him of his money, his raiment, and his goods, and wound him, and depart, leaving him half dead. Very clearly there is no neighbor-love in that. Next we observe a priest coming along, on his way from Jerusalem to his country home; but, though he sees full well the straits to which the unfortunate man has been reduced, he "passes by on the other side." Just as clearly there is no neighbor-love in that. Then, after the priest has gone out of sight, a Levite makes his appearance. As he comes up to the victim of the robbers' violence, he pauses a few moments to look at him, and we begin to think that he will do something for him; but, after all, he also "passes by on the other side." Just as clearly there is no neighbor-love in that. After he has gone, a Samaritan on horseback rides up; and as soon as he perceives the poor man's plight, he dismounts, sets to work for the reviving of the half-dead one, by pouring oil into his wounds, and wine into his mouth, then lifts him up on to the saddle, and bears him to an inn, where he sees that he is well cared for at his expense. Then, when he departs on the morrow, he leaves with the host a sum sufficient for the immediate wants of his *protégé*, and this blank check, as I may call it, to be filled in at the discretion of the landlord, to whom he was evidently well known: "Take care of him; and whatsoever thou spendest more, when I come again I will repay thee." Now, here, the lawyer himself being the judge, — here was true neighbor-love. Therefore, teaching him out of his own mouth, Jesus said to him, "Go and do thou likewise. The suffering whom thou canst relieve, the ignorant whom thou canst instruct, the degraded whom thou canst elevate, the oppressed whom thou canst protect, wherever he may be, and whatever be his nationality, barbarian, Scythian, bond or free, *he* is thy neighbor. Go, therefore, and do to him as the Samaritan did for the wounded traveller."

Let us, therefore, analyze as far as we may the actions of this Samaritan, and see if we can get any fuller apprehension of the meaning of this "likewise."

I. In the first place, then, it is clear that the kindness of this man was of the spirit, and not merely of the letter. Here was one main point of difference between him and the priest and Levite. They needed a specific injunction, but he wanted to carry out a great principle. Had they found in the law a command to this effect, "If thou shalt see a man lying half dead upon the highwayside, thou shalt not pass him by unheeded, but shalt surely help him," I think that they would have exerted themselves for his deliverance. But because the precept ran, "Thou shalt love thy neighbor as thyself," and did not define who their neighbor was, or what precisely they were to do for him, they imagined that they were under no obligation to do any thing whatever on his behalf. In the mind of the Samaritan, however, love meant the doing of every thing within his power, for all who required his help; and therefore, without asking any questions or making any excuses, he gave the poor man all the assistance he could.

This distinction must be clearly seen by every one, and, indeed, it is apparent in all departments of human activity. Thus, in the workshop, you have on the one hand the man who gives only his hands to his employer, and does mechanically only what he is hired to do, — no less, indeed, but no more, — and on the other you have the ready and obliging artisan, who finds much to do which no contract can specify, and cheerfully does that without requiring to be asked. In the counting-house there is, on the one hand, the lad who is always stickling about the performance of this or that piece of work because it is not in what he calls "his department," and who gets himself heartily hated for his pains; and, on the other, the active and obliging youth, who does what he sees needs to be done, whether it is his own proper work or not, and whose sole ambition it is to promote the happiness of all around him, and advance the interests of his employer. So important is this distinction as a criterion of character, that, if I were required to decide concerning a man's moral principle, I would not examine so carefully what he is in respect to what ethical writers have called the determinate virtues, which are marked off by a well-defined boundary from their opposite vices, but I would investigate very thoroughly what he is in regard to those virtues which are indeterminate, the measure of a man's devotion to them being left to the promptings of his own heart. A man cannot be a thief or a liar without crossing a well-marked boundary between right and wrong; but he may be a selfish churl without knowing it, because in regard to benevolence the law is left indefinite, being, indeed, like an algebraic formula, expressed in terms so general that they need to be translated by the occasion into definite particulars. Where the law is so broad as to be applicable to all circumstances, there is always a danger that some will feel no obligation to obey it in any circumstances; and only the heart which has imbibed the principle or spirit of the law will feel its force continually. Here, then, let us examine ourselves, and see what manner of men we are. If we do that only which is formally prescribed, and if, where the law leaves a blank to be filled up by circumstances, we act as if there was no law at all, then we have yet to learn what true benevolence is; nay, more, we have yet to learn what kind of a book the New Testament is: for it is not a list of distinct precepts, each of which is applicable to only one case; but it is a book of living principles of universal application, and he who really understands them, and has a heart to feel their obligation, will be at no loss to find occasion for their manifestation. To read it as if it were a set of rubrics, with minute directions for every detail of conduct, will make us Pharisees: to read it as a book of great principles that are to have free course through all our actions, even as the blood has through the body, will make us the disciples of Him "who went about doing good." Instead, therefore, of waiting for any minute definition in the letter, like that which this lawyer expected when he said, "Who is my neighbor?" let us show, that, taught by the Holy Spirit, and stimulated by the example of the Lord Jesus, we have learned to see that every sufferer whom we can assist has a claim of neighbor love upon us which we cannot repudiate without injuring him and dishonoring God.

II. In the second place, we may perceive that this man's benevolence was not hindered by any prejudices of nationality or religion. The injured traveller was an entire stranger to him, but he did not say within himself on that account, "He has no claim upon me." He was, besides, a Jew. So much, indeed, is not said in the parable, because Jesus was speaking to Jews, and therefore they would suppose that one of their own nation was meant unless another nationality had been specifically ascribed to him. He was, then, a Jew; and the feud between his people and the Samaritans, because it was a religious one, between people that were neighbors, and agreed in certain points while they differed on others, was exceedingly bitter: yet he did not exclaim, "Let him die, for all I care!" No: he was a man, in great straits, and all other things were forgotten by him in the presence of these two. In other circumstances he might have enjoyed a debate with him about the rival claims of Moriah and Gerizim, or perhaps he might have allowed his prejudice to carry itself so strongly as to make him pass him without any salutation; but in the presence of his misery he loses remembrance, for the time, of such matters. Nationality is swallowed up by humanity, and sectarianism is put to flight by religion, as he dismounts to minister to a suffering fellow-man.

Now, here, again, we are furnished with a test as to the genuineness of our own neighbor-love; and by its application we may discover that our benevolence is often chilled, if not, indeed, absolutely killed, by some prevalent influences. These may be described as caste, denominationalism, and a certain prudishness which we may call purism.

There is, first, caste. That is commonly supposed, indeed, to be a heathenish thing, having no existence in our land of liberty and equality. But that is a popular delusion. The word may be foreign, but that which it signifies is home grown. There are Brahmans and Pariahs here, as really as in Hindostan. There are families brought up among us to believe that those who live in poorer houses or have darker skins than themselves exist for their benefit; and, as a consequence, they treat them with despite. Their dignity would be lowered if they were to attend to sufferers in such humble circumstances; and so, like the priest and the Levite, they pass them by on the other side. But true love knows nothing of any such distinctions. Rich and poor, white and black, Caucasian and Mongolian, are alike to her, when they are touched by the sanctifying hand of affliction; or, if she makes any difference between them, she gives the preference to the lowliest as having fewest friends. She believes that greatness, like wisdom, "is ofttimes nearer when we stoop than when we soar;" and in her ear the gratitude of the humblest whom she has relieved is sweeter far than the hollow flattery of worldly pride.

Then there is denominationalism. Now, let it not be supposed that I dispute the principle, that, while we should do good to all men as we have opportunity, there is an "especially" in the case of those who are of the household of faith; or, that I deny that a church should have a peculiar care over its own poor. On the contrary, I admit both of these propositions. But I altogether deny that a Christian's benevolence should be restricted within the bounds of his own denomination, or even of the Church of Christ. We are Christians first, before we are denominationalists; we are men before we are Christians: and I have an utter abhorrence of that system which refuses to help those who cannot pronounce "shibboleth" as we do, or who have not yet found their way to the foot of the cross. Had this Samaritan insisted, that, before receiving his assistance, the poor traveller should have assented to the pre-eminence of Gerizim over Jerusalem, he would only have insulted the misery which he was offering to alleviate. But before the majesty of suffering, all such sectarianism disappeared; and it should be so among ourselves. When a man's house is on fire, we do not stay to bid him repeat the Apostles' Creed before we begin to help him to extinguish the flames; and it seems the paltriest of all proceedings, to restrict our benevolence to any class of religionists. The great thing we have to do in a case of suffering is to relieve it; and it is not without the deepest suggestiveness, that the relief here was given by a man who belonged to a sect which Christ himself, on another occasion, declared to be clearly in the wrong. So that, in his view, we are left to infer that heterodoxy showing love is a better thing than orthodoxy manifesting indifference.

The last thing tending among us to counteract benevolence is what I have called purism; and it is characteristic of those who have set themselves up as guardians of the public morals, so that they can not or will not help those who have brought their suffering upon themselves by their sins. Now, here, again, I am as far as possible from saying that benevolence should be exercised so indiscriminately as to bestow a premium upon vice; and I must confess, that in this city, and in these days, a wise caution should be exercised when we seek to do good to others. Either we should ourselves make personal inquiry into each case, or, through the medium of the Charity Organization society, we should make sure that we are dealing with a real necessity, and not helping to maintain one of those professional "bummers" who prey upon the gullibility of the people. I have nothing to say against such discrimination in our benevolence; but what I want to condemn is the spirit of those who say in the face of deepest misery, "Well, he has brought it upon himself. He has made his own bed, let him lie upon it as best he may. It is only what he deserves." Such language might be appropriate in the mouth of an angel, — only there is not one of them who would use it, — but it is dreadful in the mouth of a sinful man. "What he deserves!" Has

not the great dramatist said, " Use every man after his
deserts, and who should 'scape whipping?" And what
and where should we now have been, if God had acted
toward us on such a principle? Thus, for all so earnest as it seems in virtue's cause, this purism is at heart
a Christless thing. Be it that the man has brought it
upon himself; is he for that to die unhelped, while we
stand by and piously moralize over his misdeeds? It
will be time enough to give our moral lesson when his
misery is alleviated, and we may then hope that it will
be heeded; but to give a lecture when the cry is for
help, is something like giving a serpent for a fish, or a
scorpion for an egg. Thus again we come back to the
queenly majesty of love, for wherever she exists she
makes a way for herself. No fashionable barriers will
stop her progress; no denominational boundaries will
hedge in her efforts; no guilt, even, will seal up the
fountain of her beneficence. Over all such obstacles
she will triumph; and, be the sufferer who he may, she
will see in him a *man* wearing the nature which the
Son of God has consecrated by his incarnation, and
ransomed by his blood; and, for his sake, she will
relieve him.

III. In the third place, it is obvious that this man's
benevolence was not hindered by any considerations of
personal convenience. He might have said within himself, as he looked at the rapidly westering sun, "I must
be in Jericho on urgent business, by a certain time."
Or he might have reasoned after this fashion: "If I am
found near this poor man, I may get into trouble, and
be accused of robbing and maltreating him." Or, more
plausibly still, he might have thought, "These cruel
robbers cannot be far away, and they may attack me

also: therefore I must hasten on as rapidly as possible." Or, in sordid avarice, he might have argued that he could not afford to do all that was required; and so, like the priest and the Levite, he too might have passed by on the other side. But, no! he could do nothing but help this poor, helpless man. It made no matter what should come to him. His business might take care of itself for the time; he might be accused of the robbery; he might even be robbed, himself; it might cost him a good deal before he was done with it: but, whatever came, this man should be helped. Thus he forgot himself in the presence of the traveller's distress, and set himself at once to revive and relieve him.

Now, by this, again, we may try our own benevolence; and when we apply to it this testing acid, I fear that much of what looks like finely polished charity will prove to be no better than burnished selfishness. Many do kindnesses, that they may be seen and honored of men. They will give, if the giving will secure them some coveted position, or in some way else, as the phrase is, "bring grist to their own mill." Some will give money to buy themselves off from personal exertion. Others will give their personal exertion to save their money. But in the instance before us, both were given; for, what genuine neighbor-love does, it will do thoroughly. Self will save always what is dearest to self, but love is ready to sacrifice up to the extent of the necessity which it seeks to meet. And blessed be God, there is such love among us! I have seen it in the wealthy Christian, whose money and whose time were largely given to the service of suffering humanity. I have seen it in the poor Christian, who out of compassion has taken into his home an orphan child, and done for it in every respect as for his own.

I have seen it, too, where one would scarcely expect to find it, as when some despised "woman of the city" gives herself up to the tending of a guilty sister whose misery was deeper than her own. Alas that a case like that should put to shame the selfishness of many who claim to be the followers of the Lord Jesus!

IV. In the fourth place, it is evident that this man's benevolence took its form from the nature of the misery which he sought to relieve. He did the very things which the sufferer needed to have done for him, and he did these at once. He might, indeed, have put himself about in many other ways, under the idea that he was helping the unfortunate traveller; but nothing could have met the case save the method which he adopted. He had no stereotyped mode of showing mercy, which he sought invariably to follow; but he did in each case just what each required. Now, this is very important, because, for lack of attention to it, many people's benevolence, though it may be very well meant, is a total failure. In "Ivors," which is one of Miss Yonge's best stories, you may remember that there is a gouty old admiral who is continually saying most caustic yet true things; and among other remarks bearing on the point now before us, he is represented as affirming that "There is a great mania abroad at present for doing good, and wonderfully little common-sense in setting about it." This witness is true; and in few things is the lack of common-sense more apparent than in the neglect to adapt the efforts which are put forth, to the necessities which they are designed to meet. Thus, a man has been wonderfully successful in one or more instances by using a particular method, and forthwith he becomes so enamoured of it that he uses it on every sort of occasion; but in the vast majority of cases it fails, because it is not adapted to more than one class of instances. In the fortifications on the Dardanelles, there are said to be some guns which are so built in, that they can hit a vessel only at one point; and so they are useless except at the moment when a ship is passing that point. Now, the benevolence of the man of whom I am now speaking is like one of these guns. It can meet only one class of cases; whereas it ought rather to be like the swivel-gun upon the turret-ship, which sweeps the horizon round and round. Even as, in perfect consistency with the general principles of medical science, the remedy must be changed to meet the disease, so our efforts in practical beneficence must take their shape from the evils which we mean to mitigate. The path which I take in going after him who is out of the way must be regulated by the situation of the wanderer, else I shall never find him. And so in every other case. Thus the surroundings of each instance of suffering must determine the form in which it is to be best met by benevolence; and so the principle of love is kept from being stereotyped, and every case draws out new inventiveness. And what is true of individuals is also true of different ages and nations. The charities of the past will not meet the exigencies of the present, and the kind of instrumentality called into existence by the evils of a hundred years ago will not meet the new miseries of to-day. Thus the questions suggested in this particular by the parable before us are, " What interpretation is given to this 'Go, and do thou likewise,' by the requirements of our own times? Where in these days shall I find the counterpart of this poor, half-dead traveller? and what for me will correspond to the oil and the wine and the money which his benefactor gave? What does this 'Go, and do thou likewise,' mean now and here for me?" These questions, each one must grapple with and settle for himself; and, having found an answer to them, he must seek to meet the new necessity with means as admirably adapted to their purpose as were those which this Samaritan adopted. One will find this poor traveller in the little Arab of the streets, and will seek through the Children's Aid Society or the Home for the Friendless, or other kindred agency, to rescue him from a future of crime, and prepare him for becoming a good and useful citizen and an earnest Christian. Another will see him in the poor victim of drunkenness; and through the Christian Home for Intemperate Men, or some similar house of mercy, he will endeavor to secure his emancipation from the slavery of appetite. Another will find him in the freedman struggling up towards Christianity and education, and will help him in his ascent. But what need I more? To identify this Samaritan in modern times, would take me round the entire circumference of human misery. You have but to open your eyes to see him anywhere; and, when you recognize him, see to it that you open your hearts and your hands for his assistance.

V. But now, as supplementary to the teaching of the parable, I add, that, if our benevolence would be of the highest order, we must exercise it out of regard to Him who died to show mercy to ourselves. I do not, of course, imagine that such a thought was in the mind of this Samaritan, even as Jesus has portrayed him. But I do see the great heart of Christ himself throbbing through this story. Was not he himself, in a very exalted sense, the good Samaritan to the human race? And, as he points to Calvary, has he not a right to say, as none other can, "Go, and do thou likewise"? Here is the grand motive power, under the influence of which that command is to be obeyed: "Ye know the grace of the Lord Jesus Christ, who, though he was rich, for your sakes became poor, that ye through his poverty might be rich." As he laid down his life, that we might be delivered, so let us make cheerful sacrifice of every thing, — money or time, or even, if need be, life itself, — for the sake of the suffering among our fellows. Thus our humanity will rise into Christianity, and our benevolence will be baptized into the name of the Lord Jesus.

I conclude with the story of an incident in the life of my grandfather, which I have often heard from my father's lips. It was more than a hundred years ago, when wheeled conveyances were rarely used in the rural districts of Scotland, and the custom was to convey grain to the mill in a sack laid over a horse's back. The good man was making such a journey once, over a rough bridle-path; and the horse stumbled, so that the sack fell off. The weight of years was on his shoulders, and he could not replace the load. As he was perplexed, and wondering what to do, he saw a man on horseback in the distance, and had just made up his mind to ask him for assistance, when he recognized in him the nobleman who lived in an adjoining castle; and then his heart sank again within him, for how could he request *him* to help him? But he did not need to ask him, for he was noble by a higher patent than any monarch could confer; and, when he came up, he dismounted of his own accord, saying, "Let me help you, John." So between them they put the load again upon the horse; and then John, — who was a gentleman too, though he did wear "hodden gray," — taking off his broad Kilmarnock bonnet, made obeisance, and said, "Please your lordship, how shall I ever thank you for your kindness?" — "Very easily, John," was the reply. "Whenever you see another man as sorely needing assistance as you were just now, help him; and that will be thanking me."

So, as we contemplate the sacrifice of Christ on our behalf, we cry, "What shall I render unto thee, O Lord, for all thy benefits toward me?" and there comes this answer: "Whensoever thou seest a fellow-man needing thy succor as much as thou wast needing mine when I gave my life for thee, help him, and that will be thanking me." "Inasmuch as ye do it unto one of the least of these my brethren, ye do it unto me."

XVI

THE FRIEND AT MIDNIGHT
Luke 11:5-13

THIS parable is introduced by Luke in connection with his account of the manner in which the Lord answered the request of his disciples, that he would teach them to pray, "as John also taught his disciples." They had seen him at his private devotions, probably had even overheard his supplications to his Father, and had been thereby made to feel how far they were from knowing any thing about such prayer as that which he had offered. Hence they asked to be instructed in the matter; and in response he gave them, both as a model and a form, that beautiful cluster of petitions which he afterward repeated in his Sermon on the Mount, and which we are accustomed to call "the Lord's Prayer." Then, as some among them may have mentally interjected the objection, "But we have prayed frequently, and have received no answer," he told this simple story to encourage them to continue in humble, fervent, believing, and patient prayer. The case is clearly a supposition; and the parable, like that of the good Samaritan, which we have already considered, is illustrative, and not typical or symbolical. We must not say that the friend at midnight represents God, or that the manner of the applicant at his door shows how we are to proceed in making supplication to God, or that the newly arrived stranger denotes any particular class, or that there is any special significance in the loaves. This story is merely an illustration, on which an argument is founded; and it is of immense importance, that we have a correct idea of what that argument really is.

First, however, let us have the case supposed clearly before us. It is midnight. A friend has arrived from a distance, and he to whose house he has come has nothing to set before him. In his extremity he goes to a neighbor, and knocks at his door to state his necessity, and to ask for help. But the sleepy response is, " Trouble me not: the door is now shut, and my children are with me in bed. I cannot rise and give thee." The suppliant, however, is not to be thus denied; so he thunders away shamelessly, even impudently, at the door, until, in sheer despair of getting any rest otherwise, and simply to get rid of what he deems a nuisance, his neighbor rises, and gives him what he wants. " I say unto you," says the Lord, " though he will not rise and give him because he is his friend, yet because of his importunity " — or rather, as it ought to be rendered, " shamelessness," or, more strongly still, " impudence " — " he will rise and give him as many as he needeth." Then the Lord proceeds to give the *Magna Charta* of prayer in the familiar words, " And I say unto you, Ask, and it shall be given you; seek, and ye shall find; knock, and it shall be opened unto you. For every one that asketh receiveth, and he that seeketh findeth, and to him that knocketh it shall be opened." To this he appends a comparison between an earthly father's dealings with his children, and those of our heavenly Father with his, thus: " If a son shall ask bread of any of you that is a father, will he give him a stone? or if he ask a fish, will he for a fish give him a serpent? or if he shall ask an egg, will he offer him a scorpion? If ye then, being evil, know how to give good gifts unto your children, how much more shall your heavenly Father give the Holy Spirit to them that ask him?"

Now, these last verses, as I believe, furnish the key to the argument in the parable. Like them, it reasons from the less to the greater, or, rather, from the worse to the better. It does not mean to represent God as gruff and disobliging, like the neighbor newly roused out of his earliest sleep; neither does it recommend the suppliant to use with God such shamelessness or impudence as his friend employed with him. But the suggested inference is this: If the impudence of that midnight knocker prevailed even with an angry and annoyed man so much, that he arose and gave what was requested, how much more will the humble, reverent, believing, and persevering prayer of a true child of God prevail with the infinitely kind and loving Father to whom he makes petition? Over against the irritated and reluctant man, only half awake, he places the calm, loving heavenly Father, "who slumbers not, neither sleepeth;" while, in contrast with the impudence of his troublesome neighbor, he suggests such earnest pleading with a Father as that which they had just seen in himself, or as he had recommended in the form which he had given them. And the conclusion which he draws is: If the appeal in the former case was ultimately successful, how much more is it likely to be in the latter! He is far from encouraging us to trust in boldness or irreverence or impudence in prayer, as so many misunderstand his words. We shall not be heard for our frequent speaking, any more than for our "much speaking." He would not have us trust in our prayer at all, but in the loving, fatherly heart of Him to whom we pray. Neither the place of prayer, nor the manner of prayer, nor the frequency of prayer, will avail. The answer will not come because of any of these things, but simply because God loves to give his people that which they request, if it be for their good; and so, when we come to him, our thought should be rather of his grace and wisdom than of any merit in our supplications, or of any attribute in them that will constrain him, so to say, to comply with our petitions. We are to wait on God in reverence and faith, biding his time, and trusting in his mercy. For, if a surly man ultimately yields to impudence, much more will the good God give the humble, reverent suppliant that which he desires.

I am the more anxious to set this clearly before you, because of many prevalent errors on the subject in these days. The tendency among multitudes, in regard to prayer, is to put more stress on the sort of prayer that is offered, than on the fact that all real prayer is offered to a loving God, who is better to his people than an earthly father is to his children; and the notion of too many is, that, if they will only keep at it long enough, they will ultimately, and by sheer force of importunity, prevail, as a teasing child wears out the patience, and sometimes even dethrones for the time the wisdom, of his parent. But here is no enforcement of importunity of that sort; rather, by implication, the impudence of this needy neighbor is condemned, and over against it is set such filial devotion as that which Jesus manifested when he was praying to his Father. "Wait on the Lord," — that is the lesson. Wait upon him because he is the Lord, and not a surly man who cannot be troubled with your prayer; and, because he is the Lord, wait upon him in humility, in faith, in patience, and with such reverence as is due to Him who is the King of kings and Lord of lords.

But some may say, "We have tried thus to wait upon him, and though we have waited long our prayers are still unanswered: how, then, can we reconcile this experience of ours with the unqualified promise in these words, 'Ask, and ye shall receive; seek, and ye shall find; knock, and it shall be opened unto you. For every one that asketh receiveth, and he that seeketh findeth, and unto him that knocketh it shall be opened'?" Now, what answer can we give to these troubled spirits? Must we admit that God has been unfaithful to his promise? Nay, for he is the Faithful One. What, then, shall we say? The answer will take us into the consideration of the conditions of successful prayer; and as on this subject, especially in its relation to the cure of diseases, there are current among us so many views which savor more of presumption than of faith, it may be well to discuss it with some degree of fulness. To that, therefore, I shall devote the remainder of this discourse.[1]

Let it be remembered, then, that the words here uttered by the Lord Jesus are not the only ones which he has spoken in regard to prayer; and that, to have a comprehensive conception of the matter, we must take into consideration all his other utterances concerning it. The recognized rule in the explanation of a statute is, that we should expound it all in the light of what is called the interpretation clause; and that, whenever we have a universal term by itself in one place, and have it repeated in the same connection, with certain qualifications, in other places, we are to understand it as

[1] The substance of what follows was contributed by the author as an article to the Princeton Review.

being always so conditioned in that connection. Now, to the universal terms here employed, there are some very important conditions attached elsewhere; and in the light of these must this promise be interpreted. Thus it is said by James, "Ye ask, and ye receive not, because ye ask amiss, that ye may consume it upon your lusts;"[1] and again, "But let him ask in faith, nothing wavering; for he that wavereth is as a wave of the sea, driven by the wind and tossed."[2] To the same effect are the Saviour's own words, "Therefore I say unto you, what things soever ye desire, when ye pray, believe that ye receive them, and ye shall have them."[3] More important still is the qualification in the words, "If ye abide in me, and my words abide in you, ye shall ask what ye will, and it shall be done unto you."[4] And again, in the Old Testament, "Delight thyself also in the Lord, and he shall give thee the desires of thine heart."[5] Nay, more: in the immediate neighborhood of one of the universal passages already quoted is the following: "And when ye stand praying, forgive if ye have aught against any; that your Father also who is in heaven may forgive your trespasses: but if ye do not forgive, neither will your Father which is in heaven forgive your trespasses."[6] Moreover, it cannot be forgotten, that in the Bible itself we have mention of prayers offered for certain things which the suppliants did not receive: thus David fasted and wept and prayed for the life of his little child, and the child died after all; while Paul desired that his thorn in the flesh might be taken from him, and received an answer indeed, but yet not the very thing which he requested. From all this, then, it is evident that this universal promise is to

---

[1] Jas. iv. 3.   [2] Id., i. 6.   [3] Mark xi. 24.
[4] John xv. 7.   [5] Ps. xxxvii. 4.   [6] Mark xi. 25, 26.

be understood as qualified by some indispensable conditions which connect themselves, first, with the character of the suppliant; second, with the nature of the thing requested; and, third, with the purpose and prerogative of God himself. By attending a little to each of these, their importance will be manifest.

In the first place, then, the success of prayer is conditioned by the character of the suppliant. Not every kind of asking is acceptable prayer. That which men desire simply for the gratification of malice, or the pampering of appetite, or the satisfying of ambition, or the aggrandizing of selfishness, God has nowhere promised to bestow; and unless there be in us the spirit to subordinate every thing to the honor of Jehovah, we have no warrant to expect an answer. Beneath every genuine prayer there must be evermore the disposition which is expressed in the doxology, "for Thine is the glory:" otherwise, the reproof of James will come in with fearful pungency, "Ye ask, and ye receive not, because ye ask amiss, that ye may consume it upon your lusts."[1]

Again, the wish that simply flits across the soul, as the shadow of the cloud glides over the summer grass, is no true prayer. It must take hold of the spirit, and gather into itself all the energy and earnestness of the man. The popular idea, indeed, is that prayer is a very simple matter: but, in reality, it is the highest exercise of the soul, and requires for its presentation the concentration of all its powers; and the English prelate was right when he said that "no man is likely to do much good in prayer who does not begin by looking upon it in the light of a work to be prepared for, and persevered in, with all the earnestness which we bring to bear upon subjects which are, in our opinion, at once

[1] Jas. iv. 3.

most interesting and most necessary."[1] To the same effect are the words of Coleridge. "Believe me," said he to his nephew, two years before his death, "to pray with all your heart and strength, with the reason and the will, to believe vividly that God will listen to your voice through Christ, and verily do the thing that pleaseth him at last,—this is the last, the greatest achievement of the Christian's warfare on earth.—Teach us to pray, Lord."[2]

But no one can long persist in such prayer without faith; and so at this point the Saviour's qualifying word, "believing, ye shall receive," is appropriate. The earnest petitioner knows that he is not beating the air. His faith is not in his prayer, but in his God; and the stronger that faith is, the more earnest will be his perseverance. Even though he knows that the blessing is coming, nay, just because he knows that it is coming, he will, like Elijah on Mount Carmel, go again and again, until in the little cloud he sees the beginning of the answer.

But more important even than any of these conditions in the character of the suppliant is that laid down by Jesus, when he says, "If ye abide in me, and my words abide in you, ye shall ask what ye will, and it shall be done unto you." The man who is abiding in Christ has his eye purified so that he clearly perceives what things he ought to ask; while at the same time he is in that state of preparation which renders the granting of his prayers a blessing to him, and not a curse. We need, therefore, to be in a high condition of holiness before we can have fulfilled to us the promise, "Ye shall ask

---

[1] Bishop Hamilton; quoted by Liddon, in Some Elements of Religion, p. 172.
[2] Coleridge's Complete Works, vol. vi. p. 237.

what ye will, and it shall be done unto you." We must not take the first part of that declaration, and divorce it from the second: it is only in the measure in which we are abiding in Christ, and his words are abiding in us, that we have any right to expect that our prayers shall be answered. Behold how this was seen in Abraham when he took it upon him to speak unto the Lord. It was the meeting of friend with friend. On the one hand Jehovah said, "Shall I hide from Abraham that thing which I do?" and, on the other, Abraham said unto the Lord, "Peradventure ten shall be found there;" and the answer came, "I will not destroy it for ten's sake." We are apt to imagine, at first thought, that all this was the manifestation of mere earnestness; but out of what did that earnestness spring? It sprung out of the closeness of Abraham's walk with God; that is, out of his abiding in God, and of God's words abiding in him. So it was with all the others spoken of in the Bible as successful suppliants. Daniel, the beloved, had his eyes opened, in answer to his prayers, because he was so exalted in character; and he who saw the great Apocalypse was the disciple who leaned upon the Master's breast at supper, and had drunk in most of his spirit. Successful prayer is thus the fruitage of a holy character; and it is only when we delight ourselves in God, that we can calculate upon receiving the desires of our hearts. It is thus, indeed, a great thing to pray; and, when all these things are taken into consideration, we need not be surprised that so few, comparatively, of our requests are answered. The cause is not in God, but in ourselves; for, tried by these tests, the best of us must confess that we have rarely prayed at all.

But a second class of conditions connect themselves

with the nature of the thing requested. That which
we ask must be in accordance with God's will. Beneath
every genuine supplication, there is the spirit of resig-
nation breathed by Jesus himself in his Gethsemane
anguish: " Nevertheless, not as I will, but as Thou wilt."
We are ignorant and short-sighted, and very often ask
for things which would be hurtful to us. We cannot
see the end from the beginning; and so, frequently,
that which at present seems to us desirable would ultimately prove injurious. When, therefore, we ask for
such a thing, God does with us precisely as we do with
our own children, and keeps it from us for our good.
There are many instances of this in Scripture, and it is
so common in human experience that even Shakspeare
has referred to it in these lines: —

> "We, ignorant of ourselves,
> Beg often our own harms, which the wise powers
> Deny us for our good: so find we profit
> By losing of our prayers."

Nor is this ignorance only partial, and confined to
certain petitions. "Ye know not what ye ask," is true,
in a very deep sense, even of the simplest request which
is presented to God. Who can tell all that is involved
in the granting of a single desire? It seemed a little
thing to the sons of Zebedee, to ask that they should
sit, the one on the right hand, and the other on the left
hand, of the Master in his kingdom, — a thing to be
granted as easily as one sets a chair for another in a
room; but, in reality, it involved in it the drinking
of a cup of agony, and the submitting to a baptism of
fire, of which at the moment the two apostles did not
dream. Now, the very same ignorance which James
and John manifested regarding the meaning of their

prayer, exists in us all regarding the effect which the granting to us of the very thing we ask would have upon us. We cannot tell what bearing on ourselves, or on our households, or on our church, or on our neighborhood, the giving to us of the very thing we ask may have. We ask for worldly prosperity; but perhaps it is denied us, because God sees that if we had it, we should become full, and deny him. We ask for deliverance from that physical weakness which makes to us, it may be, every work a burden; but no strength comes, — perhaps because God sees that only by some such chronic disability he can keep us at his feet. And so with other things. God is no mere blind, indulgent father, who gives his children every thing they ask. He is wise and kind, and has, withal, the discrimination of omniscience; so he gives only that which will be best: and, if we were to view the matter rightly, we should see as much reason to be thankful to him for a refusal as for an answer to the letter of our prayers.

But this condition, connecting itself with the nature of the thing asked, is nearly akin to the third class of conditions which spring out of the purpose and prerogative of God himself. This is a view of the case which has not been sufficiently attended to by Christians. "The hearer of prayer" is not the only relation in which God stands to his people. He is their Father as well; and he is, besides, the moral Governor of the intelligent universe. Therefore he uses his prerogative in answering prayer for moral purposes; and the action which he takes on the petitions of his children is a portion of that discipline to which he subjects them, and by which he trains them into strength and holiness of character. Or, it may be, that the kind of answers which he gives is determined by the influence which the suppliant's example may have on others. He may give what is asked, in order that they who ask it may be convinced of the folly of their request. He may deny that which is besought, in order that by the denial he may open the suppliant's eyes to the need of higher blessings, and stimulate him to ask for these. Or, he may give something else than that which is craved, because, while it will be equally valuable to the petitioner, it will be an encouragement and assistance to many others.

There are illustrations of all these in the word of God. Thus, when the children of Israel in the wilderness cried for supplies, it is said that "he gave them their request, but sent leanness into their soul."[1] So, again, when the tribes desired a king, he gave them Saul, that, through the infliction of that monarch's arbitrary and capricious tyranny, they might be convinced of the wickedness of their desire. Never was there a more devout and sincere suppliant than he with whom God talked face to face; and yet, when he pressed his suit to be permitted to enter Canaan, Jehovah answered, "Let it suffice thee: speak no more to me of this matter,"[2] in order that all people might know from this denial, even to Moses, how dreadful a thing sin is in the sight of the Lord. For a similar reason, probably, it was, that David's prayer for the life of his child was not granted. And, when Paul thrice besought the Lord for the removal of his thorn, the answer came not in the healing of his body, but in the strengthening of his spirit; that believers in every age might be able to appropriate the promise, "My grace is sufficient for thee: my strength is made perfect in weakness."

It is thus apparent that the promise of answer to

[1] Ps. cvi. 15.   [2] Deut. iii. 26.

prayer, though given in universal terms in some passages, is qualified by the wisdom and love of Him who gave it; and that he will keep it only in so far as it shall be for the highest welfare of his people that he should. While declaring, in general phrase, that he will give what his children ask, God yet, to speak after the manner of men, reserves to himself a certain discretionary power, so that he may either deny that which is requested, or bestow something else, according as he sees what shall be best in all the circumstances of each case. His great design, in the administration of his moral government, is to advance the interests of the gospel, and through that to promote holiness and happiness among men. Now, the hearing of prayer by him is only a means to that end. It is not an end in itself. God does not exist simply and only to answer prayer. He is the Governor of the world, and the Father of his people; and his hearing of prayer is only one among many means which he employs for the discipline of his people and the training of them into holiness.

Now, if these views are sound and scriptural, then there may be deduced from them three inferences of great practical value.

In the first place, we may see how impossible it is for us to discover the results of prayer, by any merely human test. How, for example, shall we determine when a true prayer is offered? If so much depends on the character and spirit of the suppliant, how can any one, who is unable to read the heart, tell when the request which a seeker presents is such as God can approve? How, again, can any external observer take cognizance of such spiritual considerations as those which must enter into the determination of the questions whether, and in what form, a prayer has been answered? Where are the delicate instruments which shall indicate or measure the results, on the character of the suppliant, which are produced sometimes by the denial and sometimes by the granting of his requests? Therefore we cannot classify results here, and argue from them, as we do in statistical investigations. The demand which was made some years ago, for a scientific test of prayer, betrayed on the part of those who made it ignorance of the fact that prayer lies not in the plane of physical science, but in that of moral and spiritual things; and indicates a spirit not unlike that of the Israelites of old, when they tempted God, and said, "Is the Lord among us, or no?" In the wards of the hospital, the physician deals with each patient according to his disease, his temperament, his constitution, and his history. He does not give each what he requests. He may even give to one the very thing which he has just denied to the patient next him. And he does all that from considerations altogether beyond their knowledge, and perhaps, also, above their comprehension. He is there, not simply to grant their requests, but to heal their diseases. So with God and his people. He treats each one as he requires; and grants his prayer, or refuses to grant it, according as it will best promote his spiritual welfare. But how can men, who look merely on the outward appearance, take cognizance of considerations which are patent only to the eye of God? No mere human test can distinguish a true prayer from a false one; and if it cannot judge of the cry which comes out of the lips of a man, how can it analyze the answer which comes out of the heart of God?

But, as a second inference from this whole subject, it may be seen, that, to be successful suppliants, we must be holy men. "The secret of the Lord is with them that fear him, and he will show them his covenant."[1] Character, as God sees it, gives its quality to prayer; and they who are nearest akin to God in holiness get the most frequent answers to their requests. Yet this is the consequence of their holiness, and not the reward of it. Their purity of heart has clarified their spiritual perception, so that they see plainly what they should ask for, and asking that they are not disappointed. Thus the prevailing prayer of the closet is that of the "righteous man," and the measure of personal holiness is the measure also of the power of petition. You hear of the great results that have been wrought by prayer, in the history of men and institutions; and few more striking things are written anywhere on that subject than those to be found in "Praying and Working," by Dr. Stevenson of Dublin. But beware of supposing that nothing but asking is involved in such successes. The asking was of a peculiar kind: it was that of men who lived much with God, and were doing much for God, and whose characters, in the life of every day, illustrated the gospel of the Lord Jesus. It was that, moreover, of men who were diligently seeking, by the use of appropriate means, to answer their own prayers; and not by one spasmodic leap can we vault into their privilege. It belongs only to their holiness and activity; and through growth in these alone shall we grow into their success. But if we seek it only for the success's sake, or only to be like those who have been successful, we shall ignominiously fail. They sought it from God, that they might give it to God; and those who would imitate them must do the same.

As a final inference from these considerations, it may be noted how necessary it is that prayer should be

[1] Ps. xxv. 14.

characterized by entire submission to the will of God. The undertone of every supplication should be, "Thy will be done." There is a warrant for stretching earnestness up to this point, "Father, if it be possible;" but that must always be combined with the "nevertheless, not as I will, but as thou wilt." That is a prayer which is always answered; and the answer to it can bring ultimately nothing but blessing to him who breathes it sincerely, though in the immediate future there may be betrayal and crucifixion. So let the Christian go his way, undistracted by the unguarded things which spiritual enthusiasts have said about the power of prayer; and, having faith in God, let him leave every request with him, sure that in the end he shall either get that which he seeks or something better. Thus, in the words of the good Leighton, "True prayers never come weeping home;" and again, "This is the excellent advantage of the prayer of faith, that it quiets and establishes the heart in God. Whatsoever be its estate and desire, when once he hath put his petition into God's hand, he rests content in holy security and assurance concerning the answer, refers it to the wisdom and love of God how and when he will answer; not doubting that whatsoever it be, and whensoever, it shall be both gracious and seasonable. But the reason why so few of us find that sweetness and comfort that is in prayer is because the true nature and use of it are so little known."

XVII
THE FOOLISH RICH MAN
Luke 12:13-21

THE character of a man is often indicated by the direction which his thoughts take when he is listening to a religious exhortation. Commonly, indeed, the speaker gets all the blame if he cannot hold the attention of his auditors to the subject which he desires to impress upon them. But, frequently, the true cause is to be found in the fact that the soul of his hearer is inthralled by some overmastering passion. Here, for example, the greatest of all preachers, even the Lord Jesus Christ himself, while speaking of such important matters as the danger of hypocrisy, the comfort that comes from the knowledge of the universality of the providence of God, and the duty of confessing the truth before men, relying on the promised help of the Holy Spirit, is interrupted by the ejaculation of one of the company to this effect: "Master, speak to my brother, that he divide the inheritance with me." The topic thus introduced had nothing whatever to do with those which the Lord had just been handling. The interruption, therefore, was unseasonable. It was even impertinent, inasmuch as it thrust the personal squabbles of individuals, about property, on the attention of those whom he wished to think of topics immensely more important. It was, besides, an attempt to traffic in the eminence which Christ had acquired as a teacher, by enlisting him on the side of one of the disputants in a family quarrel, much as men in prominent positions nowadays are pestered with applications from every quarter to give their influence to enterprises which are to profit individuals who care nothing for them, save that they think they can make something out of their names and position.

It was, therefore, with some degree of severity, that the Lord replied, "Man, who made me a judge or a divider over you?" There were properly constituted tribunals in existence for the settlement of all such disputes, and to them the complainant might apply. The Lord had no jurisdiction in the case. He was not authorized by those who alone could give him the position of a judge, to deal with such matters; and if he had consented to take action in them, he would have been held as setting himself up as the rival and antagonist of the legal courts of the land. Therefore, just as he declined to settle categorically the question about tribute, he here refused to listen to the complaint which had been so intrusively thrust upon his attention. It was no part of his mission to meddle directly with legal or political affairs. He came for the regeneration of individuals, and through that alone did he desire or design to affect the public life of the nation. Therefore he would be no judge in such a matter as this man brought before him. The man might, or might not, have right on his side: the courts would determine that. But whether he had, or not, one thing was clear, — the mere making of this demand by him, at such a time, and in such a manner, showed that he was moved by covetousness; and so, rising from the individual case, the Lord addressed himself to the evil of which it was a manifestation; and, turning to the multitude, he said to them,

"Take heed, and beware of every form of covetousness," — for so, according to the best manuscripts, the clause should be read.

But what is covetousness? It is not simply the desire of property. For that is one of the instincts of our nature; and the effort to acquire wealth plays a most important part in the education at once of the individual, the nation, and the race. At first, indeed, such is the influence of our depravity, the desire for property may develop the direst selfishness: but it is undeniable, that, in proportion as a people obtains it, it rises both morally and socially; whereas, where no property exists, you have neither laws, literature, civilization, nor religion. The attempt to acquire riches stimulates frugality, develops forethought, and encourages that kind of self-denial which subordinates present enjoyment to future good; while, again, the possession of property leads to the respect of the rights of others. So close, indeed, is the connection between these two things, that, wherever property ceases to be respected, there you have an end of law, and an absolute reign of anarchy and terror. The men who took for their creed the infamous dictum, that "property is theft," saw the legitimate outcome of their principles in the Parisian commune; and when now their apostles are preaching their favorite doctrine even in our own land, it is well that we should be reminded of the consequences to which such teachings lead.

The desire of property, therefore, with a view to its right and legitimate use, is not only not covetousness, but is lawful and right. As Robert Hall has said, "If there were no desire for wealth, there would be no need of it. It would soon cease to exist at all, and society would go back to a state of actual barbarism."[1]

---

[1] Hall's Works, vol. i. p. 147.

Covetousness, therefore, is neither the having of money, nor the desire to have it for the uses to which it may be rightly put; but it is the desire of having it simply for the sake of having it, — the making of that which is at best a means of ministering to life or comfort or enjoyment or usefulness, into the great end for the gaining of which we live.

Now, there is always a danger, in our depraved natures, lest we should allow that which ought to be kept subordinate, to become the controlling motive of our existence; and because money is so closely identified with our daily lives, and so needful for the supply of our common and ordinary wants, that danger is specially great in reference to its acquisition. Besides, the fact that in our modern society a man is too frequently estimated by the magnitude of his wealth only increases the peril: so that we have peculiar need of the warning, "Take heed, and beware of every form of covetousness," — which simply means, Beware of setting up the possession of property or riches as the chief good, to which every thing else is to be made subservient. Let not the acquirement of wealth become the absorbing ambition of your life. Set not your heart on possession as the great object of your desire. Do not live simply to make money and hoard it up; but use what property you may acquire, for the promotion of those higher and more spiritual ends, the attainment of which ought to be the great aim of your existence.

That is the meaning of the Saviour's caution, and he enforces it with this consideration: "For a man's life consisteth not in the abundance of the things which he possesseth." The clause thus rendered is, in the original, somewhat involved, and is rather difficult to translate. It is thus given literally in the margin of the

Revised Version: "For not in a man's abundance consisteth his life from the things which he possesseth;" and some have taken it to mean, that a man's life does not depend on the surplus of what he has above what he needs; while others would take it as denoting that life, in its higher sense, does not consist in possession, but in character. In the former case, the words simply enunciate the truth that little is needed to support life, viewed as mere animal being and well-being. As William Arnot has expressed it in his little volume on "The Race for Riches:"[1] "A very small portion of the fruit of the earth suffices to supply a man's necessities. The main elements are a little food to appease hunger, and some clothing to ward off the cold. These, as a general rule, the poor man obtains; and what more can the rich consume? In this matter God has brought the rich and the poor very near to each other in life, and at death the slight difference that did exist will be altogether done away." This is doubtless, in the main, true; and it accords readily enough with some aspects of the teaching of the parable which the statement on which we are now commenting was meant to introduce. But still it seems to me to fall sadly beneath the high level of our Lord's general treatment of the subject of life, and therefore I greatly prefer the other interpretation. Life, in all its breadth and depth of significance, as the proper exercise and enjoyment of a rational, spiritual, and immortal being, such as a man is, does not consist in possession, but in character; and the true riches are the riches of the soul toward God. "A man's life," as distinguished from that of a beast, does not depend on wealth. His happiness, his usefulness, his honor, may be secured without riches; and as, before

---

[1] pp. 45, 46.

God, he is estimated by what he is, rather than by what he has. Money is not the chief good. There are many things which it cannot purchase, but which yet may be acquired and possessed by those who are poor in this world's possessions. Of this sort are health, happiness, character, usefulness, and especially that acceptance with God, that relationship to Christ, "in knowledge of whom standeth eternal life," which we call salvation. There are wealthy men who are destitute of all these things; and there are many among the poor who possess them all, being "rich in faith, and heirs of the kingdom of heaven." With a fact like that before us, therefore, we can easily see that "a man's life," in its noblest sense, as the life of one worthy to be called a man, "consisteth not in the abundance of the things which he possesseth."

Now, it was to illustrate and enforce this truth, that the Lord spake the parable of the foolish rich man. The story is in itself so plain as to need little or no explanation. A certain land-owner, already possessed of so much that he is called a rich man, saw an unusually large crop upon his fields, and began at once to consider how he should dispose of it. He had no thought, indeed, of doing any thing with it but keeping it to himself; but even to do that, he felt that he would require larger accommodation than he possessed. So he determined to pull down his barns, and build greater; and then, as if already his purpose had been carried out, he rejoiced in anticipation over the "good time" which he would have, for he exclaimed, "I will say unto my soul, Soul, thou hast much goods laid up for many years; take thine ease, eat, drink, and be merry." But alas! he had forgotten to take God into his reckoning, and at the very time when he was gleefully calculating on this future enjoyment, the decree came forth from the Eternal, "Thou fool, this night thy soul is required of thee; then whose shall those things be which thou hast provided?" That is the story, and the Lord adds the moral thus: "So"—that is, such a fool, and so great—"is he that layeth up treasure for himself, and is not rich toward God."

The essence of the lesson, thus, is the folly of this rich man; and therefore the true interpretation will be found in the answer to the question, Wherein did his folly consist? To the consideration of that question, therefore, let us now address ourselves.

And here, in the first place, the folly of this man appears in the fact that he completely ignored his responsibility to God in the matter of his possessions. He speaks of "*my* fruits" and "*my* goods," and the Lord describes him as laying up treasure "*for himself.*" No doubt he had cultivated his ground, and sown his seed; but, after all, the greatest factor in the production of his wealth had been God, who had sent his rain and sunshine, and so caused his crops to grow luxuriantly. Yet he speaks throughout as if he had all the merit of his prosperity, and gives God no praise; while the idea that any portion of the increase of his fields belonged to God seems never to have entered into his mind. But does this man stand alone in this particular? Are we not all too sadly in the same condemnation with him? How many among us glory in the fact that they are, as the phrase is, self-made men? Have we never heard the boast in the mouth of a successful merchant, that he is the architect of his own fortune? and are we not all too prone to take to ourselves the sole credit for any property we have acquired, or for any eminence we have reached? Yet it is just as true in every department of life, though perhaps not quite so apparent, as it is in agriculture, that the chief factor to success in it is God. He gave the original aptitude and ability to the man; his providence furnished the means of cultivating both of these, and opened up the avenues to prosperity; and it will commonly be found that the critical turning-points of life, which led directly to the results over which we felicitate ourselves, were due entirely to him, and came altogether irrespective of our own arrangement. Why, then, should we take the whole credit to ourselves? Would it not be more appropriate for us to say, "Not unto us, O Lord, not unto us, but unto thy name give glory, for thy mercy and for thy truth's sake"?

But the restriction to himself of the honor of his success led directly to the complete appropriation by this man of its fruits. He regarded them as exclusively his own. He acted as if he felt that God had no claim to any part of them whatever. Far from looking upon himself as God's steward, he took every thing for himself. Therefore he never thought of consulting God about the disposal of his property. He asked no advice of any one: he simply "spake with himself." "My goods are my own, and I shall do with them as I please,"—that was the language of his heart; whereas, if he had been animated by a right spirit, he would have said, "My fruits are thine, O God: show me what thou wouldst have me to do with them." Now, am I uncharitable when I say that there are too many in these modern times who resemble the man in the parable in this also? Multitudes never pray to God about their business at all. Some may pray that he would send them prosperity; but when the prosperity comes, how few there are, comparatively speaking, who lay their wealth at his feet, and ask him to direct them in disposing of it! Disposing of it! alas, that is the last thing they ever think of. Their one aim is to keep it, and, if possible, to increase it. Accumulation is their great ambition; and if they spend at all, they spend, too many of them at least, on their own indulgence, and not in the furtherance of those good and noble objects with which the glory of God and the welfare of men are identified. We cry out against those defalcations on the part of trusted officials in banks and other commercial houses, which have been so frequent among us in recent years; and I would not say a single word either in vindication or in extenuation of such iniquity. It is as wicked as it is said to be, and deserves the severest punishment; but how many of those who are loudest in its condemnation are themselves guilty of similar defalcation before God, inasmuch as they have kept for themselves, and spent on themselves, the wealth which he has intrusted to them for the welfare of others and the glory of his name? The creed of the communist is the extreme protest against this extreme of selfishness, and, like all other extremes, it is itself as bad as that against which it protests; but if the New-Testament doctrine of stewardship were universally acted upon by those who are possessed of property, communism would cease to exist. Property has its responsibilities, as well as its rights; and if its responsibilities were more fully acted on, its rights would be more sacredly respected. The communist says to the capitalist, "What is yours is mine, and I will come and take it by force." That is theft. But the Christian says, "What is mine is *God's;* and I will use it, under his direction, for the good of others." That is stewardship; and in that alone is the antidote to the troubles which have so long agitated the countries of the Old World, and which, alas! are making their appearance now among ourselves. It is an awful folly for the man of wealth to ignore his responsibility to God for the use which he makes of his wealth. The crash of 1793, and again of 1871, in Paris, might have taught him that if he had cared to learn. God grant there may not come to him a more terrible lesson in the outburst of a volcano beneath his very feet in this new land!

But, in the second place, the folly of this man appears in the fact that he ignored the claims of other men upon him for his help. He had no idea, apparently, that there was any other possible way of bestowing his goods than by storing them in his barns. As Augustine, quoted by Trench,[1] has replied to his soliloquy, "Thou *hast* barns, — the bosoms of the needy, the houses of widows, the mouths of orphans and of infants;" these are the true storehouses for surplus wealth. It is right to provide for those who are dependent upon us; it is prudent to lay up something in store against a possible evil day: but after that, the storehouse of wealth should be benevolence. By scattering it in useful directions, it will be most effectually preserved; and there are not a few among us to-day, who, in the reverse of fortune that has come upon them by recent disasters, can say, "I have still at least that which I gave away: it was given to the Lord, and he has taken care of that." I have somewhere read that a lady once went to call upon a friend near the close of autumn, and found her emptying her closets, and exclaiming, "Oh, these moths!

---

[1] Notes on the Parables, p. 334.

these moths! they have consumed almost every thing that I laid away in the beginning of the summer." The visitor expressed her sorrow, but said she did not know what it was to have a garment moth-eaten. Whereupon her friend asked for the specific which she used, and to her surprise received for answer, "I gave away to the poor, months ago, all the garments for which I had no longer use; and there was no difficulty in preserving the remainder from the moths." The true storehouse for our surplus is benevolence. That is a barn which is large enough for all that we can put into it; and, rightly bestowed in that barn, our treasures are where "neither moth nor rust doth corrupt, and where no thieves break through to steal." Benevolence clips the wings of riches, so that they do not fly away; while, at the same time, it sweetens the breath of society, and deprives the agitator of the stock in trade wherewith he infuriates the "sand-lot" audience to deeds of violence and confiscation. He who has is, in a very important sense, a debtor to him who has not. As I have elsewhere said,[1] "What I have that another has not, is to be used by me, not for my own aggrandizement, but for the good of that other, as well as for my own. It is committed to me as a trust, and is to be expended by me for the benefit of others as well as for myself. The greatness of exceptional endowment, of whatever sort it may be, carries with it an obligation to similar exceptional greatness of service. This is the gospel principle. It makes the powerful man the protector of the weak; the rich man, the provider for the poor; the learned man, the teacher of the ignorant; and the free man, the emancipator of the enslaved. Thus, by so much the wealthier a man is, if he acts on this

[1] Contrary Winds and Other Sermons, p. 191.

principle, it will be just so much the better for the poor, for whom he is a trustee." That is the only principle that can preserve us from constant imbranglement between class and class in society; and they who ignore it are not only dishonoring God, but are foolishly furnishing the fuse for unscrupulous men to use in the production of some dynamite explosion that may shake the nation to its centre.

But, in the third place, the folly of this man is seen in the fact that he imagined that material things were proper food for his soul. The mere animal life of the body may be supported by such goods as this man was about to lay up, but the soul needs something better than these. Its true food is God himself; and hence Jesus, in the moral of the parable, calls the man who has that "rich toward God." The Psalmist tells us, that, when the Israelites lusted after flesh to eat, " God gave them their request, but sent leanness into their soul," [1] — words which plainly imply, that, while the body may be pampered with its material food, the soul may be really starving. So, again, in reply to Satan, the Lord. quoting from Deuteronomy, said, "Man shall not live by bread alone, but by every word of God;" [2] and when his disciples, having left him hungry, came back to the well, and could not get him to eat, he replied, "I have meat to eat that ye know not of;" "My meat is to do the will of him that sent me, and to finish his work." [3] That is the true food of the soul. All else for it is worse than the husks which the swine did eat were to the prodigal.

But we may get at the same conclusion in another way. Thus we speak of a man's being rich in intel-

[1] Ps. cvi. 15.   [2] Matt. iv. 4.   [3] John iv. 34.

lectual resources, meaning thereby that he has the means of satisfying, to a large extent, the cravings of his mental nature; while, when we say of another that he is deficient in intellectual resources, we wish it to be understood that he has in himself nothing to fall back upon in the hour when he is cut off from all material delights. Now, carrying this mode of speech up to that moral and spiritual department which is the highest in our complex humanity, we see at once that he is rich who has a good conscience, a will in unison with God's, and joy in the contemplation of Jehovah; while he is poor whose soul is burdened with a sense of guilt, which he cannot remove, and whose heart is filled with horror and dismay at the prospect of standing naked and open before the eyes of Him with whom he has to do. True riches — or, in other words, the true food of the soul, by which alone it can be nourished and satisfied — are to be found in God alone. Reconciliation to God, peace with God, likeness to God, and fellowship with God, — that alone can fill the heart of man. God for us in the work of his Son, God with us in the orderings of his providence, God in us in the indwelling of the Holy Spirit, and God before us in the hope of heaven, — that is the true food of the spirit of man; and to think of sustaining it with material fruits and goods and possessions, is as absurd as it would be to try to satisfy the hunger of the body with a diamond, or to quench the thirst of the body with a pearl. As the poet has expressed it, —

> "Attempt, how monstrous and how surely vain!
> With things of earthly sort, with aught but God,
> With aught but moral excellence, truth, and love,
> To satisfy and fill the immortal soul.
> Attempt, vain inconceivably! attempt

> To satisfy the ocean with a drop,
> To marry immortality to death,
> And with the unsubstantial shade of time
> To fill the embrace of all eternity!" [1]

This was the folly of the rich man here. Let us take care that it be not also ours; for "God has made us for himself, and our souls must be ever restless till they rest themselves in him."

But now, finally, the folly of this rich man is apparent from the fact that he had entirely ignored the truth that his material possessions were not to be his forever. When the decree went forth, "This night thy soul shall be required of thee," he could not prevent its being carried out. All his wealth could not bribe the death-messenger that came to summon his soul into the presence of its God, or avail to lengthen his life on earth a single hour. And when he went, he could not take his riches with him; for, as the Spanish proverb has put it with a horrible distinctness, "There are no pockets in a shroud." "How much did he leave?" asked one man of another, in the street-car, as they were talking of a millionnaire whose death had been announced in the morning paper. "*All he had*," was the solemn and suggestive answer. Let these two things stand out in lurid distinctness on this subject: wealth cannot buy off death, and when we die we can take none of it with us; and then you will understand how supremely foolish it is for a man to live simply and only for its accumulation.

But another thought is suggested here. Then "whose shall those things be which thou hast provided?" Ah, me! if some of those wealthy men who

[1] Pollok's Course of Time, Book IV.

have gone in recent years from this busy, bustling city, into the world beyond, could come back for a moment, and see what fightings there have been over their fortunes; how the details of their own idiosyncrasies have been dragged out into the light, to prove, if possible, that they had not sense enough to make their wills; how the most painful secrets of their lives have been proclaimed upon the housetop; how the skeleton in their closet has been handled and laughed over by the profane and unfeeling crowd; and how their sons and daughters and relations, out to the farthest limit of consanguinity, have wrangled over their portions, — I think they would say within themselves, "What consummate fools we were, to spend our days on earth in laying up treasures to be squandered thus in the courts, and to be quarrelled over by a hungry crowd, as wolves howl over carrion!" And if they had to live again, they would try, I think, to be their own executors, and to use their possessions in a way that would bless the world and glorify their God. There has been, as I cannot help thinking, a grim irony in God's providence, in cases like these; and as I read the reports of the surrogate's court from time to time, I am reminded of the words, " He that sitteth in the heavens shall laugh; the Lord shall have them in derision." At all events, they prove conclusively the short-sightedness and folly of those whose sole delight in life was the adding of dollar to dollar.

But a deeper thought is here suggested: "Whose shall those things be?" Whose were they all along? They were God's, and should have been used for God. You remember, in that most glorious scene in David's glorious reign, when he brought out what he had gathered for the building of the temple, and consecrated it all to God, and his people willingly followed his example, he used these remarkable words: "All things come of thee, and of thine own have we given thee: *for* we are strangers and sojourners, as were all our fathers; our days on the earth are as a shadow, and there is none abiding."[1] Mark the force of that *for* in this connection. Men come and go, but God is the immortal owner of all things; and in giving to him of our possessions, we but give him of his own. Friends, if there were more acknowledgment of that truth among us, there would be more liberality like that of David, and our missionary and benevolent societies which are continually laboring in the rearing of the great spiritual temple of his Church would not be so often in straits with their balances so largely on the wrong side of the ledger. Think on these things, I beg of you, and the Lord give you understanding in all things.

We see now how the moral of this story is established. "So is he that heapeth up treasure unto himself, and is not rich toward God." The first great thing for us is to be rich toward God; and that will keep us from giving undue importance to earthly treasure, — nay, it will teach us how to use that treasure, and show us that we may keep it best by spending it for God. That is the gist of the whole matter.

I ought now, therefore, to proceed to consider the question how these riches toward God are to be acquired and increased. Here, however, your time forbids me to enlarge. James gives one answer when he speaks of God as having chosen the poor of this world rich in faith;[2] and Paul supplements his statement when he exhorts Timothy to charge them that are rich in this world, that they be "rich in good works."[3] Faith in

[1] 1 Chron. xxix. 14, 15.   [2] Jas. ii. 5.   [3] 1 Tim. vi. 18.

Jesus Christ enriches us, by giving us the blessings of forgiveness, peace, holiness, and heaven; and good works, wrought as the outcome of gratitude for these blessings, enrich us with present happiness and future reward. These are things which the world cannot give or take away. These are things which are the possessions of our soul, and of which death cannot deprive us. The one of them is a present heaven, and the other will be an enrichment of the heaven that is in the future. Lay up these treasures for yourself, then, for no power can take them from you. And if you make that spiritual accumulation your supreme care, covetousness will find no lurking-place within your heart; for the wealth of earth will be valued by you only for the good works which it will give you the means of performing, and so the gold that is material and uncertain may become, in a wondrous way, transmuted into the riches which are spiritual and abiding. Here is something better than the philosopher's stone, for it turns material gold into immortal riches.

XVIII

THE BARREN FIG TREE
Luke 13:6-9

IT was a common belief among the Jews, that the coming of special calamities on a man was a proof that he had been guilty of peculiarly aggravated sin. In spite of the teaching of the argument of the Book of Job upon the subject, that doctrine held its place in the popular creed; and we meet with it on more than one occasion among those with whom our Lord came into contact in his public ministry. Nor was it a mere harmless superstition: for it tended to generate, in the hearts of those who cherished it, both uncharitable judgments of others, and Pharisaic opinions of themselves. If they who specially suffered were thereby proved to have specially sinned, then it followed that those who had been signally exempt from calamity were thereby shown to be particularly excellent. It was therefore, we may be sure, with such condemnation of the sufferers, and such appreciation of themselves, that, at the very moment when the Lord was upbraiding his hearers with their inability to discern the signs of the times, certain of those who were present told him of the massacre by Pilate of some Galilæans, while they were in the act of offering sacrifice in the court of the temple. They complacently took credit to themselves for exemplary holiness, while they implied that the victims of Pilate's cruelty were guilty of unusual wickedness. But the Saviour gave them to understand that in all this they were only confirming his statement as to their inability to read the signs of the times. For those unfortunate worshippers whom Pilate slew had, in a very true sense, died for the nation. Their fate was a warning of that awful judgment which was impending over the whole people; and the same thing was true of those who had been killed not long before in Jerusalem, by the falling on them of a tower in Siloam. The fact was, that, unless they repented, they should all perish "likewise,"—not simply also, but in like manner; for Trench [1] is undoubtedly right when he says that "the threat is, that they shall literally in like wise perish," and adds, "Certainly the resemblance is more than accidental between these two calamities here adduced, and the ultimate destruction which did overtake the rebellious Jews, as many as refused to obey the Lord's bidding and to repent. As the tower of Siloam fell, and crushed eighteen of the dwellers at Jerusalem, exactly so multitudes of its inhabitants were crushed beneath the ruins of their temple and their city; and during the last siege and assault of that city there were numbers also who were pierced through by Roman darts, or, more miserably yet, by those of their own frantic factions, in the courts of the temple, in the very act of preparing their sacrifices, so that literally their blood, like that of those Galilæans, was mingled with their sacrifices, one blood with another." Thus, what the news-tellers reported as evidence of aggravated wickedness in the case of the sufferers, Jesus interpreted as a warning to the nation as a whole; and it was to enforce that lesson yet more plainly and

[1] Notes on the Parables, pp. 346, 347.

pointedly, that he spoke the parable of the barren fig-tree.

It runs to this effect: "A certain man had a fig-tree planted in his vineyard; and he came and sought fruit thereon, and found none. Then said he unto the dresser of his vineyard, Behold, these three years I come seeking fruit on this fig-tree, and find none: cut it down; why cumbereth it the ground? And he answering said unto him, Lord, let it alone this year also, till I shall dig about it, and dung it: and if it bear fruit, well; and if not, then after that thou shalt cut it down."

There is nothing in the terms of this simple but solemn allegory requiring minute explanation. It was no uncommon thing for the owner of a vineyard to plant a fig-tree in it; and the expectation that it should bear fruit there was warranted by the exceptional attention which was bestowed on it in common with all within such an enclosure.

So, again, if for three consecutive years after it had come to maturity, such a tree should bear no fruit, it might fairly be accounted barren, and would be removed, not only as being itself useless, but also as taking up ground which might be more profitably occupied by something else. It is easy, therefore, to understand why the owner of the vineyard should have said of such a tree, "Cut it down." Nor is it difficult to comprehend the feeling which would urge the gardener to say, "Let it alone this year also." He had taken great pains with it; he had done for it all that he could think of: and, though it had all been vain, he could not cut it down without giving it another chance. So he begged for it one more year of grace, during which he would use stronger measures than ever; and, if these should fail, then he would cut it down without compunction. It is all very natural. It might have been a conversation last autumn, in some modern garden in this neighborhood, between a master and his servant, about some particular fruit-tree; and yet, natural as it is, it is used here by the Saviour as a symbol of the most solemn spiritual truth.

For, taking the key which is furnished to us by the occasion on which the parable was spoken, the interpretation is easily opened up. The fig-tree is the Jewish nation. The vineyard is the enclosure of privilege, within which that nation was secluded from all others, and which insured to it the unspeakable advantage of a revelation from God through the prophets. The coming of the lord of the vineyard, seeking fruit, represents the Divine expectation of holy character from the people, as the outcome of the exceptional position in which he had placed them. The three consecutive years must not be pressed into significance, as denoting any special epochs in Jewish history, or as designating the years of our Lord's public ministry. Rather, they represent the whole course of the history of Israel, the results of which were spiritual barrenness and Divine disappointment. Then came the fiat, "Cut it down: why cumbereth it the ground?" which symbolizes the decree for the destruction of Jerusalem, and the removal of the Jews from their vineyard privileges, preparatory to, and in order to, the calling of the Gentiles. But the carrying out of that is delayed at the intercession of the vineyard-dresser, who represents the Lord Jesus himself, and whose mediation secured a longer day of grace for the Jews, with the promise of his concurrence in their doom, if, after all, they should be still unfruitful.

The primary application of the parable is thus to the

Jewish nation; and the exposition which I have just given is its interpretation, properly so called. But the principles which underlie that interpretation are for all time, and we may very profitably spend the remainder of the discourse in considering their bearing on ourselves. They are, briefly, these: That much will be required of those to whom much has been given; that, if those to whom much has been given fail to meet that which is required of them, sentence of destruction will be pronounced against them; and that, though the execution of this sentence may be deferred at the intercession of Christ, it will certainly be carried out if there be no repentance and amendment manifested.

I. Now, looking at the application of these principles to ourselves, we may see, in the first place, that God has placed us in the most favorable circumstances for the bringing-forth of fruit. The privileges of the Jews were small in comparison with those which we enjoy. True, they had the oracles of God; but the system under which they lived was mainly typical, prophetic, and preparatory. God manifested himself to them, but he did so in a manner that was shadowy and pictorial rather than substantial and real. The light which they enjoyed was that of the early dawn: ours is that of the noonday sun. They had the prophets, we have the Son of God. They had typical sacrifices, we have the great propitiation. They had a temple material and symbolical, we have the temple spiritual and true. Let any one read the Epistle to the Hebrews; and, as he discovers how point after point is made by the writer in the course of his demonstration that Christ is the mediator of a better covenant, which was established on better promises than that of Sinai, he will understand how true it is, that our privileges are as much greater than those of the Jews of old, as those of the Jews were than those of the Gentiles by whom they were surrounded.

Nor is this all: when we contrast our situation in this free land with that of almost all the other nations of the earth, even at the present day, we shall see reason to conclude that no people, with but one possible exception, enjoy such spiritual advantages as those which, by the favor of God, we here possess. The children here are born into an atmosphere which is already highly charged with Christianity. They have the best educational facilities. The Bible is early in their hands. Many of them are trained in Christian homes. Still more of them are taught in Christian Sunday schools. There are no legal disabilities attached to their adherence to Christianity. It is not a crime, as it has sometimes been in other lands, and as it is still in some, to have a Bible. We have absolute liberty of worship; and there is no privilege of citizenship depending on any form of religious belief, or on the observance of any particular religious ordinance. Never were greater Christian advantages enjoyed by any people than we now and here possess. Truly " the lines have fallen unto us in pleasant places, and we have received a goodly heritage." Surely, if God could say with truth, in that age of the world's history, regarding Israel, "What could have been done more to my vineyard that I have not done in it?"[1] he might so speak, with even more force, of all that he has done for us. We glory in our institutions. We call ourselves the envy of the nations. We fondly regard ourselves as the pioneers of progress. But let us never forget that responsibility is proportional to privilege.

[1] Isa. v. 4.

II. For God expects exceptional fruit from a tree on which he has bestowed such exceptional advantages, and that is the second point to which I would here give prominence. If we *have* so much more than other nations, we ought to *be* just so much better than they. For the fruit in this case is that of character. It is commonly supposed, indeed, that fruitfulness in the Christian life is to be shown by the success of our labors in bringing others to the knowledge and acceptance of Christ, and there are many who would measure Christian fertility simply and only by usefulness. Now, usefulness is exceedingly valuable, and it is the duty and the privilege of every one who has found Christ for himself, to bring others to him; but, as an accurate expounder of the New Testament, I cannot allow you to rest in the idea that usefulness is the only fruitfulness. This point is so important that I must ask your special attention to it. Let me quote to you a few passages where the word "fruit" occurs : " The fruit of the Spirit is in all goodness and righteousness and truth ; " "The fruit of the Spirit is love, joy, peace, long-suffering, gentleness, goodness, faith, meekness, temperance ; " "Giving all diligence, add to your faith virtue, and to virtue knowledge, and to knowledge temperance, and to temperance patience, and to patience godliness, and to godliness brotherly kindness, and to brotherly kindness charity; for if these things be in you, and abound, they make you that ye shall neither be barren nor unfruitful in the knowledge of our Lord Jesus Christ ; " " Ye have your fruit unto holiness." [1] Now, putting all these together, it becomes apparent that fruitfulness is, first and before all things else, in character, in holiness, in what we are rather than in what we do, and only in

[1] Gal. v. 22, 23; 2 Pet. i. 5-8; Rom. vi. 22.

what we do so far as that is the genuine outcome and spontaneous revelation of what we are. Usefulness is the result of character, and must never be lost sight of; but character is first, and in that the fruit of our position in God's vineyard is chiefly to appear. Righteousness, meekness, fidelity, — in a word, moral excellence springing from our faith in Christ and our devotion to him, — that is the fruit which God expects to find in us as the occupants of his vineyard. Has he seen that in us? or, in spite of all our privileges, are we just like other people in other lands, — selfish, mammon-loving, unscrupulous, unrighteous, eager to take advantage of others, and seeking only to please and profit ourselves? The question is all-important; for on the answer which must be given to it will depend our immortal welfare as individuals, and the permanence and prosperity of the nation.

III. For now observe, in the third place, that God pronounces sentence of destruction on all who, having had such privileges, bring forth no fruit. In his discourse on the true vine, Jesus says, "Every branch in me that beareth not fruit he taketh away;" and again, "If a man abide not in me, he is cast forth as a branch, and is withered; and men gather them, and cast them into the fire, and they are burned."[1] So again, in the Sermon on the Mount we have these words: "Every tree that bringeth not forth good fruit is hewn down and cast into the fire."[2] The statement is unmistakable, and in the providence of God there have been many illustrations of its truth. What could be more marked, indeed, in this connection, than the case of the Jews themselves? They were the people of God's possession, the objects of

[1] John xv. 2, 6. [2] Matt. vii. 19.

his peculiar regard. He brought them out of the land of Egypt, and planted them in Palestine; he sent unto them his prophets; he trained them by the discipline of his providence; he dwelt among them in the mystic shechinah glory of the holy of holies. If ever any nation might have looked for exemption from the operation of a law, it was surely that of the Jews. But no, they came under its most rigid sweep; and just because they had received so much, they were all the more severely dealt with for their guilty barrenness. Their temple was razed to the foundations, their capital was destroyed, their country was given to others, and they themselves were scattered among the nations, even until this day.

We may see a similar instance in those seven Asiatic churches to whom the Book of Revelation was addressed. They, too, had rare privileges and ample warning; but they failed to rise to their responsibility, and the candlestick of each has long since been taken out of its place, so that the very regions which they occupied have come under the influence of Mohammedanism, and need to be Christianized anew. More modern instances may be found in the cases of those lands which, like Spain, Italy, and France, refused to accept the blessings of the Reformation when it was in their power to do so, and have been contending with difficulties ever since. But in thinking of these we may not forget ourselves, for the law holds of individual churches and individual men, as well as of nations; and if we wish to secure permanent prosperity and existence as a congregation, we must remember that we can do so only by maintaining constant fruitfulness in works of faith and labors of love, and holiness of character. When these disappear, and barrenness sets in, then there will come the sentence, "Cut it down." The history of the past will not compensate for the sterility of the present. We cannot live upon a reputation, any more than the Jews could save themselves because they were able to say, "We have Abraham to our father." The church's life depends on the present members of the church, and only through their fruitfulness can its permanence be insured. The same is true of individuals. When they cease to grow, they cease to live; and barrenness is at once the symptom of death, and the reason why they die.

IV. But observe, in the fourth place, that this sentence pronounced on the barren fig-tree is not at once carried into execution. The vine-dresser interceded, and the lord of the vineyard acquiesced. So God has forbearance for a time, even toward those who are doomed to destruction, if haply they may yet repent and return to him. The flood is foretold; but between its announcement and its coming a hundred and twenty years elapse, during all of which God's Spirit is striving with man, to bring him, if possible, to a sense of his guilt and danger. And here, in the case of the Jewish nation, even after their crucifixion of the Lord Jesus, there was a respite of forty years, during which, in all the power of their Pentecostal baptism, the apostles and early Christians were at work to lead them to repentance. Now, it is an interesting fact brought out here, that for all such respite as interposes, in any case, between evil desert and its immediate punishment, men are indebted to the intercession of Christ. If he had not been provided as the Lamb slain from the foundation of the world, the race would have died when Adam sinned; and it is a solemn thought, that the continued existence even of those who ridicule his love, and blaspheme his name, is due to the intercession of Him whom they revile.

But a respite or reprieve is not a pardon. It is only a postponement; yet, because it is a postponement, men are apt to think that God has lost sight of them, and will not hold them to an account. Thus the forbearance of God is misinterpreted as if it were indifference, and the sinner under it is tempted to go more recklessly into wickedness. If, when a man is in the act of committing his first theft, some unusual thing were to happen, and the thief were to be surprised into the acknowledgment of God's omniscience, he would regard that as a Divine interposition; but because nothing like that occurs, he takes the absence of it as an evidence of the Divine indifference. So men judge of God as if he were such an one as themselves; and "because sentence against an evil work is not executed speedily, the hearts of the children of men are fully set in them to do evil."[1] But there is no Divine indifference in the case. The stroke of justice is only arrested for a season, and its arrest is due to the mediation of the great High Priest. Take care, therefore, lest you fall into the mistake made by those of whom Peter speaks,[2] who, because all things continued as they had been, leaped to the conclusion that they would always be as they were, and so regarded that forbearance which was meant to give space for repentance as an actual manifestation of indifference, if not even of approval. But there is no indifference; and if the fruitless man repent not, the day of the Lord will come to him also as a thief in the night, and he will suddenly be destroyed, and that without remedy.[3]

[1] Eccles. viii. ii. [2] 2 Pet. iii. 3–10. [3] Prov. xxix. 1.

For the guilt *after* such forbearance, and *against* it, will be greater than it was before, inasmuch as, with the addition of the day of grace, there is combined an increase in the efforts on the part of the vine-dresser to promote fertility. Mr. Arnot, whose own early labors make him a specially good authority here, has written thus: "The two chief applications employed in husbandry to stimulate growth and fruitfulness are digging and manuring. These, accordingly, the dresser of the vineyard undertakes to apply, in the interval, to the barren fig-tree. I think something may be gained here by descending into particulars. One of these agricultural operations imparts to the tree the elements of fruitfulness, and the other enables the tree to make these elements its own. Digging gives nothing to the tree, but it makes openings whereby gifts from another quarter may become practically available. The fertilizer contains the food which the plant must receive and assimilate, and convert into fruit; but if the hardened earth were not made loose by digging, the needed aliment would never reach its destination. Similar processes are applied in the spiritual culture. Certain diggings take place around and among the roots of barren souls, as well as of barren fig-trees. Bereavements and trials of various kinds strike and rend, but these cannot by themselves renew and sanctify. They may give pain, but cannot impart fertility; the spirit, much distressed, may be as unfruitful as the spirits that are at ease in Zion. These rendings, however, are most precious as the means of opening a way whereby the elements of spiritual life conveyed by the Word and Spirit may reach their destination. The Lord who pours in the food for the sustenance of a soul stirs that soul by his providence, so that grace may reach the root and be taken in."[1] But if, after all that, the soul still refuses to unite itself to Christ, of course its guilt is all the heavier; and then comes the limit of forbearance, beyond which there is neither respite nor remedy.

V. That is the last lesson in the parable. May God enable us to lay it well to heart! If you ask me where precisely that limit of forbearance is, I cannot tell. The great truth is, that there is such a limit; and it ought to be our effort to keep away from it as far as possible. But how shall we do that? How better than by turning now in repentance and faith to God by Jesus Christ, and so becoming part and parcel of the true and living vine, whereof he says, "I am the vine; ye are the branches"? Do not tempt the Lord by putting his forbearance to the test, as if you would see how far and how long it will stretch; but go at once, and show that you account that "the long-suffering of God is salvation," and so the goodness of God will lead you to repentance. It is not yet too late. As the good, mild Leighton has expressed it, "Any of you that are stirred to any real desires of fruitfulness to him, I dare give you warrant to be confident of his not only forbearing upon such a desire, but of his favorably accepting of it as a good sign, yea, as already a beginning of fruit. But in case of people remaining barren after all, the end will be to be cut down. And to every fruitless and godless person amongst you, it is not long to that day: it will be upon you ere you are aware. As John preached, 'the axe is laid to the root of the tree; therefore every tree that bringeth not forth good fruit is hewn down, and cast into the fire.' God is taking his axe, as it were, and fetching his stroke at you;

[1] Arnot on the Parables, pp. 385, 386.

and you know not how soon it may light, and you be cut down, and cut off from all hopes forever, never to see a day of grace more; cut down, and cast into the fire to burn, and that never to end. Oh for some soul to be rescued, were it even now! Oh, to-day, to-day, if ye will hear his voice, harden not your hearts!"[1] Obey that call, my brethren, and you need not trouble yourselves about the precise position of the limit of God's forbearance; for thereby you will pass at once within the circle of his complacency.

[1] Leighton's works, Nelson's edition, p. 547.

XIX

THE GREAT SUPPER
Luke 14:16-24

THIS parable had its occasion in the remark of one, who, with a number of like-minded friends, had been invited to meet the Saviour, at the table of one of the chief Pharisees, on the sabbath day. It seemed a courteous kindness to the Lord, to ask him to eat bread with such a company; and yet the spirit at once of the host and of the guests is revealed by the Evangelist in these words: "it came to pass . . . that they watched him." They were not only curious to see what he would do, and to hear what he would say; but they were also on the alert to take advantage of any thing out of which they might manufacture some accusation against him. But the Lord, with that divine tact which he invariably manifested, began the attack himself, and, instead of contenting himself with acting on the defensive, boldly showed them to themselves with such unsparing fidelity, that they were utterly overthrown. Thus when a poor, diseased man came in, and made mute appeal for healing, he did not wait to be criticised, but "taking the bull by the horns," asked, "Is it lawful to heal on the sabbath day?" and when no one ventured to speak, he at once proceeded to cure the afflicted one, and sent him away rejoicing. Then, marking the jealousies which came out in their contendings for precedence at the table, he read them a lecture on their conduct, and commended to them that humility which was willing to take the lowest place, so that, when moved at all, it was moved only to a higher. After that, glancing at the appearance of the guests, and perceiving that they all belonged to the upper class of the population, he recommended them, when they made a banquet, to invite those who could not ask them to their tables in return, and to look for their recompense "at the resurrection of the just." Thus he disarmed criticism, and silenced opposition, by addressing himself directly to the conscience: thereby setting an example which might be profitably followed by his ministers, when they find themselves before an audience that is watching for an opportunity to trip them up; for conscience rightly addressed is always on the side of the preacher, and helps him to a victory.

In the present instance, all that came out of the antagonism of his adversaries was an empty commonplace, apparently in harmony with what he had been saying, but really no more than a bit of conversational padding, designed to fill up a somewhat painful pause, and meaning nothing in particular. Jesus had said, that if they invited to their feasts the poor, the maimed, the lame, and the blind, they should be recompensed at the resurrection of the just; and the feeble outcome was, that one of his hearers exclaimed, "Blessed is he that shall eat bread in the kingdom of God." He said nothing, you observe, of the condition on which the Lord had declared that they would be recompensed, but contented himself with a fervent ejaculation about the happiness of those who should feast in the kingdom of God; much as if one, on hearing a present duty faithfully enforced, should indulge in a fervent outburst about the blessedness of heaven. It was pure sentimentalism, holy humbug, or — to use the expressive modern word — absolute cant. The man was talking about that of which he knew nothing. The kingdom of God, in his view, was eating and drinking; and there was withal no doubt in his mind that he would be in it. But then, it was still a long way off; and this flourish about its blessedness might turn the current of conversation away from the disagreeable channel in which it had been flowing.

Instead of that, however, it only furnished occasion for the utterance of this parable, which went still deeper in than any thing that had gone before, and showed to the whole company the nature of the privileges which they were at the moment enjoying, and the magnitude of the danger in which there and then they were standing. This man had spoken of the kingdom of God, as if its coming were not to be until the resurrection of the just; but Jesus shows him that it had come already, and that, while they were praising its blessedness in the future, they were despising its invitations in the present. He had also complacently taken it for granted, that he would be at the banquet of the kingdom; and Jesus warns him that they who rejected its invitations would never taste its provision.

Thus this also is a parable of warning like that of the barren fig-tree; and it has in it, besides, a predictive element, foretelling, as it does, not only the rejection of the Jews, but also the calling of the Gentiles. In many of its features, it bears a strong resemblance to the parable of the royal marriage-feast, contained in the twenty-second chapter of the Gospel by Matthew, which we have already considered; but they are clearly distinct. In both, indeed, the gospel blessings are symbolized by

a feast, to which men are invited, and from which they
rudely absent themselves. But *this* was spoken at an
early date in the Saviour's ministry: *that*, in the very
Passion Week. *This*, as we have seen, was addressed
to the guests at a feast: that, probably, in the temple, to
the multitude. In *this*, the invited ones are content with
making excuses: in *that*, they treat the messengers with
violence. In *this*, the despisers of the invitation are
merely excluded: in *that*, they are destroyed, and their
city burned. When *this* was spoken, the antagonism
to the Lord had not gained such headway as it had
acquired when *that* was uttered, and so it has a milder
aspect than the other; while the episode of the man
without the wedding garment has here no place.
Clearly, then, though similar, they are distinct; and
therefore we may be able to bring out the characteristic features of that now before us, without going
over ground which we have already traversed.

The story may be briefly told as follows: A wealthy
inhabitant of a great city made preparations for a splendid feast, to which, after the fashion of the country, he
invited many of his fellow-citizens some time before
the day which had been fixed for its celebration. But
when the set time came, and the servant was again sent
forth to remind them of the feast, those who had been
invited made most frivolous excuses, and declined to
come; whereupon the lord of the banquet indignantly
sent his servant out to bring in from the streets and
lanes the poor, and the maimed, and the halt, and the
blind; and when these were not sufficient to fill the
tables, he commissioned him to go forth again, this time
outside of the city altogether, to the highways and
hedges, and to bring in all whom he could find, that
the house might be crowded; adding, — and in this we

have the pith of the story, — "I say unto you, That none of those men which were bidden shall taste of my supper." Now, let us attend to the interpretation; and, that we may not repeat what we have already said on the parable of the marriage-feast, we shall take it under a series of separate particulars.

I. There is, first, the feast. This is the gospel which God has provided for mankind sinners. Great preparation had to be made before it was available for men. The law which we had broken had to be satisfied; the penalty which we had incurred had to be endured; the obedience in which we had failed had to be rendered. None of these things, however, could be done by man for himself. To accomplish them, therefore, it was needed that the second in the glorious Trinity should take human nature into union with his deity, should tabernacle for a season on the earth, should be crucified and buried, should rise again from the dead, and enter into glory; and it was on the ground of the perfection and infinite sufficiency of the work of this our Substitute, that the invitation went forth, "Come, for all things are now ready." This was the preparation, and the gospel thus procured for us is a feast.

It is so in respect of the excellence of the provision which it sets before us. Pardon of sin, favor with God, peace of conscience, renewal of the heart, access to the throne of grace, the comforts of the Holy Spirit, the exceeding great and precious promises of the Scriptures, and a well-grounded hope of eternal life, — these are the blessings which crown the gospel board, and they are absolutely invaluable.

It is a feast in respect of abundance, for the supply is inexhaustible. On one memorable occasion of which

we read, the wine began to fail; and there have been
repeated instances among men, where the number of
the guests has more than exhausted the provision which
had been made for their entertainment: but that has
never happened, can never happen, here. Numbers
without number have already partaken of these precious
blessings; but they are still as abundant as they were
at first, for, like the bread that came from the hand of
Christ upon the mountain-side, they multiply with the
multitudes that need them, and, after all, there will be
something over. In our Father's house there is not
merely bread enough, but there is always bread "to
spare."

It is a feast in respect of fellowship. Men do not
make a banquet for solitary enjoyment, but that they
may have the society of others with them while they
partake of its rarities. And it is not otherwise here.
The blessings of the gospel are for social, and not
simply for private, life; and what circle of earthly
friends can be put into comparison with that into
which we enter when we seat ourselves at the gospel
table? There we have communion, not only with the
best and wisest of earth, but with the redeemed before
the throne; for

> "The saints on earth, and all the dead,
> But one communion make;
> All join to Christ, their living Head,
> And of his grace partake."

We sit down here with Abraham and Isaac and Jacob,
in the kingdom of our Father; yea, our fellowship is
with the Father, and with his Son Jesus Christ.

Finally, it is a feast in respect of joy. The giver of it
and the guests at it rejoice together. The great Father

says of each redeemed sinner there, "This my son was dead, and is alive again; was lost, and is found." The Divine Son sees "of the travail of his soul, and is satisfied." The Holy Spirit delights in the presence of those whom he has renewed and sanctified. And the joy of each guest in the possession of the blessings set before him is redoubled by the gladness of all the rest; for "true grace hates all monopolies, and loves not to eat its morsels alone," but rejoices in the number of those who with it are participators in the bounty of God.

Truly, then, may the gospel be symbolized as a feast; and as we look upon the provision which God has made for all our spiritual wants in Christ, we may see the fulfilment of the ancient oracle: "And in this mountain shall the Lord of hosts make unto all people a feast of fat things, a feast of wines on the lees; of fat things full of marrow, of wines on the lees well refined."

II. But now let us look, secondly, at the invited guests. In the parable, the servant sent with the first invitation stands as the representative of all those who were commissioned in God's name and on his behalf to the Jews, to prepare them for the advent of the Messiah. We must not restrict the reference either to John the Baptist, or to any one of the prophets, but must regard it as including all who in any way pointed the Jews to the coming Deliverer as "the Lamb of God," who was to take "away the sin of the world." The servant sent at supper-time to say to the invited guests that all things were now ready is clearly the Lord Jesus Christ himself, whom, when the fulness of the time was come, "God sent forth, made of a woman, made under the law, to redeem them that were under the law." [1] And when the more influential of the Jewish nation ignored this invitation, the servant sent forth to the poor and maimed and halt and blind, in the streets and lanes of the city, represents the Lord Christ and his apostles, who turned to the outcast and neglected classes among the Jews, — the publicans and sinners, — after their message had been repudiated by the spiritual rulers of the people; while he who was commissioned to go out to the highways and hedges outside of the city, and instructed to compel those whom he found there to come in, symbolizes the first preachers of the gospel to the Gentiles. The gospel was thus proclaimed first to the officials of the Jewish nation, next to the outcast and degraded among the Jews, and finally to the Gentiles; and the fulfilment, or exposition proper, of this part of the parable, may be recognized in a moment by every intelligent reader of the book of the Acts of the Apostles.

But while this is the literal interpretation of the parable, the point which it is most important for us now to remember is, that the invitation to this feast is given to every one in whose hearing the gospel is proclaimed. That is a great privilege; but it is also, as we see, a great peril, and it becomes us to realize at once the advantage and the responsibility of the position in which we stand. *We* have received this invitation, "Come, for all things are now ready." To us also it is said, "Yet there is room;" and on us have been put forth all those sweetly constraining influences which are designed to "compel" men "to come in." This, therefore, is not a matter of mere antiquarian interest,

[1] Gal. iv. 4, 5.

or of curious exegetical importance. It concerns our own spiritual and immortal welfare; for, though the invitation is given through the instrumentality of a servant, — the preacher, — it comes from the great God himself; and, on that account, it is not to be trifled with, or despised. In the court language of Great Britain, when a subject receives an invitation to the royal table, it is said that her Majesty "commands" his presence there. And, similarly, the invitations of the King of kings to his gospel banquet are commands, the ignoring of which constitutes the most aggravated form of disobedience. What, then, shall we do with this invitation? That is for us the most important of all questions, and ought to have our earliest and most devoted attention; for it is an invitation from God, and our answer must be given to him. Remember, then, that we have been bidden to this great feast; and that will raise in your view the interpretation of this parable, from a question of curious exposition, up to one of personal and eternal importance.

III. This leads me, however, in the third place, to look at the reception given by those first invited, to the call which had been addressed to them. "They all with one consent began to make excuse." There had been no previous understanding between them. They did not act as they did, in consequence of any preconcerted agreement among themselves. The word "consent," as you observe, is not in the original; and its introduction here is apt to convey an erroneous impression. The meaning rather is, that, animated by one spirit, moved by one impulse, under the influence of the same disposition, they all began to make excuse. What that spirit was, is very clear. Each of them considered some worldly thing as of more importance to him than the enjoyment of the feast; and that is just saying, in another way, that they all treated the invitation as a matter of no moment. They did not think it worth their while to put themselves to any inconvenience for its acceptance. By a little forethought, each of them might have made such arrangements as would have enabled him to go; and, if they had cared to be present, they might all have been there with ease. But the real truth was, that they did not care to be present; and that was the secret explanation of their conduct. These excuses, therefore, were all *pretexts*. They were statements of what was true, but they did not give a true statement of the whole case. These men did not go to the feast, simply because they did not care to go. They were in the position of those Jews to whom the Lord himself said, "Ye *will* not come unto me, that ye might have life." For, if they had really desired to go, none of the things here mentioned would have kept them away. Perhaps they deluded themselves into the belief that they were acting in good faith; but if they had gone deeper down into their hearts, they would have found that they were deceiving themselves, and putting forth as excuses things, which, if they had been earnestly determined to go to the feast, would not have kept them for a moment.

And their self-delusion, if it were so, was all the more insidious because the things which they alleged in excuse were all proper enough in themselves, and such as, when kept in their own places, no fault could be found with. There was no harm in going to see a piece of ground which one had bought, or in proving in harness five yoke of oxen which one had purchased; and the law of Moses gave exemption from liability to military service to a man for a year after his marriage. But, allowing each of these its due importance, could any of them for a moment be put into comparison with the invitation to this banquet? The proving of the oxen, and the seeing of the piece of ground, might well enough have been postponed till another day; and no bride, worthy of the name, would have objected to the absence of her husband for such a great occasion. Therefore it is manifest, that, though the statements made might all be perfectly true, they were still frivolous, and altogether inadequate as excuses, betokening that those who made them were wedded to other things, and cared nothing either for the banquet or its lord. Hence we conclude that this part of the parable must be read in connection with the twenty-sixth verse of this chapter, which almost immediately follows it: "If any man come to me, and hate not his father and his mother, and wife and children and brethren and sisters, yea, and his own life also, he cannot be my disciple." Jesus will have the whole heart. If therefore, it is set on any thing else, it cannot be given up to him; and every excuse that is offered for withholding it, whether the excuse in itself be true, or not, does not give the real reason for his rejection. That must be sought in the fact that the heart is set on something else, which it is not willing to part with, even for him. It is the old story. "*One thing thou lackest;*" but that one thing is every thing, for it is the love of the heart. Let us see to it, therefore, that we keep the heart for Christ; for unless we give him that, we shall never taste of his supper.

IV. But we are thus brought to the fourth thing suggested by this parable; namely, that those who persistently decline to come to the feast shall be forever excluded from its enjoyment. The rejecters of Christ are themselves eternally rejected by Christ. The primary application of this principle was, of course, to the Jews; for, after they would not receive the Saviour, the apostles and first preachers of the gospel were commanded to turn to the Gentiles. But now the privileges which the Jews enjoyed are possessed by the Gentiles, and the same principle holds in reference to them; for, if they refuse the invitation to the feast, they too will be excluded from it. Privilege thus, as we have so often had occasion to remark, involves peril: and if we neglect the great salvation, there is not for us, any more than for the Jews, any possibility of escape; for, as one has solemnly said, the concluding portion of this parable " implies the impossibility of future restoration of those who have received and refused the gospel invitation in this life."[1] Much has been said in these recent days regarding the condition of those who pass from earth without having heard of Christ and his salvation. But even in their case, as I read the New Testament, there is no continuance of probation after death; for the language of Paul, "The invisible things of Him from the creation of the world are clearly seen, being understood by the things which are made, even his eternal power and Godhead, so that they are without excuse;" and again, "As many as have sinned without law shall also perish without law," — seems to me conclusive on the subject. But, whatever may be said concerning them, there can be no hesitation — among those, at least, who receive the statements of the Lord Jesus Christ himself as authoritative — concerning the fate of such as, having heard the gospel, neglect or despise or reject it. These are terrible

[1] Abbott.

words in themselves: "I say unto you, that none of those men which were bidden shall taste of my supper," but they are yet more terrible as coming from the lips of the loving and tender Lord Jesus. They are like the kindred words of the dresser of the vineyard, in the parable of the barren fig-tree: "Then, after that, thou shalt cut it down." And if that be the sentiment of Him who died for men, what man has any right to cavil at or condemn it? Until one is willing to be himself crucified for the salvation of those who reject Christ, he has no right to find fault with this declaration made by Christ. Where shall we find gentleness, self-sacrifice, and consideration for the human race, such as Christ has manifested? If there had been any possibility of averting this doom from impenitent unbelievers, we may be sure that he would have availed himself of it on their behalf; but if he speaks in this fashion, then their destruction must be inevitable. Yes, and it must be not only in harmony with justice, but with love. Now, we have heard the gospel, we are constantly hearing it. Let us beware, therefore, lest, by neglecting the great salvation, we become examples of its terrible realization. Think not, I beseech you, to gain admission to the banquet after the door is shut; for, has not Christ himself said, "Many will say to me in that day, Lord, Lord, have we not prophesied in thy name, and in thy name have cast out devils, and in thy name done many wonderful works? And then will I profess unto them, I never knew you. Depart from me, ye workers of iniquity."[1] Ah! it is a terrible thing to hear the gospel, if we do not accept it and obey it.

V. Finally, this parable reveals to us the fact that, notwithstanding the rejection of this invitation by multi-

[1] Matt. vii. 22, 23.

tudes, God's house shall be filled at last. The servant was sent into the streets and lanes of the city, and the highways and hedges of the country, to bring men in. That, as we have seen, symbolizes the call of the degraded outcasts among the Jews, and, following thereupon, the call of the Gentiles at large; but it implies also that the tables shall be furnished with guests. Yes, heaven shall be fully occupied with God's redeemed people, and the saved shall not be few. One of the greatest of French preachers — Massillon, to wit — has a marvellous sermon entitled, "On the Small Number of the Elect;" but, in spite of much that is solemn and true in the discourse, I cannot agree with the sentiment implied in its title. Hitherto, indeed, in the world the Church of Christ has been in the minority; but when the supper of the Lamb shall be celebrated above, it shall not be so. The saved shall vastly, and many times over, outnumber the lost, and the house of God shall be filled. Only the few first stragglers, as it were, from the streets and lanes and highways, have yet taken their seats; but the messengers of the Lord of the feast are busy over an ever-widening area, carrying the invitation to an ever-increasing multitude. Thus far the few only have accepted it; but by and by the nations shall flock in to the feast, "as the doves to their windows." When the number of the elect shall be accomplished, it shall be seen to be no mere fraction of the race, but the great majority of mankind; and the place of perdition shall be to heaven only as the prison is to a populous community. Whether, therefore, we be saved or lost, shall make little difference, so far as the furnishing of heaven with guests is concerned; but it will make an awful difference to us. We shall not be missed, amid the numbers without number that people heaven, but oh, how much we shall miss! God's purpose shall be accomplished, whether we accept the invitation of the gospel or not. If we accept his grace, it shall be accomplished in our salvation; but if we ignore his invitation, it shall be accomplished in our everlasting exclusion from the feast.

But why should we thus entail destruction on ourselves? "*Yet there is room.*" Come, then, my hearer, and avail thyself of the gracious opportunity. Once again the Saviour says, "Hearken diligently unto me, and eat ye that which is good, and let your soul delight itself in fatness. Incline your ear, and come unto me; hear, and your soul shall live: and I will make with you an everlasting covenant, even the sure mercies of David." But listen again, for he adds, "Seek ye the Lord while he may be found, call ye upon him while he is near."[1] There is coming a day when he will not be found. The opportunity is precious, but it is fleeting; therefore embrace it while it lasts, — yea, embrace it now.

[1] Isa. lv. 2, 3, 6

XX

THE LOST SHEEP
Luke 15:1-7

IN our exposition of the parable of the great supper, we saw that the poor, the maimed, the halt, and the blind, in the streets and lanes of the city, to whom the lord of the feast sent his invitations to the banquet, after the respectable citizens had insulted him with their excuses, represented the despised classes among the Jews, to whom, after he had been treated with contempt by the scribes and Pharisees, Christ would go with his message of salvation. That parable, therefore, contained in it a threatening of judgment to the Pharisees, and a promise of mercy to the degraded.

[1] In the summer of 1872, shortly after the beginning of my pastorate in New York, I preached a series of six discourses on the fifteenth chapter of the Gospel by Luke. These were almost immediately afterward published in a small volume entitled, The Lost Found, and the Wanderer Welcomed; and of that a new edition was issued from the press some two years ago. In view of these facts, my first impulse, when I came to this point in my present course of expository sermons on the parables of our Lord, was to omit the consideration of this chapter altogether. But on mature reflection I have come to the conclusion that it would be a mistake to pass silently over these matchless allegories now, merely because I have formerly expounded them. I have determined, therefore, to make a re-study of them all, not going into such minuteness of detail as I did in the little work to which I have referred, but still endeavoring to bring out as distinctly as possible the truths which they suggest and illustrate, with such additional light as the experience of these intervening years and the illumination of the Divine Spirit have given me upon them.

Now, in the opening verses of this chapter, we learn that already, not long after the parable had been delivered, its threatening was in course of being carried out, and its promise in course of being fulfilled. The Lord had, in a very large degree, turned away from the exclusive and self-righteous portion of the nation, and had begun to address himself specially to the outcast and despised, with such success, too, that the Evangelist says, " All the publicans and sinners were drawing near unto him to hear him." Nor is it difficult to account for their being thus attracted by him. He did not despise them as others did; and while he never said a word that could lead them to make light of their sin, and his own purity was a constant protest against their wickedness, yet by his message of salvation he awakened hope within them, and by his winning love he drew them after him to follow in his steps. He taught them to respect themselves, by showing them that they were the objects of the Divine solicitude; and he helped them to rise above themselves, by breathing his own Spirit into them: so that, as they listened to his words, they too might say, like the officers who, being sent to apprehend him, were themselves apprehended by him, "Never man spake like this man."

But, singularly enough, the scribes and Pharisees who had themselves rejected Jesus were exasperated by his tenderness to the outcasts whom they despised. They would not go in themselves, yet they were irritated and annoyed to see such persons welcomed by the Lord; and they made his treatment of them a new reason for antagonism to him. Therefore they said with a sneer, "This man receiveth sinners, and eateth with them." They meant it in scorn, but it was in reality the great glory of the Lord; and even their sneer, uttered in contempt, has become a jewel in the crown which now he wears.

Such exclusiveness as theirs, however, was not to go unreproved; and in order to show them how thoroughly they were out of sympathy with the inhabitants of heaven, and what like their cold cynicism looked in contrast with the welcome which God gives to the returning sinner, he spake these three parables, which have ever since been regarded by his disciples with peculiar interest. Behold how, out of evil, God ever bringeth good! We owe the parable of the prodigal son to the taunt of the Pharisees and scribes. The sandal needs to be cut in order to give out its richest fragrance; and no diviner words ever issued from the Redeemer's lips than these which he spoke in answer to a sneer. The cross of Christ was God's reply to the world's iniquity, and the story of the prodigal's reception is the reproof which Christ administered to the contempt of his assailants when they despised him for his kindness to the publicans and sinners.

The parables in this chapter are three, but the purpose pervading them is one. They were all designed to show the Pharisees how unlike God they were in the spirit which they manifested when they taunted Jesus with the reception of sinners; and so they all illustrate the joy that is in heaven over a penitent's return to God. The first two show the scribes and Pharisees what they ought to have felt, by describing the joy of a shepherd over the recovery of a lost sheep, and the joy of a woman at finding a piece of money which she had lost; the third teaches the same lesson by portraying the happiness of a father in receiving to his home again the son whom he had lost, and in the episode of the elder brother there is held before the Pharisees a faithful mirror in which each one of them might see himself.

But while, undoubtedly, that is the great drift of the parables, they, at the same time, teach other correlated truths with great power. They all agree in representing the sinner as having been lost by God, and in portraying the ecstasy of God on finding him again. But the first two show us, in addition, God's search for that which he had lost; while the third sets before us the result of that Divine search in the sinner's own return to God. The first two have their starting-point in the heart of God; and in them we see the yearning of that heart over that which had been lost, prompting him to use urgent means for its recovery. The third has its starting-point in the heart of the sinner. In it we have a picture of his departure, his wandering, his degradation, and his return. Thus one in purpose, these parables are different in detail. But they do not describe different classes of sinners, as if some were found by God after a long search, and others returned of their own accord to find God for themselves. Rather they are different views of what happens at different times to the same sinner, and the full truth concerning the conversion of any sinner is to be attained by combining all the three. Such is the wonderful nature of conversion, that no one parable can adequately illustrate it; and therefore here we have three given us, that, in the union of them all, we may have a complete understanding of its nature. When the prodigal comes to himself, and says, "I will arise and go to my Father," the parable of the lost sheep tells us that already the Good Shepherd has been there to seek him; and that of the lost coin informs us that already the woman has been there with her lighted candle and her dislodging broom to seek for the piece which she had lost.

But, leaving these general topics, let us look a little at the parable of the lost sheep. It is in itself so simple, so natural, and yet so pathetic, that it makes its way at once to the heart of every reader. Indeed, it might have been often enacted in the pastoral country in which it was first spoken; for its author says, "What man of *you* having an hundred sheep?" and all who are familiar with shepherd life will recognize its truthfulness at once. Now, the argument implied in the parable is this: If the recovery of a lost sheep is recognized by you as an event so joyous as to warrant the owner of it in calling his friends and neighbors together to rejoice with him because he has found it, much more is the recovery of a lost soul by God a cause of gladness to him and all beside him; and if you do not participate in that delight, then are ye out of harmony with the inhabitants of heaven, among whom "there is joy over one sinner that repenteth." It is an argument from the less to the greater, having as its suppressed premise the question once before upon the lips of the Lord, "How much is a man better than a sheep?" and its reference to the joy of the heavenly inhabitants was a reproof — all the stronger because it was a tacit one — of the cynicism of the scribes and Pharisees over his reception of publicans and sinners.

But, while that is the main lesson and proper interpretation of the parable, there are many other things in it which cannot be neglected without serious loss. Let us, therefore, examine it more carefully.

I. And first let me ask you to look at the loss. "What man of you, if he lose one sheep." We have here vividly set before us the fact that the sinner has been lost by God. Usually in the exposition of this parable, so far as it refers to the sinner, attention is directed to his hapless condition. We are reminded of the helplessness of the wandered sheep, running hither and thither, "bleating up the moor in weary dearth," and ever liable to be assailed by wild beasts, or to fall headlong over some rugged precipice, or into some fearful pit; and we are told that in all this we have a picture of the sinner, who has gone away from God, and cannot find his way back, while he is a prey to spiritual adversaries of every sort. Now, that is all true; but it is not the truth taught here. For the loss here is sustained not by the sinner, but by God; and in *that* fact we have the infinite pathos of these parables. *He* is the shepherd whose sheep has wandered off. *He* is the woman whose piece of money has disappeared in the darkness and *débris* of the house; *He* is the father whose son has gone away, and become lost to him. Now, I know that it is perilous to press a human analogy to its utmost, when we are speaking about God. I admit also, that, strictly speaking, God cannot be said to lose any thing. But still, somewhere and somehow, the figure of these parables has a real significance. We can not, we dare not, eliminate from this losing of the sheep, of the money, of the son, all reference to the feelings of God toward the sinner. They mean, that, in the separation between him and the man, which sin has caused, Jehovah has lost something which he had formerly possessed, and highly valued. They mean, that, to God, the sinner is as something lost is to him to whom it belonged; and these parables let us see how anxious he is, and what efforts he will make, to regain it for his own. At first there was a human voice in the choral anthem of his praise; but when man sinned, that voice dropped out, and He marked its absence with as much of sadness as Deity can feel. Nay, there was a special reason why God should miss human allegiance, even though, in other respects, its loss should seem no greater than that of one sheep out of a hundred; for man alone, of all his creatures, was formed in God's image. In him alone could Jehovah see the complete, though miniature, representation of himself; but when he sinned, that image was defaced, and God lost that which was to him so dear. Or, to put it more simply, when man fell, God lost the honor and service of human lives, the affection of human hearts, and the joy of human fellowship.

Nor let it be supposed, that, in giving prominence to this thought, I am insisting on something which is of no importance; for in this feeling of loss on the part of God, I find the explanation of the great sacrifice which he has made for human redemption. We do not like to lose any thing. No matter how apparently trivial that which we have lost may be, we will search again and again before we give it up as irrecoverable; and the more we value it, the more earnest will be our quest. If it be an animal, or a sum of money, we will go hither and thither ourselves, and engage others in the search, that by all means we may be successful. If it be a son, all the depths of our hearts will be stirred within us as we set out to track his wanderings; and we will never give up our efforts until we come either on himself or on his grave. Now, there must be something like that in God; for he has made us in his own image. I say not, indeed, that the loss of his human children caused him positive unhappiness; and yet, after all, why need I be so chary? Do not the Scriptures speak of him as grieved? Do they not represent him as soliloquizing thus: "How shall I give thee up, Ephraim? How shall I deliver thee, Israel? How shall I make thee as Admah? How shall I set thee as Zeboim? Mine heart is turned within me, my repentings are kindled together."[1] Let me take courage, then, and say, that, feeling the loss which he had sustained in being deprived of man's affection and obedience, God yearned in eager earnestness for the recovery of that which he so missed. We can speak of God only in human words, and these must lose some of their earthly meaning when applied to him. Nevertheless, it standeth here most sure, that, when man sinned, God lost that which he valued very greatly; and that the sense of this loss impelled him to seek after the salvation of sinners. "He *so* loved the world, that he gave his only begotten Son." What is that but just another way of saying that he so missed man's affection and fellowship, that he gave his only begotten Son? He sought our salvation not merely for our sakes, but also for his own; and thus the consciousness of loss corresponds, at the one end of the matter, with the rapturous joy which is felt at the other when the sinner repenteth.

This view of the subject may well give careless sinners food for serious reflection. You are God's. As his creatures, yea, as his sons, you are his. But you have gone away from him after your own paths, seeking your own ends; and he *misses* you. He on whom the universe depends, and who, it might be supposed, cares nothing about you, — *he* misses you. He yearns for your affection. He desires your return. Yea, he has used means of the most costly sort to find you out, and to bring you back. Why will you continue to be indifferent to him? Why will you perversely misrepresent him as one who takes no interest whatever in your wel-

[1] Hos. xi. 8.

fare? Believe me, you can give him no higher joy than by returning unto him, while at the same time your repentance will secure your own eternal happiness.

II. But it is time now to look at the search and recovery. "Doth he not leave the ninety and nine in the wilderness, and go after that which is lost until he find it? and when he hath found it he layeth it on his shoulders rejoicing." Many questions rise out of these words, which are more easily asked than answered. Whom do these ninety and nine represent? What is meant by the leaving of *them*, and going after that which is lost? and when may the lost be said to be truly found? The ninety and nine are said, in the seventh verse, to be "just persons which need no repentance." Now, some have supposed that there is here a reference to the Pharisees and scribes. They would make it an ironical expression like that other, "They that are whole need not a physician, but they that are sick. I came not to call the righteous, but sinners, to repentance;"[1] and they would interpret the leaving of the ninety and nine as a vindication of himself by Jesus for leaving the exclusive and self-righteous and going after publicans and sinners. This gives a good and consistent enough meaning, and I have been greatly inclined to adopt it as correct; yet two reasons weigh with me so strongly as to lead me to prefer another. These are: First, it is positively said here that these ninety and nine need no repentance: therefore it is implied that they have never sinned. Second, it is affirmed that "joy shall be in heaven over one sinner that repenteth, more than over ninety and nine just persons which need no repentance:" therefore it is im-

[1] Matt. ix. 12.

plied that there is some joy over the ninety and nine.
But that cannot be true if they represent the Pharisees,
since it is impossible to conceive that any inhabitant of
heaven could rejoice in any degree over them. Therefore, although the view which I prefer is not without its
own serious difficulties, I am disposed to regard the
ninety and nine as descriptive of the angels who have
kept their first estate, and who ceaselessly serve God
before his throne.

If, then, that representation be correct, the leaving
of the ninety and nine will signify the leaving of heaven
by the eternal Son, when, at the era of the incarnation,
he who was "rich, for our sakes became poor," [1] and set
out in search of that which was lost. And the search
itself will include every thing which the Lord Jesus
did by his own personal ministry on earth, by his death,
resurrection, and ascension, and by the mission of his
Spirit, as well as every thing which he is now doing by
the preaching and labors of his ministers, for the recovery of sinners. All the way from the bosom of the
Father to the tomb of Joseph, Jesus came to seek and
to save that which was lost; and while that was the
goal which he had in view at the last, he was all the time
giving illustrations of his great work as he went along.
He was seeking his sheep which he had lost, when he
sat by the well of Sychar, and talked with the woman
of Samaria; when he called Zacchæus down from his
perch among the leaves of the sycamore-tree; and when
he bade Matthew follow him from his toll-booth. He
died that the path might be opened up for him to go
farther still in his loving search; and he had the same
object in view when he shed forth his Spirit on the day of
Pentecost, and inspired his servants to proclaim his truth

[1] 2 Cor. viii. 9.

with power. He has been continuing his search ever since: and still in the events of his providence, whereby he rouses the careless to reflection; in the labors of his ministers, who proclaim his message, and speak to the hearts of their fellow-men; and in the strivings of his Spirit, whereby often, when they can give no explanation of the matter, men's minds are strangely turned in the direction of salvation, — he is going after that which was lost. Yea, he is here to-night prosecuting his search, as once again, through the exposition of this parable, his love and earnestness and tenderness are set before us. Nor will his search be concluded until time shall be no longer. Oh! in view of this unceasing work of the Good Shepherd, may we not sing, in the words of the old hymn, —

> "Wearily for me thou soughtest,
> On the cross my soul thou boughtest,
> Lose not all for which thou wroughtest"?

But when is a sinner found by Christ? The answer is: when, on his side, the sinner finds Christ. The finding of the lost sheep is, as you see, spoken of in the parable as corresponding with the repenting of the sinner. When, therefore, the sinner turns to God, he is found and recovered by God; or, borrowing here a side light from the third parable in this chapter, when the prodigal comes to himself, and says, "I will arise and go to my Father," he is precisely at the point indicated in the first parable by the shepherd's finding his sheep and laying it on his shoulder. What is seen from the heavenly side is Christ laying his hand upon the sinner as he says, "I have found that which was lost;" but what is seen from the earthly side is the sinner laying his hand on Christ as he exclaims, "I have found my deliverer." Yet these are not two things so much as different sides of the same thing, and they are both present in every conversion. Nor must we lose sight of the tenderness of the Good Shepherd as he is here described. He does not strike the sheep, or speak to it in words of harshness; but he lifts it gently on to his own shoulders, and carries it back to the flock. So it is with Jesus and the sinner. He does not upbraid him with his waywardness and folly; he does not cast his ingratitude and disobedience in his teeth: but with gentleness he receives him to his heart, and fills him with happiness and joy. "A bruised reed shall he not break, and the smoking flax shall he not quench."[1] You need not be afraid of him, O sinner; for he is saying to you now, "Come unto me, and I will give you rest."

III. The last thing in the parable is the joy over the recovery of that which had been lost. "And when he cometh home he calleth together his friends and neighbours, saying unto them: Rejoice with me, for I have found my sheep which was lost. I say unto you, that likewise joy shall be in heaven over one sinner that repenteth, more than over ninety and nine just persons which need no repentance." The home-coming here can hardly be identical with the finding of the lost one, but must rather be understood of the introduction of the saved one into heaven at last. Yet the joy over his recovery is not delayed till then, though then it shall be intensified and increased. An illustration may make this perfectly plain. Suppose that one of your children has wandered away from home, and that a trusted member of your family has set out in search of him. He is

---

[1] Isa. xlii. 3.

away a long time, and your heart grows weary as it looks for tidings day after day in vain. At length there comes a telegram from a distant city with the information that the lost one has been found, and that both will be home again ere long. Of course the mere receipt of that message gives you joy, irrepressible and ecstatic. But when the loved one enters your dwelling once again, your joy becomes more emphatic and demonstrative than ever. Now, your gladness at the receipt of the telegram corresponds to the joy that is in heaven over a sinner's repentance; while your higher delight over the reception of your child into your home symbolizes the joy which shall be felt when the saved sinner is received into glory.

But why should there be *more* joy over the repenting sinner than over the unfallen angels? The question is important, for that is the chief point of difference between the first and second parables here. As we shall see when we come to it, the joy of the woman in the next parable demands society to make it complete, even as it is said here that the shepherd calleth "together" his friends and neighbors; but in the moral of that parable this general joy is brought into prominence, whereas in that of this one it drops out of notice, and stress is laid mainly on the fact that the joy is greater over the recovery of the lost than over the retention of the unfallen. And to understand how that may be, we have but to recall familiar experiences of our own. The mother regards with a peculiar interest the child that has been nigh unto death and brought back again as from the grave. The greater the peril one has passed through, the greater the joy over his ultimate safety. One Bible has as much in it as another, and to the devout soul any copy of the Scriptures will be an object of interest; but I am sure Dr. Andrew Bonar regards with special delight that Bible which he accidentally let fall into Jacob's well, and which, after having been for long years lying there, was at length fished up and restored to him by his friend Dr. Wilson of Bombay. A ship-launch is a glad occasion; and as the crowds behold the vessel, gayly decked with flags, slip down the ways into the water, they rend the air with cheers; but there is another kind of joy in the hearts of those whose loved ones have been on board a steamship that is long overdue and has been given up for lost, when she is signalled off the port, and they hasten down to the wharf to receive those for whom they had almost mourned as for the dead. Such experiences as these, human though they be, may help us to understand the joy that is in heaven, and chiefest of all there in the heart of God himself, over one sinner that repenteth. Such a joy, O sinner, you may occasion there. Repent, therefore, now: and as the news is told on high, a thrill of gladness will vibrate in the hearts of the redeemed; angels will share the high delight, and God himself will own the rapture of the moment as he says, "This my son was dead, and is alive again: he was lost, and is found."

I conclude with the repetition of one of the most touching lyrics founded on this parable which I have seen, though my imperfect acquaintance with the dialect of the colored people, in which it is written, may prevent you somewhat from feeling the power of its exquisite pathos.

> De massa ob de sheepfol',
> Dat guards de sheepfol' bin,
> Look out in de gloomerin' meadows
> Wha'r de long night rain begin:
> So he call to de hirelin' shepa'd, —
> "Is my sheep, is dey all come in?"

THE LOST SHEEP

Oh, den says de hirelin' shepa'd,
"Des's some, dey's black and thin,
And some, dey's po' ol' wedda's,
But de res' dey's all brung in, —
But de res' dey's all brung in."

Den de massa ob de sheepfol',
Dat guards de sheepfol' bin,
Goes down in de gloomerin' meadows,
Whar de long night rain begin;
So he le' down de ba's ob de sheepfol',
Callin' sof', "Come in, come in," —
Callin' sof', "Come in, come in!"

Den up t'ro' de gloomerin' meadows,
T'ro' de col' night rain and win',
And up t'ro' de gloomerin' rain-paf
Wha'r de sleet fa' pie'cin' thin,
De po' los' sheep ob de sheepfol'
Dey all comes gadderin' in, —
De po' los' sheep ob de sheepfol'
Dey all comes gadderin' in.

XXI

THE LOST COIN
Luke 15:8-10

THE story told in these verses is thoroughly true to Eastern life. Even to this day, as I have been informed by one, who, from long residence among them, is perfectly familiar with the domestic habits of the people of Palestine, the cherished heirlooms of a Syrian woman consist, for the most part, in pieces of money. They are her own exclusive property, with which her husband may not interfere; and, having descended to her from her mother, they are handed down by her in turn to her daughters. They are commonly worn in the hair, the larger pieces generally hanging from the ends of the braids. Thus one might easily fall out of its place; and, if it did so, it could not be recovered without a search.

For there was not in Eastern dwellings, in the Saviour's day, the same scrupulous attention to cleanliness that we love to see in so many homes among ourselves. The floors were frequently covered with rushes, which, being changed only at rare intervals, collected a vast amount of dust and *débris*, among which a coin might be very readily lost. Add to this, that Eastern houses are constructed in such a way as to keep out the light and heat of the sun as much as possible. Dr. Edward Robinson speaks of his having passed a night in the Lebanon, in a house in which there was "no window, and no light except from the door;"[1] and, in general, the windows are few, while even these are shaded with such lattice-work as tends to exclude rather than admit the light. Hence when a comparatively small article, like a piece of money, was lost in such a place, the lighting of a lamp, and the sweeping of the house, were the most natural means to be used for its recovery. Moreover, as the coin formed presumably a part of the dowry of the woman, in which all her descendants had an interest as well as herself, we can easily understand how its loss and recovery would be almost equally an object of interest to them all. It was quite natural, therefore, for her to call her female friends and neighbors, — for so the phrase is in the Greek, — to rejoice with her over the finding of her lost heirloom; for they, as having similar treasures exposed to similar dangers, would be able to enter fully into her feelings.

The parable is thus realistically true, even in its minutest details; while yet it has in it that idealistic universality which makes every reader feel that it might have happened to himself. It is a painting of an interior, such as Wilkie and Teniers loved to portray, with this added feature, that we have here the motion and progress, which no picture can reproduce; while it is all so natural, that we seem for the time to be ourselves taking part in the search, and joining in the gladness wherewith its success is celebrated.

But beautiful as it is, even as a picture, this parable is no less striking as the material analogy of the spiritual truth with which the Saviour was dealing when he spake it at the first. It carries its interpretation on its

---

[1] Biblical Researches, vol. iii. p. 44.

face; and is in the main a repetition, with emphasis, of the parable of the lost sheep. Both of them set before us a loss, a search, a recovery, and a resultant joy. In both the argument is from the less to the greater; and in both the application is to the objection which the Pharisees and scribes raised against Christ for receiving sinners, and eating with them. The lesson plainly is, that, if a woman has such gladness over the finding of a lost piece of money that she cannot but call upon her friends and neighbors to rejoice with her, much more ought all right-thinking persons to rejoice with God over the recovery of lost sinners. And that joy is felt among the inhabitants of heaven, over one sinner that repenteth.

This is the full exposition of the parable. But to enforce that would be only to repeat what we have already advanced in our consideration of the story of the lost sheep; and therefore to-night we shall turn your attention to some things suggested here, which, though not strictly and properly belonging to exposition, may yet fairly enough find a place in the homiletic treatment of the subject, provided it be clearly understood that we regard them, not as a part of the interpretation of the parable, but simply as edifying truths, which are recalled to our minds by the special features of the story itself.

I. Look, then, first, at the thing lost. It was a coin. It was not simply a piece of precious metal, but that metal moulded and minted into money. You remember how, when the enemies of Jesus sought to insnare him by asking whether it was lawful to give tribute to Cæsar or not, he said to them, "Show me a penny;" and when one had been produced, he asked, " Whose is this image and superscription?" They replied, "Cæsar's." Whereupon he answered, "Render therefore unto Cæsar the things which are Cæsar's, and to God the things which are God's."[1] Now, reading this parable in the light of that narrative, we think of the coin as stamped with the king's image, and designed not only for a medium of exchange, but also for a testimony to the royalty and right of him whose likeness was impressed upon it. What a beautiful thing is a new piece of money! How sharply cut are the letters which are imprinted on it! How finely relieved the likeness of the monarch! And how bright its polished surface! Can we help being reminded by all this of the human soul, when first it came new-minted from the Creator's hand? It had enstamped upon it his image in knowledge, righteousness, and holiness, and was designed by him to be a willing witness-bearer to the rightfulness of his authority and the stability of his throne. He made man after his own likeness, and this coin in its original condition may image forth to us the human soul in its primal dignity and beauty.

But *the coin was lost*, and that may suggest to us that the great purpose for which man was created has been missed by the sinner. For any good which the piece of money, so long as it was lost, was to its owner, it might as well have been non-existent. And similarly the sinner is, so to say, of no use to God. He gives no glory to God; he is of no service to him, so far, at least, as the promotion of his honor and the acknowledgment of his authority are concerned. He does not "like to retain God" in his knowledge. His heart is estranged from God's love; his life is devoted to another lord: he is lost.

[1] Luke xx. 24, 25.

Yet he is not absolutely worthless; *for the coin, though lost, has still a value.* If it can be recovered, it will be worth as much as ever. It may be blackened with rust, or soiled with mud, or covered over with dust; but it is still silver, — nay, it is still minted silver. Even so the human soul is valuable though lost. It has in it the silver of immortality; and, depraved though it be, its intellectual powers, its moral freedom, its soaring ambition, and its upbraiding conscience tell not only of its former grandeur, but also of its present importance. Sinful as he is, man is the most valuable being in the world. There is nothing equal to him; nothing, almost, that we can name as second after him. There is a wide, yawning, impassable gulf between him and the highest of the lower animals. He has a dignity to which they can lay no claim. He has a character which is unique and peculiar to himself. In spite of modern theories of development, there is in every human being a moral nature which marks him man and not brute, together with such feelings after the future life as stamp him immortal; and this is the silver of the coin that once bore, distinct and well defined, the lineaments of Jehovah's image.

But *the coin may be recovered,* for it was lost in the house. The woman did not let it fall as she was crossing the wild and trackless moor, neither did she drop it into the depths of the Galilæan lake. Had she done either, she would never have thought of seeking for it, for she would have regarded it as irrecoverable. But knowing that it had fallen from her in the house, and that it must be somewhere within its walls, she made vigorous search in the certainty that it could be found. Now, that reminds us that the soul of the sinner is recoverable by God. It is capable of being restored to its original dignity and purity. It has in it still possibilities as great and glorious as ever.

There are many things which are to human view irremediable, and must be left as they are. No human alchemy can bleach into its primal whiteness the blackened snow which has been trodden into miry slush upon the city streets. No artistic ingenuity can replace the downy skin upon the peach which has been rubbed against the ragged wall. No manufacturing skill can restore to the violet the velvet softness of its leaf after it has been crumpled up and withered. But the soul of man, even in its most depraved condition, is capable of being renewed, and may yet become a pure and holy denizen of heaven. For "who are these in white robes? and whence came they?" These are "they who have washed their robes, and made them white in the blood of the Lamb," souls renewed by the power of God's Spirit, through the work of his Son. The lost sinner, therefore, may be recovered. So no one needs despair, or think that he is beyond the possibility of salvation; neither should any one among us regard the most abandoned as hopeless: for the coin went a-missing, not in the dark depths of the inaccessible ravine, but within the four walls of the house. What an antidote to personal despondency, and what a spur to flagging energy in our efforts for the benefit of others, have we in this delightful thought!

II. But now let us look at the search, and we may find some equally important truths recalled by that to our remembrance. The loser here is also the seeker; and, as it was natural that the shepherd should go after his sheep, it is equally natural, that, in this case, the woman should make search for the coin. We may not, therefore, press into undue significance the fact that prominence is given here to a woman, or seek to bring more out of the parable than it really contains. Yet it is hardly possible, for me at least, to read it, in the connection in which here it stands, without having recalled to my mind the agency of the Holy Spirit in the conversion of a soul. In the first of the parables, the shepherd reminds us of Him who is emphatically the Good Shepherd; and we had no hesitation in applying what is said there to his seeking and saving that which was lost. In the third of the parables, the reception of the prodigal by his father connects itself, in the mind of every reader, with the loving Fatherhood of God, as manifested in the welcome which he gives to the returning sinner. And therefore there is no impropriety in associating what is here said of the woman, with the agency of the Holy Spirit in the recovery of a sinful soul. Mr. Arnot, indeed, will not allow us to take such a view, even though we do not put it forward as involved in the proper interpretation of the parable. He affirms, that, since the shepherd who lost the sheep represents the Lord Jesus, the woman who lost the piece of money must represent him too. But if that argument have any force, then we must go farther, and affirm that the father who lost his son must also represent Christ. But that is a view which no one will accept. The truth is, that which was lost, whether we call it sheep, or coin, or son, represents the sinner who was lost by the *Godhead;* and if in the shepherd we are reminded of the Son, and in the father we have God the Father suggested to us, there can surely be no impropriety in hinting that the action of this woman may remind us of the work of the Holy Ghost in the regeneration of a sinner.

This woman lighted a lamp, and swept the house, and searched diligently until she found the piece which she had lost. Now, the lighting of the lamp suggests to us the illuminating agency of the Spirit in bringing the truth to bear upon the soul. The truth which he employs for the conversion of a sinner is the word of God, all of which has been given by his own inspiration; and the special portion of that word which he uses in his saving work is the wondrous story of the cross. "The truth as it is in Jesus;" the fact, that "God so loved the world, that he gave his only begotten Son, that whosoever believeth in him should not perish, but have everlasting life;"[1] the faithful saying that "Christ Jesus came into the world to save sinners,"[2] — this is the light which he employs. No new revelations does he now bestow. He uses still this old gospel, — the good news of salvation through Him "who died for our offences, and rose again for our justification." In a word, the truths which centre in the cross of Calvary are those which the Spirit employs for the conversion of men. It was so on the day of Pentecost; it has been so in every period of true spiritual revival; it has been so in every individual conversion. They say that in some of our large millinery establishments many needles are lost in the course of the day; and that, in seeking to recover them, a young woman, instead of going down upon the carpet, and wearifully picking them up one by one, takes a powerful magnet, and, holding it near the floor, goes all around the room, attracting to it each minutest particle of steel, and so recovering all. So, in searching for lost souls, the Holy Spirit goes through the world, employing the magnet of the cross. Everywhere he seeks to draw men to

[1] John iii. 16.   [2] 1 Tim. i. 15.

him by the attraction of his love, and constrains them "to live by the faith of Him who loved them, and gave himself for them."

But not all at once, — at least, as a general rule, — do men attend to and believe this truth of the gospel. The magnet will do its work wherever there are no neutralizing elements near; but so long as the soul is sunk in depravity, or engaged in worldly pleasures, or absorbed in earthly pursuits, it feels not the charm of the Redeemer's love. Hence means must be used to destroy the counter attractions of the world, which keep men from being sensitive to the love of Christ. Or, taking our language from the parable, if the light of the lamp fall immediately upon the coin, it is then and thereby found; but if the piece of money, having been dropped on a rush-covered floor, has rolled away, and become covered by the straw and *débris* of weeks, these must be removed before the light can reveal it to the seeker's eye. But then comes the sweeping of the house. There are providential disturbances in business, or there are family bereavements or personal afflictions, or there is the awakening of the conscience by the hearing of some solemn discourse; and, as the result of these or of some other of the manifold expedients which God the Holy Spirit can employ, there is a general upturning of the soul, like that which is created in the home by the annual house-cleaning; and, just as, on such occasions, many things which had been hidden for a long time come out into view, and compel you to settle what you will do with them, so, in the soul's disturbance, the long-neglected questions about sin and salvation come up, and the man is impelled to cry, "What must I do to be saved?" Then, as some Evangelist exclaims, "Believe on the Lord Jesus Christ, and thou shalt be saved," he turns in penitence and faith to the Redeemer; and that moment the Holy Spirit finds and recovers the lost soul.

In this view of the case, then, every time a sinner is brought face to face with trial, every providential unsettlement that disturbs him, or, to use Jeremiah's expression, every "emptying from vessel to vessel"[1] to which he is subjected, is a new sweeping of the house by the Holy Spirit in his search after him for his salvation. Do not, I beseech you, O sinner! misunderstand God's dealings with you in these dispensations. The more severe they are, they are only the more impressive revelations of his earnestness in seeking for your highest welfare. They are but, as it were, the result of his diligence in searching after you; and, if now this is revealed to you for the first time, oh, let him find you as, with devout reverence and genuine repentance, you exclaim, "Lord, I believe: help thou mine unbelief."

III. Turning now to the joy over the recovered coin, we find here one of the distinctive features of this parable. In the story of the lost sheep, while the social character of the shepherd's gladness is certainly referred to, the specialty of his delight lay in the fact, to which prominence is given in the appended note of interpretation, that it was greater than over the ninety and nine which had never gone astray. Here, however, the emphasis is laid on the circumstance that the woman "called together her friends and neighbors, saying, Rejoice with me; for I have found the piece which I had lost," while no reference is made to the nine pieces which she had always possessed; and the note of exposition simply reads, "Likewise I say unto you, There is

[1] Jer. xlviii. 11.

joy in the presence of the angels of God"—that is, substantially, in the hearts of God and of his angels —"over one sinner that repenteth." We have seen already, in our introductory remarks, how it came that the woman's female friends were likely to have special sympathy with her in her delight. But gladness everywhere is diffusive. We cannot have the highest kind of joy if we must keep it to ourselves. There are certain sorrows which must find vent in tears, else death will be the result; and in this connection we must all remember the words in Tennyson's beautiful song, "She must weep, or she will die." But there is something similar, also, with the opposite emotion of delight. There are joys which, if we may not share them with others, will seriously injure ourselves. The pent-up feeling will choke us; but the expression of it to others will give relief to ourselves, while, if they are in any way like-minded with us, or deeply interested in our welfare, it will make them also sharers of our ecstasy. Nor is this all: the sight of their gladness will redouble our own, and add to our permanent happiness. Every reader of ancient history remembers the "*Heureka*" of Archimedes after his great discovery; and there is probably no one among ourselves, who has not had times in his own experience, when, eager for sympathy in his joy, he has gone long miles to make it known to those who would understand and participate in his delight. We want to be congratulated by those who can appreciate and intelligently join with us in the gladness of the hour.

Now, here, again, we find in ourselves a feature of our resemblance to God. For his joy also, if I may venture to say so, needs society to give it perfection; and the fact that there are those beside him to whom he can make known the story of each repenting sinner, and who, in some degree, realize the occasion of his delight, intensifies his gladness, and diffuses among them a new happiness. The celestial inhabitants who share with God his joy over a repenting sinner are the holy angels; part of whose education, if I may so say, consists in their perception of the gradual development of the Divine plan for the salvation of men, and the continued evidence of its success. Nor let any one suppose that this is a mere fancy of our own, for which there is no foundation in Scripture apart from the words of this parable; for Paul has said that "God hath created all things by Jesus Christ, to the intent that now unto the principalities and powers in heavenly places, might be made known, *through the church*, the manifold wisdom of God."[1] Now, as the church exists in the world for the salvation of men, these words must mean that through it God is showing, in the recovery of human souls, his manifold wisdom to the principalities and powers of heaven; and that in the appreciation of his success, by those who know something of the difficulties with which he had to contend, and which he overcame, he has his highest joy. When Sir William Thomson let down his grappling apparatus from the deck of the "Great Eastern," into the dark depths of the Atlantic, and succeeded in bringing up therewith the cable which years before had been lost, there was, we may be sure, a thrill of unutterable gladness in his own heart; but when his fellow-electricians, who understood so well what skill was needed to devise the means which he had used, crowded round him to express their great delight, nothing more was needed to make his joy complete. So, if we may compare human things with divine, the per-

[1] Eph. iii. 9, 10.

ception of his wisdom in the means which he has devised for the recovery of lost men, and the appreciation of his success in the use of those means, by the principalities and powers of heaven who are nearest him, and know him best, is the very acme of the Divine delight; and we can well understand how Paul, in speaking of the way of salvation, calls it "the glorious gospel of the *happy God.*"[1] For it is not only a revelation of his glory, but also a minister to his happiness. But I can go no farther here; and I must leave it to yourselves, under the guidance of the Holy Spirit, to think out the thought to which I have given such stammering and hesitating utterance. Yet, if I have in any degree brought out to you the meaning of the Saviour's words, what an overwhelming rebuke it was to the Pharisees, to be shown how utterly out of sympathy they were with God and his angels when they sneered at Jesus for receiving sinners and eating with them! The highest in the celestial principalities would have counted it an honor to be employed in just such work as Jesus was performing, and they were even at the moment contemplating it with sympathetic interest; while the scribes — for all so righteous as they thought themselves — stood by and sneered. My brethren, let us take warning from their case; and whenever we catch ourselves looking with contempt at missionary work among the lowly, let us see therein the leaven of Pharisaism in our hearts, and take means to purge it out.

I cannot conclude, however, without staying a few moments longer to give emphasis to two thoughts, which may gather up for us the lessons of this parable. The first is, that the recovery of any sinner, though he has been lost to God, is possible. No one is beyond

---

[1] 1 Tim. i. 11. The word is μακαρίου.

hope here. No abandoned one, however sunk in depravity, needs despair of salvation; and no worker in the service of Christ needs regard the conversion of any one as hopeless. Paul said, "After me, any one;" and you remember the story which William Jay tells of John Newton to this effect: "When I one day called upon him, he said, 'I am glad to see you, for I have just received a letter from Bath, and you may know something of the writer,' mentioning his name. I told him I did, and that he had been for years a hearer of mine, but he was a most awful character, and almost in all evil. 'But,' says he, 'he writes now like a penitent.' I said, 'He may be such, but if he be I shall never despair of the conversion of any one again.' 'Oh,' said he, 'I never did since God saved me.' "[1] In that hopefulness for the conversion even of the very worst, lay, I am persuaded, much of the secret of Newton's power; and herein also, I believe, will be found much of the explanation of the success of those who, from being themselves among the chief of sinners, have become the most earnest of evangelists. Let us, therefore, in our work despair of no one, and let no sinner regard himself as beyond recovery. Christ is able to save "unto the uttermost." The piece of money went a-missing in the house, and so it could be found. I have rarely seen this truth presented with such power as in the well-known lines entitled "Beautiful Snow." I do not know who wrote them; I cannot tell, either, what truth there is in the story that was told on their first publication, of their being found in manuscript among the personal effects of a poor outcast woman who died in a hospital in Cincinnati: but they are all exquisite, and I reproduce here these three stanzas, that

[1] Autobiography and Reminiscences of Rev. William Jay, p. 275.

they may rivet in your memories the truth on which I am now insisting : —

> " Once I was pure as the snow, but I fell,
> Fell like the snow — but from heaven to hell;
> Fell to be trampled as filth of the street,
> Fell to be scoffed, to be spit on and beat;
>   Pleading — cursing — dreading to die,
> Selling my soul to whoever would buy;
> Dealing in shame for a morsel of bread;
> Hating the living, and fearing the dead.
> Merciful God! have I fallen so low?
> And yet I was once like the beautiful snow.
>
> Once I was fair as the beautiful snow,
> With an eye like a crystal, a heart like its glow;
> Once I was loved for my innocent grace, —
> Flattered and sought for the charms of my face!
>   Father — mother — sisters, — all,
> God and myself, I have lost by my fall;
> The veriest wretch that goes shivering by
> Will make a wide sweep lest I wander too nigh;
> For all that is on or about me, I know,
> There is nothing that's pure as the beautiful snow.
>
> Helpless and foul as the trampled snow,
> Sinner, despair not! Christ stoopeth low
> To rescue the soul that is lost in sin,
> And raise it to life and enjoyment again.
>   Groaning — bleeding — dying for thee,
> The Crucified hung on the cursed tree!
> His accents of pity fall soft on thine ear.
> ' Is there mercy for me? Will he heed my weak prayer?
> O God! in the stream that for sinners did flow,
> Wash me, and I shall be whiter than snow!'"

Take to thyself, O sinner, the message of these lines, and make for thyself the prayer with which they conclude. No matter how aggravated thine iniquities have been, or how deeply depraved thy spirit may be, there is mercy now for thee. Thou mayst be accepted and renewed if only thou wilt betake thyself in penitence to God in Christ; for still the proclamation is in force, "Let the wicked forsake his way, and the unrighteous man his thoughts; and let him return unto the Lord, and he will have mercy upon him, and to our God, for he will abundantly pardon. For my thoughts are not your thoughts, neither are your ways my ways, saith the Lord. For as the heavens are high above the earth, so are my ways higher than your ways, and my thoughts than your thoughts."[1]

Finally, let us learn that the most Godlike work in which man can engage on earth is that of seeking to save the lost. These two parables might fitly be inscribed with these words as their title, "The Seeking God." They tell us of the Divine yearning after and search for the lost soul of man, and the Divine joy over its recovery. But they put special emphasis on the search. The great work and happiness of Godhead are connected with the salvation of lost souls. Do you want to be like God? Do you want to be a sharer in the loftiest joy which even Deity can know? Then go forth to seek and to save that which is lost. Care not what sacrifices it may involve, or what discomforts it may entail upon you. Never mind though it may require you to go to dens of infamy or haunts of sin. These are not so far beneath you as this evil world was beneath the eternal Son of God when he came to earth for us men and for our salvation. Go, and he will take care of you, and give you success. John Gough, in one of his stirring orations, tells us how a fashionable lady who had dropped a diamond ring upon the street did

[1] Isa. lv. 7–9.

not hesitate to thrust her ungloved hand into the gutter, that she might seek for and recover her precious ornament; and shall not we, believing in the protecting grace of God, expose ourselves, if need be, to contact with moral and spiritual impurity, if only we may be instrumental in recovering the immortal jewel of a human soul, and restoring it to Him to whom of right it belongs? The great English novelist has no more pathetic chapter in his writings than that which tells how the big, burly, honest sailor set out from his boat-house on the Yarmouth shore to seek his lost Emily; and when we shall feel about sinners as he did about her, when we shall go forth in a search after them as earnest, as persevering, and as loving as his was, then we shall "begin to be disciples" of Him who, "though he was rich, for our sakes became poor, that we through his poverty might be rich;" and in our success we shall know something of the joy that is in heaven "over one sinner that repenteth."

XXII

THE PRODIGAL SON
Luke 15:11-24

ONE of the greatest preachers of the gospel that ever lived has left behind him a book, almost as widely known as "The Pilgrim's Progress" which came from the same hand, which he has called "Come and Welcome." We have often had occasion to dwell upon the "*come*," and to repeat from this pulpit the gracious invitations which God in Christ has addressed to sinners of mankind; but to-night our attention will be directed ultimately to the "*welcome*" which he gives to sinners on their return to him, as that is illustrated to us in this, which has, by common consent, come to be regarded as "the pearl of the parables."

Like those by which it is immediately preceded, it was designed originally to rebuke the cold-hearted and self-righteous exclusiveness of the scribes and Pharisees; and to show them, that, in despising Jesus for receiving sinners and eating with them, they were altogether out of harmony with Him in whose presence there is joy over one sinner that repenteth. But it differs from them in that, while they illustrate the earnestness with which God seeks the lost sinner, it describes the result of that search in the voluntary return of the sinner himself. They view the matter from the Divine side, and let us see the efforts which

God has put forth through the incarnation of his Son, and the agency of his Spirit, to recover that which has been lost. This looks at the history, if I may so call it, from the human side, and shows us the sinner rising and returning to his Father. Yet, as we said in our last discourse, these are not so much two separate things as two ways of looking at one and the same thing. Admirably has Mr. Arnot said here, "It is not that some of fallen human kind are saved after the manner of the strayed sheep, and others after the manner of the prodigal son; not that the Saviour bears one wanderer home by his power, and that another, of his own accord, arises and returns to his Father. Both these processes are accomplished in every conversion. The man comes, yet Christ brings him; Christ brings him, yet he comes."[1]

Again, in the two preceding parables, little or nothing is said as to the sinner's departure from God, and his misery and degradation in his estrangement from God. The loss which they describe is rather that which is sustained by God; and scarcely any hint is given, in either of them, of that which is incurred by the sinner himself. Here, however, the deplorable condition of man away from God, and in the far land of sin, is set in the forefront; and nowhere in the whole range of literature, whether sacred or secular, have we a more vivid exemplification of the awful truth that "the way of transgressors is hard" than that which is presented to us in this matchless story.

In the episode of the elder brother, too, we have something unique, and peculiar to this parable. In the former allegories, there is no jarring or dissonant note in the chorus of rejoicing over the finding of that which

[1] Arnot on the Parables, p. 428.

had been lost; but here, that, in the mirror which Jesus held up, the scribes and Pharisees might see their own likeness as well as his, we have one surly and sour dissentient, who virtually says to his father what they had said to Jesus, "This man receiveth sinners, and eateth with them."

Without lingering longer, however, on these general matters, let us look at the incidents of the story itself.

I. There is, first, a departure from home. "A certain man had two sons; and the younger of them said unto his father, Father, give me the portion of goods that falleth to me; and he divided unto them his living. And not many days after, the younger son gathered all together, and took his journey into a far country." What a heartless youth this is! He cannot wait until, in the course of events, his father dies; but he must have his portion now. His case, therefore, is not like that of him who, encouraged and commanded by his father, goes to some new land, there to carry on business for his parent and in conjunction with him, and who, regretting the necessity for his departure, carries with him the heart of a son, which beats continually in love and loyalty to his home. There would have been nothing wrong in that. Indeed, just in that way some of the noblest things ever wrought by men have been performed. But in this youth's heart there had been a very serious estrangement from his father, even before he left the homestead. He had become weary of the wholesome restraints of the parental household. He wanted to be his own master. He desired to be independent of all authority and interference. A son in name, he had already ceased to be a son in heart; and so he was eager to be gone from a place whose whole atmosphere had become to him most disagreeable. Seeing all this, his father gave him what he wanted, and let him go his way. And as it was *home* he hated, so, the farther from home he could get, he thought he would be the better off; and therefore he went into "a far country."

Now, this history has often been literally repeated; and I cannot help saying, that, if there should be here one youth meditating the taking of such a course, I would have him pause a little, and reflect on the very commonplace truth, that, go where he will, he will never find another father or another mother. Value, then, your home. Nip those unfilial feelings in the bud; and remember that Divine command, the first in the Decalogue with promise, "Honor thy father and thy mother, that thy days may be long upon the land which the Lord thy God giveth thee."

But it was not for its literal truth and pathos, exquisite as these are, that this story was told. It has a spiritual significance underlying its external incidents, and every man may see himself in this prodigal. For what is sin, but a departure from God, a determination to be independent of God, a casting-off of our allegiance to God, a taking of ourselves into our own hands, and a resolution to be our own God? That is the essence of all moral evil, and the germ of which all other iniquities are but the development. Very cunningly did Satan say to our first parents, "Ye shall be as gods;" and still this self-deification lies at the root of our alienation of heart from him, and rebellion of life against him. And see how, by the dowry of free will, God gives to man the liberty of choosing whether he will abide with him or not. Ah! it *is* an awful thing to have this power of choice; and, if we please, we have the liberty of leaving God. We may determine, if we choose, to become "lords of ourselves," and to take ourselves out of God's family. But we shall soon discover that to be "a heritage of woe." And we need not entail that upon ourselves simply to assert our liberty; for, equally by our choice, we may decide to give to God the love of our hearts and the loyalty of our lives.

But if we do determine to leave him, let us see the guilt which we incur thereby. For it is the leaving of a *Father*. Some, indeed, will have it that there was no revelation of God's Fatherhood until Christ came into the world. But surely, in the relationship between the prodigal and his father here, we have a type of that which existed between God and man, before the fall. If that be not so, then, for any spiritual significance in the phrase, we might as well read, "a certain king had two subjects;" or, "a certain master had two servants." But who does not see, that, if we so read, we should take away the whole power and pathos of the story? Hence we cannot but think that we have here a reference to God's original fatherly relationship to the human race; and while that explains why he was so anxious to get his lost children back, it also deepens the guilt of their departure from him. For, thus regarded, the sinner's offence is not merely that of disobedience to a master, or treason against a sovereign; but it is also, in combination with both of these, ingratitude to a Father. We condemn as the most culpable of all things, the casting-off of a father by a son; and we have no language strong enough to express our detestation of the conduct of Absalom to David. Yet, in God's sight, we have been doing, as sinners, the same thing; and we have given him occasion to say of us, as he did of Israel of old, "I have nourished and brought up children, and they have rebelled against me."

II. But now look at the ultimate destination of this youth. "He took his journey into a far country, and there wasted his substance with riotous living. And when he had spent all, there arose a mighty famine in that land, and he began to be in want. And he went and joined himself to a citizen of that country; and he sent him into his fields to feed swine. And he would fain have filled his belly with the husks that the swine did eat, and no man gave unto him." He is now away from all restraint. He can do as he will, and see what he wills to do. Thus it was, in all probability, with him. He became connected with evil companions. They led him gradually into wicked courses. As long as his money lasted, and they could make any thing out of him, they were assiduous in their attentions, and superlative in their flatteries. When, however, his means were gone, they left him to himself. Then famine arose; and to keep himself from starvation, he went and joined himself to — or, as the word might perhaps be better rendered, glued himself to, foisted himself upon; or, in the old Scottish vernacular, became a *sorner* on — a citizen who sent him out (oh, horror of horrors to a Jew!) to feed his swine; and so dreadful was his hunger, that he would gladly have fed on the pods of the carob-tree with which they were foddered and fattened. So he who had fretted and chafed over being a son at home, subject to the household rules, actually becomes a servant; nay, worse than that, — a degraded loafer hanging about the house of one who, to get rid of his persistent appeals, sends him out to be a swineherd. He wanted liberty;

and he **has** got the lowest drudgery, with unsatisfied hunger as its constant accompaniment.

Here, too, we may say that this history has been often literally fulfilled. There is scarcely a week that some poor, disillusioned man, who left his Scottish home to seek relief from parental restraint in this far country, does not come begging at my door for bread; for even in this life Satan often gives a scorpion in the end, for the egg that he held up before his victim in the beginning.

But we must not allow ourselves to forget, in the literal truthfulness of the story, its allegorical significance. And when we regard that, we have clearly set before us the three stages of what we may call the sinner's progress.

The *first* is *riotous joy*. We must not keep that altogether out of view. There *is* a pleasure in sin, *of a sort;* for if that were not so, men would not be found committing it at all. There *must* be some kind of exhilaration in the flowing bowl, or in the wild thrill of sensual gratification. "Stolen waters are sweet," perhaps just because they are stolen; but the sweetness does not last long, for it turns to bitterness in the belly. For a time, however, that is not perceived. So bright is the glare of the tinsel, that the baseness of the metal which it covers is not seen all at once. So loud is the noise of the revelry, that for a season "the still small voice" of conscience is not heard. So sparkling is the wine in the cup, that the coil of the adder at the bottom is not visible. But by and by, when the effervescence has ceased, the dread reality will appear; and when it comes, the sting of the serpent will be terrible.

And this brings us to the *second* stage in the sinner's progress. He has "*wasted his substance*" by his course.

Ah! how true that is! Sin is the most expensive thing possible. It wastes money. It wears the body to decay. But, bad as these things are, there are even worse behind; for it blights the intellect and withers the moral nature of the man. It weakens the will; it blunts the conscience; it hardens the heart. It dries up all the finer feelings of the soul, so that the wife turns against the husband, and the husband against the wife; the son against the father, and the father against the son; while ultimately all regard for truth and holiness and purity is gone. Never shall I forget how a wife, speaking once of the weakness of her husband's will before the fascination of strong drink and evil companions, said, "He used to be a firm and manly fellow, *but he's a bairn noo.*" Yes, a child in weakness, but alas! not in innocence; for sin had shorn the locks of his strength, and the Philistines in the shape of his own appetites had made a sport of him. Ah me! where has the Father's portion gone in such a case? Where are the good gifts of God to the soul now? and who, in sinners like these, can discern even the faintest trace of the image of God which once they bore?

But worse yet. When this degradation has been reached, there is still a lower deep into which the sinner must descend; for sin is *an enslaving thing*, and that is the last stage of his progress here. It becomes the master of the man who indulges in it, and sets him to the doing of the hardest drudgery. It hires him out, as it were, to feed swine, leaving him to feed along with them. That which was at first a joy becomes in the end a bondage. That which was at first a pleasant companion becomes at length a cruel taskmaster, who compels him to make bricks without straw, and sometimes even without clay. I have read in the memoirs of a detective, how once, having discovered his man, he joined himself to him as a boon companion, went with him to his haunts, secured his confidence by long fellowship, until at length, when all suspicion had been allayed, he got him, as a mere jest, to try on a pair of handcuffs, and then, snapping the spring that locked them, he took him, all helpless as he was, an easy prey. So sin does with its victim. It first ministers to his enjoyment, then drowns his vigilance, and then leads him away in helpless bondage to utter ruin. O ye who are setting out on this awful course, allured by glowing promises, let me beseech you to pause and ponder what shall be "*at the last,*" "*at the last,*" "*at the last!*" Oh, think of that, and leave it off before it be meddled with!

III. But let us contemplate now the prodigal's resolution and return. "And when he came to himself, he said, How many hired servants of my father's have bread enough and to spare, and I perish with hunger! I will arise and go to my father, and I will say unto him, Father, I have sinned against heaven and before thee, and am no more worthy to be called thy son: make me as one of thy hired servants. And he arose, and went to his father." As he sat in his starvation and degradation, the memory of that home which he had left in his pride and self-will came back upon him and roused him to reflection. The very abjectness of his misery led him ultimately to resolve to return to his father's house. Till now he had kept on hoping that "something would turn up;" but when the swine were preferred to him, and no man gave unto him, it was all over with him. He had then to decide between death by starvation, and returning to his father; and though

for a time shame and pride would keep him from taking
the decisive step, at length hunger overcame him, and
he said, "I will arise and go back." And it is no sooner
said than done, for "he arose, and went to his father."
He did not say, "I will wait until I am a little more
respectable." He did not allow himself to think that
he would be laughed at by those who had known him
there, or that he would, perhaps, be taunted by his
father with his folly. All these things were banished
from his mind by the stress of the emergency in which
he found himself; and he remembered only, that, while
he was perishing with hunger, there was bread enough
and to spare at home. So he started up, and, leaving
his guzzling herd to take care of themselves, he set out
on his homeward way.

This, also, has often been literally repeated in the
histories of individual men. But we may not dwell on
that; for, still seeking a spiritual significance in the
allegory, we find here the story of the conversion of
a soul. And when we view it thus, observe the deep
significance of the words, "when he came to himself."
Some would take that expression to mean, that he was
beside himself, or insane, and that now he came to a
sound mind. But if he were insane, he was afflicted
with that "moral insanity" of which we heard so much
during the trial of Guiteau, and of which Dr. Fordyce
Barker of this city said so epigrammatically and so
truly, "Moral insanity is wickedness." I rather think,
therefore, that we must interpret these words to mean
that all this while he had been *beneath* himself, and
that now for the first time he arose to the life that was
worthy of his father's son. When he came to what he
should have been before he left his home, when he saw
things in their true light, and ascended to his proper

self, he said, "I will go to my father." Now, in the same way, every sinner is living beneath his proper self. His higher nature is, as it were, dormant in him. He has a spiritual faculty which allies him with God, and which, as the holiest part of his nature, is most really and truly himself. But he is not conscious that he has it. It is virtually dead within him. He has overlaid it with trespasses and sins. He is not himself. I do not mean, of course, that his personal identity is gone, but, rather, that the noblest part of his nature is unoccupied by him. He lives, so to say, on the ground-floor of his soul-house. He has never gone up into the higher; and that part of his nature which was intended to be its crowning glory, and which allies him to heaven, is shut up and tenantless, like a dusty attic. But at his conversion he comes to his true self. New thoughts stir within his soul, new feelings vibrate in his bosom. He begins to see what before had been to him as a landscape is to one that is blind. It is not that new things are called into existence outside of him, for all things are there as they were before. The only difference is, that his eyes have been opened to see them; and the wonder of his whole subsequent life is, that he never saw them until then. He perceives now the guilt, the degradation, the danger, of sin; and determines to return unto the Lord with the expression of penitence and the prayer for acceptance.

The parable does not tell us any thing of the manner in which, or the agent by whom, this great change is wrought out in him. But elsewhere we learn that it is wrought by the power of the Holy Spirit, through the belief of the truth as it is in Jesus; and we must bear that in mind throughout our consideration of the subject. We are looking at the human side, and all that

is done on the Divine side must here be taken for
granted. Now, the first evidence a sinner gives that
his eyes are opened is in his perception of his misery.
"I perish with hunger." Never before had this youth
allowed himself to think that death by starvation was
to be the result if he remained in the far land; but so
soon as that became apparent, he took his resolution
to arise. Now, it is the same with the sinner and his
return to God. I believe that if we could narrow his
choice to one or other of these alternatives, everlasting
perdition as the consequence of sin, or eternal salvation
through faith in Christ and repentance toward God, he
would not hesitate as to his decision. But because he
persists in believing that he shall in some way escape,
even if he should persist in his course, he continues indifferent to the statements of the gospel. He imagines
that somehow or other, he hardly knows how, in spite
of all he is and all he has done, he will elude his doom;
and so he goes thoughtlessly on. He believes the Devil's
first lie, "Ye shall not surely die;" and in the faith of
that he remains in the "far land." But when, by the
working in him of the Holy Spirit, through the truth,
he comes to himself, all these deceptions are swept
away. He sees only the terrible fact, "I perish;" and
then comes the revelation of God's love to him in
Christ, the belief of which moves him to repentance.
You can do no good with him until he sees, that left to
himself, and away from God, he is eternally undone;
but, once awakened to that fact, he is eager to cry,
"'What must I do to be saved?" When he can say,
"I perish," he exclaims also, "Lord, save me!" And he
does not make long delay; but, realizing his situation
to the full, he exclaims, "I will return unto my Father,
and will say unto him, Father, I have sinned before

heaven and in thy sight, and am no more worthy to be called thy son. Make me as one of thy hired servants."

Now, taking this as representing "the penitent's progress," one or two things need to be noted as suggested by it.

In the first place, there is unreserved confession of sin. He does not soften matters, and speak of his "faults" and "failings." He does not say, "I have been a little wild." But he puts the plain truth forth in all its hideousness: "I have *sinned*." Neither, again, does he cast the blame on others. He does not say, "So-and-so led me astray;" "If it had not been for the companions by whom I was surrounded, I had never come to this;" or, "If I had only been in other circumstances, I would have kept myself from iniquity." But he takes all the blame to himself. His language is, "*I* have sinned: the guilt is mine. I have no wish to deny it, or to explain it away. I am ashamed of myself, and 'am no more worthy to be called thy son.'"

But, again, the enormity of his wickedness "before heaven" is that which most distresses him. He had brought many evils on himself; he had inflicted great injuries upon others: but that which most burdens him now is, that he has sinned against God his Father, who has done so much for him, and has even, after and above all, sent his Son into the world for his salvation. This is painful to him in the extreme, and he can do nothing but weep over it; but his tears, in the estimation of God, are of more value than glittering diamonds, for they tell him that his wandering son is now returning. This is true penitence. This is the broken spirit which is to God a pleasing sacrifice. This is the contrite heart which the Lord will not despise.

But, looking yet more minutely at these words, we

find in them a determination to personal exertion. "*I will arise and go.*" The prodigal did not wait until some one else should come and carry him to his home. He was fully persuaded, that, if he ever reached his father's house, it could only be by travelling the distance for himself: so " he arose and went." Now, it is similar with the sinner. Though the distance between him and God is not physical, but moral, yet, if he would be saved, there must be a putting-forth of his own personal agency. He does not require to rise from the place where he is, and go away to some distant country, in order to return to God. He may pass through the whole transition while yet he is in one and the same earthly spot. The "going" is spiritual. It is the restoring of his heart to God; the giving-back of his love and loyalty and service to his heavenly Father; the surrender to God of the sovereignty or lordship of himself, which he had determined at the first to keep. Now, that is his own act; and in that we have the consummation of conversion. No doubt, as I have said, the Holy Spirit is in it all. Yet the soul gives itself back to God; and we must beware, lest we delay this self-renunciation on the plea of "waiting for the Spirit." That would be just as foolish in us as it would have been in the prodigal here to have delayed until some one came and carried him home. Hence, if we wish the Holy Spirit to work in us and with us, we must ourselves make this self-surrender; and, when we have done that, we shall discover that he has been beforehand with us, and has already anticipated us with his quickening grace.

Finally, here, this resolution was promptly acted upon. "He arose, and went to his father." Just as he was, he set out on his homeward way. He did not say, "I must wash myself, and change my raiment, and then start out." If he had mused in that fashion, he had never returned; but he went as he was. So, in conversion, the sinner gives himself back to God just as he is. He does not seek to make himself better. He does not delay to work out for himself a robe of righteousness. He does not wait even for deeper feelings or more intense convictions. He puts himself *at once* into God's hands, sure that, for Christ's sake, he will make him all that he should be. This is the whole *matter*, — this *only;* but *all this:* and, if there be one hearing me to-night who is moved by the presentation of these truths to go back to his Father, let me beseech him to go back at once, and to give himself without reservation and without delay to God in Christ.

> "Just as thou art, without one trace
> Of love, or joy, or inward grace,
> Or meetness for the heavenly place,
> O guilty sinner, come!"

IV. But, that we may give completeness to our treatment of this part of the parable, let us look, lastly, at the prodigal's reception by his father. "And when he was yet a great way off, his father saw him, and ran, and fell on his neck, and kissed him. And the son said unto him, Father, I have sinned against heaven, and in thy sight, and am no more worthy to be called thy son. But the father said to his servants, Bring forth the best robe, and put it on him; and put a ring on his hand, and shoes on his feet; and bring hither the fatted calf, and kill it; and let us eat, and be merry. For this my son was dead, and is alive again; he was lost, and is found. And they began to be merry." As he draws near to the old home, we can imagine better than describe his feelings. Every thing looks just as it did when he left.

But, oh! the difference in himself! And the remembrance of the life he had been living might for a moment fill his heart with misgiving and make him slacken his pace a little, as he asked himself how he would be received. But before he has had time to answer his inner questionings, he sees a familiar form hastening down the hill to meet him; and before he knows, he feels himself infolded in his father's arms. What a meeting it was! There are no words of upbraiding from the venerable man. He can do nothing but weep out his joy on the neck of his son; and the son can only sob his words of penitence, "I have sinned against heaven, and before thee, and am no more worthy to be called thy son." But he does not ask now to be made as "one of the hired servants;" for already, in that warm embrace, he feels himself re-instated as a son, and the leaving-out of these words by him is the first filial mark we see about himself. Not seldom has this description been literally verified in the home of a returned and penitent runaway. But here it is employed mainly to illustrate the welcome which God gives to the penitent. What a long way he comes to meet the sinner! even all the way to the cross of Calvary, for that is the place where every penitent finds himself infolded in God's fatherly arms. And there is no casting-up to him there of his evil courses; for Jehovah says, "I am he that will not remember thy sins." "He kisses the past into forgetfulness." Bygones are bygones forevermore between them; and the sinner is received as gladly as if he were an angel returning from the doing of some high behest, — nay, with a deeper and diviner joy even than that.

But let us go on; for there is a feast behind, and a whole heap of blessings more. The fairest robe is put upon the recovered son; a ring is placed on his hand,

and shoes on his feet; a joyful festival is held; mirth and song resound through the happy dwelling; and, at every pause in the music, the old man's voice is heard repeating the glad refrain, "This my son was dead, and is alive again; he was lost, and is found."

Many commentators find a spiritual meaning in each of the details which are here mentioned. The robe, they tell us, is the righteousness of Christ; the ring, the token of assurance; the shoes, the badge of sonship, since no slave was permitted to have sandalled feet; the feast, the Lord's Supper. But all these seem now to me to be over-refinements. The whole description, true as it is, even in its minutest features, to Eastern life, is designed to set before us the joy with which God in Christ receives returning sinners; and it only weakens our impression of that, to dwell thus on the accessories of the story as if they had particular spiritual significance. The meaning of this part of the parable simply is, that God will receive the penitent with gladness, and, so far from taunting him with his guilt, will honor him by giving him the richest blessings which he has to bestow. He will re-instate him into the position which he had forfeited by his sin; he will give him righteousness without and within, peace of conscience, joy in the Holy Ghost, and happy fellowship with Himself; and over his return there shall be joy in heaven among the angels that surround the throne. As Trench has said, the banquet symbolizes "the festal joy and rejoicing which is in heaven at the sinner's return, and no less in the church on earth and in his own heart also;"[1] while Arnot puts it more simply thus, "The feast indicates the joy of a forgiving God over a forgiven man, and the joy of a forgiven man in a forgiving

[1] Notes on the Parables, pp. 412, 413.

God." ¹ Thus we have here again a point of contact between this parable and the two that go before it. The great purpose of them all is to illustrate the fact that there is joy in heaven over one sinner that repenteth. But the peculiarity here is, that the delight is shared by the recovered one himself; and as we have already considered the gladness in heaven over a sinner's repentance, we may conclude our discourse now by referring briefly to the joy of the penitent himself.

The new life begins in feast. The convert has "joy" as well as "peace in believing." While God rejoices over him, he rejoices in God; and in the first experience of his reception by God this gladness is peculiarly intense. When Philip preached in Samaria, and multitudes were turned unto the Lord, we read that "there was great joy in that city;" ² and when the Ethiopian treasurer had found the salvation that is in Christ Jesus we are told "that he went on his way rejoicing." ³ So it always is. Many illustrative cases might be gleaned from Christian biography in proof of this assertion, but we cannot enter now upon so wide a field. Suffice it to say that the holiest, most elevating, and most lasting gladness which the soul can know is that which springs from the contemplation of God's mercy, revealed to it and received by it through faith in the Lord Jesus Christ. Peter used not the words of wild fanaticism, but the language of sober truth, when he said, "In whom, though now we see him not, yet believing we rejoice with joy unspeakable and full of glory;" ⁴ and some among us can indorse the words of Mrs. Isabella Graham when, referring to her conversion, she says, "My views then were dark compared

[1] Arnot on the Parables, p. 440.
[2] Acts viii. 8.   [3] Ibid. viii. 39.   [4] 1 Pet. i. 8.

with what they are now; but this I remember, that, at the time, I felt a heart-satisfying trust in the mercy of God through Christ, and for a time rejoiced with joy scarcely supportable, singing almost continually the hundred and third Psalm." [1]

Such, my friends, is the banquet which God spreads for the returning sinner; but we may not forget that he makes both the church on earth and the church in heaven sharers with him in his joy. For when the penitent breaks his alabaster box over the feet of Jesus, the whole house of God is filled and fragrant with the odor of the ointment. All in it make merry (I like the homely word) over a sinner's conversion; and though, on the principle that it is more blessed to give than to receive, the highest delight is that of God, yet we must not forget the gladness of the penitent himself. Sinner, do you want to be happy? Then return to God. Away from him you must still be in want, hungering after the world's husks, which cannot always be obtained, and which, when obtained, give neither sustenance nor satisfaction; but from him you will receive abiding felicity, the joy of forgiveness, of acceptance, of assurance, of holiness, and finally, as the climax and consummation of them all, the joy of heaven. This is put in your offer now, and the only condition annexed to your reception of it is that you will "arise, and go to your Father."

[1] Life of Mrs. Isabella Graham, p. 150.

XXIII

THE ELDER BROTHER
Luke 15:25-32

IN the general household joy over the prodigal's return, there was one who refused to share. The elder son, who now, for the first time, comes into prominence, was absent in the field at the moment of his brother's re-appearance, and became aware that something unusual had occurred only when, as he drew near, he heard the sound of music and dancing. Instead, however, of going trustfully forward into the house, in perfect assurance that every thing over which his father presided must be right, he showed a most unfilial disposition by calling one of the servants, and asking him what "these things meant." Promptly and plainly, without any desire, as some allege, to sneer at the whole proceeding, and wishing simply to state the facts as they were, the domestic made reply: "Thy brother is come; and thy father hath killed for him the fatted calf, because he hath received him safe and sound." But the information thus given was exceedingly distasteful to the elder brother; and he was irritated and annoyed because, while so much had been done to celebrate his brother's return, nothing had ever been received by himself as a token of appreciation of his services. The sonship thus had degenerated in his heart, even while he was living at home, into the spirit of the hireling.

He had, indeed, never done any positive wrong. He had been thoroughly moral, perfectly respectable, and exceedingly industrious; but he had been all these, not from the loving impulse of a son, but, as it now appears, from the desire of reward; and because, treating him as a son, his father had never thought of giving him any thing in the shape of that, he was exceedingly displeased. Having had within him all the while the disposition of a hireling, he could neither understand nor appreciate the parental joy over the recovery of a son; and, like a hireling, he complained at not having received a hireling's pay, while so much was given to an erring but now penitent son. So "he was angry, and would not go in."

Thus he remained outside of the father's house, and was in a state of most unfilial alienation from his parent. But when his father learned of his determination, he showed to him precisely the same affection which he had manifested to his brother, only in another fashion. He welcomed back the wanderer; but now he went out after the departing one, and entreated him "to come in." But he was met in a very haughty and self-sufficient spirit; for the angry son replied, "Lo, these many years do I serve thee, neither transgressed I at any time thy commandment; and yet thou never gavest me a kid, that *I* might make merry with *my* friends; but as soon as this thy son was come, who hath devoured thy living with harlots, thou hast killed for him the fatted calf."

Now, in all this we cannot fail to observe how the heart of the son has degenerated into that of the servant. He dwells on the value of the work which he had performed, and complains that he has received nothing for it; but a leal-spirited son never can do too

much for his father, and works " all for love and nothing
for reward." There was here, therefore, much of the
disposition that animated Peter when he said to his
Lord, "Lo, we have left all, and followed thee: what
shall we have therefore?" and which was exposed and
rebuked, as we saw, in the parable of the vineyard laborers. And closely allied with that, there was an amount
of self-complacency which makes this man exceedingly
unlovely. He had an overweening estimate of his own
importance. He dwelt upon his model behavior ("neither transgressed I at any time thy commandment")
to such a degree that any attention shown to another
was interpreted by him as a slight upon himself; while
he who received such attentions was despised as altogether unworthy of consideration.

But these two qualities are always attendant upon
self-conceit. The Pharisees "trusted in themselves,
that they were righteous, and despised others;" and
when the Lord showed favor to the publicans and sinners, they felt as if he had insulted themselves. He
who is always thinking of his own excellences takes
offence where none is meant. One's appreciation of
another is by him interpreted as a depreciation of himself; and to make much of any one in his hearing, is
enough to provoke him to speak of that other in terms
of cutting and sarcastic scorn. Hence, here, the making of a festival over the prodigal's return draws forth
from the elder brother a complaint that he had been
neglected, and a contemptuous allusion to the prodigal's course, which altogether ignores the penitence
that prompted his return; while, at the same time, there
is a repudiation on his part of all relationship to such a
worthless fellow. His father might do as he pleased,
of course, but though he received the prodigal as a

son, that would not make him acknowledge him as a brother; and so he is careful to say, "as soon as this *thy son* was come." How little sympathy there is thus between the elder son and his father! *In* the household all those years, he had not been of it; and, for all his industry and respectability, he had no true *sonship* in his soul. Nay, if I rightly interpret the answer of the servant to him when he asked what the music and the dancing meant, there was more of sonship in the servant's heart than there was even in the son's.

But see how tenderly his father treats him. He takes no notice of the sneering innuendoes which were meant to be so reproachful, but calmly replies, "Son, thou art ever with me, and all that I have is thine." As if he had said, "Why speak of making merry with thy friends, when thou hast always had a feast in me; and as for thy brother's waste, say no more of that; for thou art none the poorer for his prodigality, since all that I have is thine." But he will go no farther in the way of entreaty than that. He will not acknowledge that he has in any degree overlooked the one son, in his joy over the return of the other, nor will he admit that he has done any thing improper in holding such a festival on such an occasion. On the contrary, he defends his procedure, and repeats his gladness, at one and the same time, saying, "It was meet" — that is, "it was fitting, it was in every respect in harmony with the dictates of nature and religion;" or, perhaps, more literally,[1] "it was necessary, I could not but, I could not keep myself from yielding to the impulse" — "to make merry, and be glad; for this thy brother" — mark the gentle reproof in the words — "was dead, and is alive again; he was lost, and is found."

[1] The Greek is ἔδει.

But, passing now to the interpretation of the parable, the question arises, whom this elder brother is intended to represent. Different answers have been given by different expositors. Some have said that he symbolizes the angels in their relation to the human race; but that cannot be entertained by us for a moment; for, as the other parables in this chapter make very apparent, the angels, so far from being envious and dissatisfied at God's reception of returning sinners of mankind, sincerely rejoice with him over the recovery of those whom he had lost. Others have alleged that the elder brother stands for the Jews, while the younger is the representative of the Gentiles; and it must be confessed that something may be said for that interpretation. For, as a nation, the Jews were most exclusive, and regarded with repugnance the very idea of the Gentiles being made partakers with them of the blessings of the covenant. Thus when our Lord, in the synagogue of Nazareth, referred to Elijah's mission to the woman of Zarephath, and Elisha's cure of Naaman the Syrian, thereby suggesting that the Gentiles were to be the heirs of the blessings which the Jews refused to accept, his hearers were so enraged, that they took him to the brow of the hill on which their city was built, and would have cast him over if he had not escaped out of their hands.[1] So, again, when Paul addressed the crowd from the castle-stairs at Jerusalem, they gave him patient audience until he spoke of his having been sent to the Gentiles, when they immediately cried out, "Away with such a fellow from the earth! it is not fit that he should live."[2] Nay, so strong was this feeling, even in the breast of Peter the Apostle, that he had to be prepared by a special vision from heaven for preach-

---

[1] Luke iv. 24–29.   [2] Acts xxii. 22.

ing the gospel to the household of Cornelius.[1] There is no doubt, therefore, that the disposition of the elder brother, as here portrayed, was manifested by the Jews in their treatment of the Gentiles. But whether that was the primary reference of this part of the parable, is another question. There is nothing in the circumstances in which it was first spoken to make that in the least degree probable. The Lord had not been alluding in any way whatever to the call of the Gentiles; and it would be most unnatural, and indeed unwarrantable, to put such a restriction upon his words.

Others, therefore, understand that the purpose of our Lord in adding this episode of the elder brother was to introduce him as the representative of the scribes and Pharisees, by whose taunt, "This man receiveth sinners, and eateth with them," these three parables were called forth. But even that interpretation is beset with difficulties. For how could it be said, with truth, that God was "ever with" the scribes and Pharisees, and that all that he had was theirs? We can understand, indeed, how they should say that they had faithfully served God, and had never at any time transgressed his commandment; for that is only in keeping with their well-known self-complacency: but that such a claim should be admitted, and that they should be represented as having God ever with them, is certainly somewhat staggering. Calvin meets that difficulty thus; and I quote his words because they fairly express the view of all those who have adopted this interpretation: "He compares the scribes, who were swelled with presumption, to good and modest men, who had always lived with decency and sobriety, and had honorably supported their families, — nay, even to obedient children, who,

[1] Acts x.

throughout their whole lives, had patiently submitted to their father's control. And, though they were utterly unworthy of this commendation, yet Christ, speaking according to their belief, attributes to them, by way of concession, their pretended holiness, as if it had been virtue; as if he had said, 'Though I were to grant to you what you falsely boast of, that you have always been obedient children to God, still you ought not so haughtily and cruelly to reject your brethren when they repent of their wicked life.'"[1] To those who accept this explanation as satisfactory, the elder brother has a primary, precise, and distinct reference to the scribes and Pharisees; and in this view, the uncertainty in which the parable leaves us as to whether or not he actually went into the house to participate in the feast becomes very suggestive, as being in itself an appeal to those self-righteous persons to whom it was addressed, to reconsider their position, if peradventure they might — as, indeed, we know some of them afterwards did — go in, and hold high festival with those whom Christ had lifted out of the grossest degradation.

But still the difficulty presses. The elder brother is regarded as a true, though temporarily erring, son; and therefore others, of whom Matthew Henry may be regarded as the exponent, take him as the embodiment of such as "are really good, and have been so from their youth up, and never went astray into any vicious course of living; to whom, therefore, the words, 'Son, thou art ever with me, and all that I have is thine,' are applicable without any difficulty, though they are not so to the scribes and Pharisees."[2]

Now, if I were shut up to the adoption of any one of these explanations to the exclusion of all the rest, I

---

[1] Calvin's Commentary, *in loco*.   [2] Commentary, *in loco*.

should without any hesitation, and in spite of its difficulties, accept that which regards the elder brother as representing the scribes and Pharisees, because it is most in harmony with the original purpose of the parable. Still I do not see that we are required to identify him with any particular individual or any special class. He is, in my view, to be regarded as the idealized incarnation of an evil disposition. He is the impersonation and embodiment of envy; and wherever, or in whomsoever, at any time, or in any degree, that quality manifests itself, there you have, for the time being, the elder brother.

In speaking of the younger son, Mr. Arnot very justly says, "In representing the human figure, an artist may proceed upon either of two distinct principles, according to the object which, for the time, he may have in view. He may, on the one hand, delineate the likeness of an individual, producing a copy of his particular features, with all their beauties and all their blemishes alike; or he may, on the other hand, conceive and execute an ideal picture of a man, the portrait of no person in particular, with features selected from many specimens of the race, and combined in one complete figure. The parable (figure?) of the prodigal is a picture of the latter kind: it is not out and out the picture of any man, but it is to a certain extent the picture of every man."[1] Now, in like manner, the elder brother also is an ideal figure; not agreeing in every minute particular with any one man, or any one class of men, but yet so representing the workings of envy, that the envious man anywhere may see himself in him, whether he be a Pharisee or a scribe standing outside of the spiritual church of Christ altogether, or a genuine but imperfect disciple

[1] Arnot on the Parables, p. 431

who is really connected with the Lord Jesus Christ. The advantage of this interpretation is, that, while it gets rid of the difficulties which meet every one who attempts to identify the elder brother absolutely with any individual or with any class, it so widens the application of this episode to the parable, that it conveys a lesson to every sort of reader. Take the elder brother as representing the Pharisee simply and only, and very few will be inclined to think that there is any thing of him in themselves. Take him, on the other hand, as the idealized embodiment of the spirit of envy, and each of us must feel that there is a great deal of "elder-brotherliness" in his own heart. In the rigid legalist, indeed, there is nothing but this spirit of envy; but there is more or less of it even in the true follower of Christ, and so the elder brother stands out here as a warning to us all.

"Who is this elder son?" The question was once asked in an assembly of ministers at Elberfeldt, and Daniel Krummacher made answer, "I know him very well: I met him only yesterday."—"Who is he?" they asked eagerly; and he replied solemnly, "Myself." He then explained that on the previous day, hearing that a very gracious visitation of God's goodness had been received by a very ill-conditioned man, he had felt not a little envy and irritation.[1] That was the true reading of the story, and it is capable of manifold application. It fits the case of the scribes and Pharisees, to whom it was first addressed, and who sneered at Christ for his reception of sinners. It fits the Jews in the Saviour's day, and even in the early Church, who looked askance at the Gentiles, and complained because unto them also

---

[1] Stier's Words of the Lord Jesus, vol. iv. p. 162; quoted by Dr James Hamilton in The Pearl of Parables, p. 164.

the gospel had been preached. It fits the disciples at Jerusalem, who, immediately after Paul's conversion, were "afraid of him, and believed not that he was a disciple." [1]

The appropriateness of this explanation was very singularly impressed on my own mind, in a manner which I can never forget. Some nineteen years ago I preached to my congregation in Liverpool, one Lord's Day morning, from this episode to the parable of the Prodigal Son, and gave the same interpretation of it as I have now presented to you. As I was leaving the church for my home, I was requested to visit a dying man whom I had seen frequently before, but who was just then, apparently, about to pass within the veil. He had been for many years a careless and irreligious man; but as I spoke with him from time to time, I marked that a great change had come over him. I had conversed faithfully and earnestly with him, of Jesus and his salvation; and he had turned in sincere penitence to his Father, and was, as I sincerely believe, accepted by him. When I entered his room that morning, I found him in great happiness, rejoicing in the near prospect of being with his Lord, and apparently perfectly happy. I talked with him a little on the things of the kingdom, and after prayer I took my leave. His brother-in-law followed me down-stairs, and said, "I cannot understand this at all. Here have I been serving Christ for these twenty years, and I have never experienced such joy as he expresses; and yet he has not been a Christian, if he be really one, for more than a few weeks." Immediately I recognized the elder brother, and I staid long enough to show him just how he looked in the light of this parable. I told him that I had been preach-

[1] Acts ix. 26.

ing about him that very morning. "About *me?*" he said. "Yes, about you;" and I then went on to explain to him the meaning of this episode, while I warned him of the danger of being angry, and refusing to go into the Father's house to share the joy over the returning prodigal. The result was that he saw his error, and was delivered from his envy. Now, that incident, occurring just at that precise time, has given a new point to the parable in my view ever since, and makes me far more anxious to get the elder-brotherliness out of my own heart than to identify the elder brother with any particular class.

The pastor of age and excellence, who is mourning over the apparent fruitlessness of his labors, and is tempted to ask why God makes a young brother in the neighborhood, of little experience and less eminence, instrumental in bringing multitudes to Christ, while he has no such results from his ministrations; the sabbath-school teacher who throws up his work in wounded self-love, because another, who has no such qualifications as he possesses, seems to be so much more successful than he; the laborer in any department of beneficence, who, because he thinks that more is made of some one else than of himself, gives way to personal pique, and withdraws altogether from the enterprise; the over-sensitive, conceited man, who is always taking offence where none is meant, and is so continually anxious for the due recognition of his dignity, that he manages to exclude himself from every society with which he is connected, — may all look here, and in the elder brother each will see himself.

But let not even these imagine that they are beyond God's acceptance. The father came out, and entreated the elder brother to go into the feast, and so God is still appealing to the envious. The door is open to them, if they will but enter; and when they consent to do so in the spirit of sons and not of servants, in humility and not in self-conceit, in love and not as hirelings, then they too will rejoice, and the festival, instead of aggravating them into misery, will be felt by them to be an appropriate expression of their gladness.

I conclude with three practical lessons from the whole subject.

In the first place, let Christians endeavor to show to sinners the same spirit which God has shown to themselves. The gentleness of God to us should be repeated by us in our intercourse with others, and we should deal with those who are going in penitence to Christ with the same tenderness as he himself will manifest to them. Parents, this parable speaks to you about the training of your children, and bids you seek their godly upbringing, not in rigorous and unbending sternness, but in tender love. Sabbath-school teachers, this parable bids you, in your earnest efforts after the welfare of your scholars, show to them the same gentleness that the father showed his son when he fell upon his neck, and kissed him; and it warns you against indulging in vituperation and reproach. Had the prodigal met the elder brother first, he might have gone away back to his iniquity, ay, even from the very gate into his father's house. So a cruel, unfeeling, taunting word may be the means of turning away from his penitent resolution one who might else have gone to Christ in genuine conversion. Pastor, there is a message here for thee also; and thou art commanded to be, in the midst of thy flock, loving as this father was to his home-coming son, and to beware lest by unfeeling or mistaken sternness thou shouldst drive away those who are seeking to enter into the fold. Oh for more of this divine tenderness among us all! Let us remember that the reputation of the gospel, and in some sort also the character of God himself, are at stake in our conduct; and let us tremble with a holy fear lest we should give occasion to his enemies to blaspheme his name, or lest we should, by our repulsiveness, scare away some poor sinner from the loving Father who is so willing to receive him. Men judge of God through us. Let us see to it, therefore, that they have from our deportment toward them a right idea of his willinghood to welcome them.

In the second place, let anxious sinners beware of judging of God's attitude toward them from that which is assumed by some who call themselves his children. They may be Pharisees, and not true sons. Or they may be real children; yet at the moment, by reason of the imperfection still adhering to them, they may be acting an unfilial part. In any case, we must not allow the character and conduct of any man, be he official in the church, or whatever else, to prejudice us against God. Men may repel us, and refuse to have any thing whatever to do with us; but God will receive us graciously, and love us freely. The respectable church-members in this respectability-worshipping age may stand aloof from us, and may make us feel that they would count themselves degraded by holding any fellowship with us; but He who talked with the woman of Samaria at the well of Sychar, and allowed the woman who had been a sinner to wash his feet with her tears, and wipe them with the hairs of her head, will in no wise cast us out. The minister of the gospel, even, may so far forget himself as to speak to us with hard and cold severity; yea, he may treat us with rudeness or injustice; but he is only a man, — perhaps a very imperfect man, — he is not *God*. And let us be thankful that God is not like him. There is a magnanimous mercy and an exalted generosity in God which we look for in vain, in the same degree at least, in any man.

> " For the love of God is broader
> Than the measure of man's mind;
> And the heart of the Eternal
> Is most wonderfully kind." [1]

And, whatever may be the nature of the actions of our fellow-men to us, we must not allow them to set us against Jehovah. He is always on the outlook for returning sinners; and before they have time to conclude their confession, he has already folded them to his heart. Do not misinterpret him, therefore, by supposing that the cold-hearted exclusiveness, which is too manifest in many who profess to be his children, is in any respect characteristic of him. Regard him as he presents himself to you in his Word. Read him as he has written himself in the mission and sacrifice of his Son; and, whatever else may be suggested to you by the disposition of his professed people, rest you sure of this, that his true character is portrayed in this parable, and that Isaiah has not misinterpreted him when he says, "Let the wicked forsake his way, and the unrighteous man his thoughts; and let him return unto the Lord, for he will have mercy upon him; and unto our God, for he will abundantly pardon." [2]

Finally, let us learn from this whole chapter, that God has a sincere, earnest, personal interest in the salvation of men. There are no obstacles now to the salvation of a sinner, on *God's side*. If any remain, they lie entirely with the sinner himself. With all the solemnity of an

---

[1] Faber.   [2] Isa. lv. 7.

oath, Jehovah has said, "As I live, I have no pleasure in the death of the wicked, but that the wicked turn from his way, and live;"[1] and even more forcibly than by that striking asseveration, Jesus Christ has set the same truth before us in this incomparable chapter of Luke's Gospel. I answer, therefore, all difficulties which inquirers may feel about such topics as election, the special agency of the Holy Spirit, the sovereignty of God, and the like, by bidding them go and read these parables. They show that God is in earnest in seeking to save lost souls. They prove that every thing about him, and done by him, is in the interest of the sinner's return. His electing love, his Spirit's work, his sovereignty, are all to be interpreted in the light of this chapter, and are all to be understood as designed to help and not to hinder the sinner's restoration. They are not stumbling-blocks placed in the way of the penitent, but they are agencies at work in removing obstacles from his path. See to it, therefore, that you do not misunderstand God. Meet every speculative difficulty arising from the doctrines to which I have referred, with this chapter, which has always been regarded as one of the "*crown jewels*" of the Christian Church. Silence every foreboding about the reception which God may give you, with these, "the first three" of the Redeemer's parables. Arise, and go in fullest confidence to your Father. He will not reject you, but will infold you in his forgiving embrace, and say over you, in infinite tenderness, and with Divine delight, "*This my son was dead, and is alive again; he was lost, and is found.*"

[1] Ezek. xxxiii. 11.

XXIV

THE PRUDENT STEWARD
Luke 16:1-12

THE interpretation of this parable has occasioned more perplexity to the commentators than any other in the Gospels, with perhaps the single exception of that of "the laborers in the vineyard." But the difficulty, at least so it seems to me, has arisen in great measure from the fact that it has too often been regarded from a wrong point of view. It is, therefore, incumbent upon us, in the very outset, to get a definite and correct conception of the circumstances in which it was spoken, and of the story which it tells.

Now, as to the first of these, it is clear from the place in which we find it here, that it was addressed to the same audience as that which had already listened to those three delightful allegories on the consideration of which we have been so recently engaged. Like them, therefore, it was called forth by certain well-known characteristics of the scribes and Pharisees. No doubt, in the opening verse of the chapter, it is introduced by the words, "he said also unto his disciples;" but, as is evident from the application of it made to themselves by the Pharisees, in the fourteenth verse, the design of our Lord was not only to warn his followers against that which was evil in the Pharisees, but also to get at the Pharisees through his address to them, if haply they might thereby be led to repentance. The two evil qualities by which that class of the people was distinguished were pride and coveteousness; and just as, in the Sermon on the Mount, our Lord passes from the exposure of the one of these directly and immediately to that of the other; so here the transition is equally rapid from the reproof of the exclusiveness which sneered at him for receiving sinners, and eating with them, to the condemnation of the worldliness which insisted on keeping to itself that with which it had been intrusted for the good of others.

Even the most cursory reader will observe that there is a point of contact between this parable and that which precedes it, in the fact, that, while the prodigal son is said to have "wasted his substance," the steward is accused of having "wasted" his master's "goods:" the design of our Lord evidently being, to teach these believers in self-righteous respectability that there are other ways of misusing the portion which God has given us, than by riotous living; and that he who appropriates as his own that which he has received for behoof of another is as really unfaithful to God as is the dissolute man who spends his substance on the gratification of appetite.

The parable thus is an exposure of covetousness, with a lesson founded thereon for the children of God.

The principal figure in the story is a steward, who, like Eliezer in the household of Abraham, or Joseph in that of Potiphar, had been intrusted by a certain rich man with the entire control of his affairs. It would seem that this master had the most implicit confidence in his servant; so that it might be said of him, as it is of Potiphar with Joseph, "He left all that he had in his steward's hand; and he knew not aught he had, save the bread which he did eat."[1] But after a time such evidence was laid before him as proved conclusively to him that his confidence had been misplaced. He found that he was being systematically robbed by a dishonest man; and therefore he called at once for a reckoning, and announced to his steward that he could not longer continue in his service. This came upon the defalcator like a bolt of lightning from a cloudless sky, and brought him at once to a stand-still. What was he to do now? It was impossible to establish his innocence. He would have to go; but whither? How could he get another situation, with this stigma upon his name? Manual labor with the spade was out of the question. "He could not dig." He had led too effeminate a life to be able to make much at that. And though he had not been ashamed to steal, he was ashamed to beg. There was nothing for it, therefore, but to steal again.

But this time he would make others sharers in his dishonesty; or, rather, he would use his dishonesty for the advantage of others, so that they might be laid under such obligations to him that they would be constrained to take some care of him. This was his plan. He sent for all who were indebted to his master, and systematically reduced their debts, which, as being still steward, — though "working his warning," as we would say, — he had yet the power to do. He bade one who owed a hundred measures of oil, make the bill for fifty; and another who owed a hundred measures of wheat, make the bill for eighty, and so on. Knowing his men, he did with each as it was most for his advantage to do, and thus insured a reception in each of their houses for a longer or shorter period, until he should have time

[1] Gen. xxxix. 6.

to turn his energies into some other direction. Thus he tampered with the accounts of his master, apparently for the immediate advantage of the debtors, but really for his own ultimate benefit.

This is a much better account of the matter than that given by those who would represent him as returning in this act of his to a course of honesty. They would explain the transaction thus: that he had been accustomed to charge for a hundred when he had really given only fifty or fourscore measures, putting the surplus into his own pocket (much after the fashion of the members of the ring, who, in the building of our City Hall, had the contractors' bills made out for one amount, but paid by a much smaller one, and, charging the community for the larger which was on the face of the document, divided the difference among themselves), but that now he charged only for the correct number. But the objection to this view of the steward's action is, that he meant to conciliate the debtors. Now, the discovery that all the while he had been robbing *them* would only have exasperated them, and would have determined them to have nothing more to do with him. For in this case they would be in the position in which the citizens of New York were when they discovered the fraud that had been perpetrated upon them; and so we may know what they would have felt at the revelation of the manner in which they had been robbed. Besides, it was his master whom this steward had wronged; not, as in this view of the matter it would have been, his master's debtors: and so far from having here a return to a course of honesty, we see only a continuance in the same kind of robbery which he had so long carried on, the simple difference being that it looked as if he were now doing it for the advantage of the debtors, though ultimately it was done, just as it had been all along, for his own benefit.

By some means or other his course became known to his master, who had perhaps, by that time, overcome the bitterness of his first indignation, so far as to be able to look at the humorous side of the affair, and who therefore, when he heard of it, said, "What an amazingly shrewd fellow he is! It would be ludicrous if it were not so criminal; and if only his probity had been up to the level of his prudence, he might have risen honestly to wealth and power."

That is the story; and before I leave it, I ask you to observe that the commendation of the steward, which was confined to the wisdom or prudence which he had displayed, was given not by the Lord Jesus Christ, but by his own master whom he had so flagrantly wronged; and if we read with the Revised Version, "his lord commended the unjust or unrighteous steward because he had done wisely," or shrewdly, we shall rid the phrase of ambiguity, and prevent any one from falling into the mistake of supposing that the commendation was from Christ.

But now, proceeding to the interpretation, I think it must be evident to every one, that this parable, like those of the good Samaritan, the friend at midnight, and one or two others, is not typical or symbolical, but simply illustrative. It is not an allegory, each figure in which is to be taken as the analogue of some spiritual character; and so, if we begin to ask, Whom does the rich man stand for? who is represented by the steward? whom are we to understand by the debtors? and so forth, we shall make a most fantastic, and, indeed, a most artificial use of the story. Many have tried this plan; but when such a biblical student as Dean Plumptre [1] has spent much learned ingenuity in seeking to establish that the steward represents the scribes and Pharisees in their teachings and ministerial functions, who had been intrusted by God, here represented by the rich man, with great privileges, to which they had been unfaithful, and ends by saying that they were commended by the Lord, who in the outer framework of the parable is one of the children of this world, we see into what absurdity we must be landed if we follow this principle of exposition. For, how can God be in any sense represented by one of the children of this world?

We must, therefore, discard all typical interpretation here; and we find the key to the purpose of the parable in the words, "For the children of this world are, in their generation, wiser than the children of light." The ancients had a proverb to the effect that "It is lawful to learn, even from an enemy;" and something like that is exemplified by the Saviour here. His purpose is to stimulate his disciples to prudence and energy in the prosecution of their high calling, by showing them how shrewd and prompt the worldling is in devising and carrying out measures to secure his earthly and temporal ends. Hence he has deliberately selected the case of one of "the children of this world." The example of a faithful servant might teach many other valuable lessons; but only that of an unscrupulous man of the world could give prominence to the earnestness and sagacity with which those of his class labor to gain their objects, and so, as it were, provoke Christians to outdo them in those qualities, while laboring for an

[1] In Ellicott's New Testament Commentary for English Readers, vol. i. p. 320.

infinitely nobler end. Thus, looking at the whole parable from the standpoint of these words, the very thing which stumbles most readers — namely, that Christ should have held up the case of a dishonest man in any respect as an incentive to his followers — becomes perfectly intelligible, and is seen to be similar to much that is current among ourselves. Thus, though my house may have been broken into, and robbed of many things which I most highly value, I may yet admire the ingenuity and dexterity shown by the burglar in the means which he took to find an entrance into my dwelling; and I may even go so far as to say to an honest but lethargic and unambitious workman that if he could only take, in these respects, a leaf out of the robber's book, he would soon rise to wealth and eminence. But all that is so far from an approval of the character and doings of the thief, that it is perfectly consistent with my gratification at his consignment to the State's prison as the punishment of his crime.

Thus the singling-out of one quality in a man for special commendation is very different from the laudation of his character or conduct as a whole. When the Saviour said to his followers, "Be ye wise as serpents," he did not thereby commend the other qualities of malignity and venomousness which are generally ascribed to these reptiles. He desired them only to imitate their wisdom. In like manner, when, in the parable before us, the Lord uses the shrewdness of this steward to point a lesson to his followers, we are not to imagine, for a moment, that he makes light of his dishonesty. His reasoning, as in the parable of "the friend at midnight," is from the worse to the better, and may be expanded thus: If a child of this world can show such wisdom in providing for his comfort when he is to lose his earthly situation, how much more ought the children of light to forecast their future, and seek to secure their eternal welfare in that coming emergency when the place which now knows them shall know them no more! Perhaps, better than all other interpreters, Neander has caught the spirit of this parable, when he distils its essence into these words: "As the children of the world aim steadily at their selfish objects, and with ever-watchful prudence seize upon the means necessary to secure them, so the children of light are to keep constantly before their eyes the relations of life to the Divine kingdom, and to press every thing into their service on its behalf."[1]

This steward subordinated all other considerations to the attainment of his end. He let no qualms of conscience, or protests of his better nature, keep him from doing that which would serve his purpose. The securing of his own personal comfort was the one great object which he had set before him, and nothing whatever was allowed to stand in the way of that. Now, the Christian professes that his great life-aim is the formation of a holy character through faith in Jesus Christ and obedience unto him. He admits also that every thing else ought to be made and kept subordinate thereto; but alas! he does not always act on that admission. Those things which in theory he calls secondary, he very often allows to become primary; and very frequently he loses sight of the interests of eternity, in his devotion to those of time. Hence the singleness of purpose with which the unscrupulous man pursues his object may well be commended to his study, and he may be taught thereby to concentrate himself and his life upon the "one thing" of pressing on toward

---

[1] Life of Christ, Bohn's edition, p. 300.

the mark "for the prize of the high calling of God in Christ Jesus."[1]

How promptly, too, this steward set about his work! As soon as he resolved, he acted. He "let no grass grow beneath his feet," and even insisted on the debtors when they came to him writing "quickly." The whole scene speaks of haste. What he determined to do, he did with his might. But if the soul's interests are infinitely more valuable than wealth, then they ought to be attended to with yet greater promptitude; and it is because so often spiritual things are made, even by Christians, to give way to material, and we procrastinate in the former more frequently by far than in the latter, that "the children of this world are in their generation wiser than the children of light."

How well adapted to his end, also, were the means which this steward employed! They were dishonest, indeed; but yet they laid his lord's debtors under such obligation, that, for their own interests, they were in a manner compelled to give him blackmail. When they had accepted his terms, they had put themselves into his power; and they had to give him something for hush-money. But how little practical sagacity Christians often show in the choice of means for the attainment of their spiritual ends! They know how necessary the services of the sanctuary are for the sustenance of their spiritual life; and yet they attend on them with irregularity, and become systematic absentees for half the day. They are aware how much the influence of intimate companionships affects the growth of holy character; and yet they cultivate the friendship of those who have no love of Christ in their hearts, simply because they enjoy their brilliant wit, or may profit by

[1] Phil. iii. 13, 14.

their business patronage. They admit that the choice of a partner in trade, or of a business or of a profession for life, has much to do with their progress in holiness; and yet they decide in such matters without any regard whatever to that fact. Now, if they did not profess to be "the children of light," there would be no inconsistency in all that; but to protest in words, that the prosecution of the Christian life is their great business on earth, and to disregard those things which are intimately connected with the success of that business, is to show, in the domain of spiritual things, a carelessness and a folly that are never manifested by worldly men in the prosecution of that which is to them the supreme good. Can we wonder that the type of Christian character is low among us at this rate? If one were to attempt to conduct a manufacturing concern or an importing trade in such a way, he would very soon find himself a bankrupt. Yet, as we have seen, it is just thus that many proceed in the formation of a holy character; and unless they alter their course, they will very soon be spiritually insolvent. Bankrupt in character! That is the most deplorable of all ruins. My brethren, let us take timely warning here; and, whenever we have to decide on matters which intimately concern our growth in holiness, let us make our spiritual welfare the determining element, lest we put serious obstacles in our heavenward way, and give a new illustration of the Lord's assertion, that "the children of this world are, in their generation, wiser than the children of light." Shame on us, that this allegation should be ever true! What have the children of this world to stimulate them, that they should surpass us in this particular? They are not under the constraining influence of the love of Christ. They have no heavenly crown awaiting them on high. They are moved only by appetite, or the love of money, or the love of fame, or the love of power; and all of these are things transient and temporary as the life of earth. Shall it any longer be said that these influences are felt by them to be stronger than we feel those to be which come from the cross of Calvary and the throne of glory? How long shall we live thus, beneath our principles? If Baal be God, let us follow *him;* but if Jehovah, then let us *follow* him. If we are the children of light, let us walk as such, and no longer allow it to be said that "the children of this world are, in their generation, wiser than we."

That is the general drift and purpose of the lesson which the Lord himself has drawn for us from the parable before us; but in the verses which follow, from the ninth to the thirteenth inclusive, we have a particular application of this lesson to the use of money: and we must attempt to show you the meaning and pertinence of these precepts in this place.

There is, first of all, this statement uttered with all authority and solemnity by the Lord: "And I say unto you, Make to yourselves friends of the mammon of unrighteousness; that when ye fail," — or, as it is in the Revised Version, "when it shall fail," — "they may receive you into everlasting habitations." By the "mammon of unrighteousness," we are very clearly to understand money; but why it has been so called by Christ, is not so evident. Indeed, I have seen no explanation of this matter which thoroughly commends itself to my acceptance; and I am not prepared with any one of my own. Perhaps the simplest, as it is cer tainly the most obvious, is because it is so frequently unrighteously acquired, and so much more frequently unrighteously regarded as the man's own possession, and not as a trust of which he is merely a steward. But, however the epithet "unrighteous" may be accounted for, the thing which it characterizes is money. Now, there is a time when that shall fail. Death says to each man, "Give an account of thy stewardship, for thou mayest be no longer steward." We can carry with us nothing out of this world. Money cannot, simply and only as money, be transferred into the world beyond. But it may be so used in this world as to add to and intensify a Christian's happiness in the next. We are familiar with the fact, in our daily lives here, that money may become the means of procuring that which is better than itself. Thus knowledge is better than wealth; yet by a wise use of wealth we may acquire knowledge. So, by a judicious employment of money as trustees for God, in communicating to the necessities of the saints, we shall secure that those whom we have thus relieved shall receive us into everlasting habitations. This use of money will not purchase our admission into heaven, but it will make friends for us there, whose gratitude will add to our enjoyment, and increase our blessedness. It will not open the gates for our entrance. Only Christ is the door. Through him alone can we gain ingress. But it will affect what Peter calls the "abundance" of our entrance, for it will secure the presence there of those who have been benefited by our faithful stewardship; and, chiefest of all, it will be rewarded with the approbation of Him who will say, "Inasmuch as ye did it unto one of the least of these my brethren, ye did it unto me." It is of grace alone, through Christ, that we are permitted to enter heaven;

but once there, the measure of reward will be graduated according to that of our faithfulness here as "good stewards of the manifold bounties of God." Those who have been helped and blessed by our service on earth will lead us up to the throne, and say, "This is he of whom we have often spoken, and to whom we were so much beholden in the life below;" and He who sitteth thereon will reply, "Well done: let it be done unto him as unto the man whom the King delighteth to honor." Thus, though money cannot be taken with us into the future life, we yet may so employ it here, in stewardship for God, as to send on treasure before us into heaven, in the shape of friends, who shall throughout eternity redouble and intensify our happiness. Here, therefore, is an everlasting advantage obtained, not by the dishonest application of that with which we have been intrusted, but by our faithful administration thereof as the stewards of the Most High; and if this truth were more thoroughly believed among us, and acted upon with any thing like the energy and promptitude displayed by this unscrupulous servant, there would be such a consecration of wealth throughout the churches as would usher in the very dawning of the millennial day.

But let us follow the course of the Saviour's thought as he adds, "He that is faithful in that which is least is faithful also in much; and he that is unjust in the least is unjust also in much." The connection seems to be this: "You may allege that you have too little of this world's goods to be much concerned with the truth which I have now announced; but that is a mistake, for fidelity does not depend upon the amount intrusted to you, but on the use to which that amount, however small, is put by you; and that, again, depends on your sense of responsibility as a steward unto God." The faithful man will be true to his trust, whether it is small or great; and the unfaithful man will be false to his trust, whether it is small or great. Character will reveal itself alike in the least and in the greatest. Hence that which is least is intrusted to us for a test of character; and fidelity therein is the gateway of our entrance into a larger trust. He who has proved himself to be reliable in a smaller sphere is raised to a higher; but he who makes an improper use of minor facilities shall not only not be permitted to enjoy greater, but shall be deprived of those which he has heretofore possessed. This is the principle on which God has proceeded in his government of the world. To him that hath, shall more be given; and from him that hath not, shall be taken away that which he hath. Hence the Lord Jesus adds, "If therefore ye have not been faithful in the unrighteous mammon, who will commit to your trust the true riches? And if ye have not been faithful in that which is another's, who will give you that which is your own?" That is to say: The money which men have here is another's, even God's. In comparison with the abiding treasures of eternity, which are the true riches, it is temporal and transient; and a time is coming when it shall fail: but if the man who has been intrusted with it has been unfaithful, and has appropriated to himself what really belonged to God, how can it be expected that God will give him the enduring wealth of the skies, which shall be his very own, inalienable possession?

And lest any one should be tempted to suppose that it is possible so to combine both the services of God and mammon, as to secure independence of God on earth, and happiness with God in heaven, the Saviour is careful to remind his hearers that character is a moral unit; that the soul can have but one real master; that, if we repudiate responsibility to God for our money, we are simply and only the servants of mammon, and that as such we shall be dealt with at the last. "No servant can serve two masters: for either he will hate the one and love the other, or else he will hold to the one and despise the other. Ye cannot serve God and mammon." Every man must serve some master. There are only two masters offered to our choice. These two masters are in every respect antagonistic to each other. God is love, mammon is selfishness; God is holiness, mammon is sin; God stands for the supremacy of the spiritual and eternal, mammon insists on the pre-eminence of the seen and the temporal. These are the only masters whom a man can serve; and being such as they are, there can be no compromise between them. It is impossible for any one to obey them both at once. You must break with the one if you would submit to the other. You may serve the one after the other; and, indeed, most of those who are now serving God have once, in some form or other, been the servants of mammon. You may serve the one in pretence, and the other in reality, as I fear some are doing now. You may serve God if so you determine, or you may serve mammon if that should be your choice; but the two are so antagonistic, the one to the other, that "ye cannot serve God *and* mammon;" and if you wish to preserve your faithfulness as a steward to God, you must forever renounce all allegiance to mammon.

The sum of the teaching of these weighty verses, then, is this: There are two kinds of riches, the transient and the true, — those which we hold in trust for another, and those which are eternally our own; of these we must speak of the former as that which is least, and of the latter as that which is greatest. That which is least is intrusted to us now and here, as a test of character; and according as we are or are not faithful in our management of that, we shall or shall not receive that which is greatest hereafter. Faithfulness in our management of that which is least requires that we should use it for God's glory, in promoting the welfare of his children and the advancement of his cause; and if we would so use it, we must keep our hearts simply and entirely for God as the supreme and only Master whom we serve. The devotee of mammon, like this unrighteous steward wise in his generation, makes every thing bend to the attainment of his worldly purpose: much more, therefore, should the servant of God subordinate every thing to the doing of his Master's will; and when he does that, he will find that out of the perishing possessions of earth, he has made imperishable friends in heaven, who shall add a feature of peculiar and ecstatic joy to the happiness of his celestial life. Men think that they have made great profit when, by their money, they have secured more than their money's worth: but here through the typical they gain the true; through that which is another's, they obtain that which shall be their own; through that which is perishing, they get that which is imperishable. What a glorious investment! and how blind to our own interests we are in neglecting to make it!

XXV

THE RICH MAN AND LAZARUS
Luke 16:19-31

PROBABLY no one of the Saviour's parables needs to be so cautiously handled as this of the rich man and Lazarus. The difficulty arises from the fact that the latter portion of it refers to the invisible world, regarding which its representations have to be taken from the visible. Now, wherever the spiritual is expressed in terms of the material, we are liable to serious error in the interpretation of that expression; and so we need here to be specially on our guard. In the exposition which I am about to give, therefore, I shall endeavor to bring into prominence the great truths which the parable was intended to emphasize, without pressing into significance those features of it which belong to what I may call the figurative framework in which it is set.

Every careful reader of the chapter as a whole will perceive at once that the story, on the consideration of which we are now to enter, is the complement of that of the prudent steward. It treats of the same general subject, and was designed to give sharper point to the moral which that had enforced, and to deepen the impression which that had produced.

True, there are between them certain verses which express some very important principles, the pertinence of which in this particular connection it is hard to discover; but the introduction of which in this place may be explained, perhaps, on the supposition that they were answers to remarks made by the Pharisees, with the view of interrupting, and, if possible, of terminating, a discourse which was felt by them to be too personal to be quite agreeable. In any case, it would be rash to affirm with many that these verses are here out of their proper context: for we can see that the assertion, "that which is highly esteemed among men is abomination in the sight of God," is fearfully illustrated by this parable; while the statement that "it is easier for heaven and earth to pass, than one tittle of the law to fail," re-appears in another form, in the words with which the story ends: "if they believe not Moses and the prophets, neither will they be persuaded though one rose from the dead." There must therefore be some subtile link of association between these verses and that which follows them, if our eyes were keen enough to trace it; but the existence of that is not at all inconsistent with the truth of the assertion, already made by us, that this parable is the companion and complement of that of the prudent steward, and has its interpreting clauses in the verses appended by our Lord to that difficult but graphic story.

To see that such is the case, you have but to look at these verses, and then read the parable. In the first of the verses we have these words: "I say unto you, Make to yourselves friends of the mammon of unrighteousness, that when it shall fail, they may receive you into everlasting habitations;" and in the parable we have the history of a man who, though he had the mammon of unrighteousness in abundance, failed to employ it in that beneficent manner, and so found himself, after death, without a friend, excluded from the habitations of the blessed. In the second of these verses the Lord says, "He that is faithful in that which is least is faithful also in much; and he that is unjust in the least is unjust also in much;" and in the parable we have unveiled to us the future life of one who was unjust in that which was least, and who as a consequence was denied the enjoyment of that which is greatest. In the third of these verses the Saviour asks the questions, "If ye have not been faithful in the unrighteous mammon, who will commit to your trust the true riches? And if ye have not been faithful in that which is another's, who shall give you that which is your own?" and in the parable we have the case of a man who was unfaithful in the use of that money which was not his but God's, and who ultimately was refused the true, abiding, personal, and inalienable riches of eternal blessedness. Thus, like that of the steward, this parable treats of the use of money; and the difference between the two is, that, while the one shows how riches laid out beneficently in stewardship for God may add to the blessedness of the soul in heaven, the other illustrates how wealth unfaithfully and selfishly employed must increase the misery of the lost in the place of perdition.

The story itself consists of a series of contrasts, with a practical application from them.

The first contrast shows us a rich man in a home of luxury and selfishness, expending every thing on his own enjoyment, so that what in other men's experience was an exceptional thing was the commonplace of his life, for "he was clothed in purple and fine linen, and fared sumptuously every day;" while over against him we have a miserably poor man, laid at his gate, wasted with want, and so helpless with disease that he could do nothing for himself, — could not even drive away from him the dogs who licked his sores. At the very gate of abundance, he "desired" to be fed with the crumbs which fell from the table of the rich man; but it is not said that he received any, and we may therefore, perhaps, conclude that he was systematically neglected by the occupant of the palace. Now, that one case is given as representing the habit of this wealthy man's life. It was a typical instance of his thoughtless indifference to the claims of others on him. Other opportunities brought before him were all ignored by him in the same way. It was his custom to "pass by" want and suffering "on the other side." Not simply therefore for his neglect in this particular case, but for the character of which that was an indication, and which was thoroughly selfish, because he had no sense of his stewardship to God, is he here held up to condemnation.

The second contrast is in the matter of their death and burial. One event, namely death, comes alike to all; and both of these men died. But no notice is taken of the beggar's burial. He was hurried away, it may be, roughly and unfeelingly, by the city officials, to the "potter's field" of the time, in some such spirit as that indicated in the words of the song, —

> "Rattle his bones
> Over the stones,
> He's but a pauper
> Whom nobody owns."

But the rich man had a funeral, ostentatious probably, and expensive, like that described by Southey with such withering scorn; and his body may have been laid in a tomb massive as a temple, and more costly than many a palace.

But now comes the third contrast. The Saviour

follows the spirits of both to Hades, the state of the disembodied, or, as the word itself properly means, the state of the unseen; but here we cease to deal with literal history, and enter into the section where difficulty especially emerges. We cannot speak of the spiritual except in words which have already acquired certain significance in the material; and every one knows that in seeking to instruct others we must conform to the modes of thought to which they have been accustomed. Now, the conception of the disembodied state entertained by the Jews of the Saviour's day was that of a place divided into two portions, one for the spirits of the just, and one for the spirits of the unjust. The former was often spoken of among them as Abraham's bosom; and the latter was regarded by them as a place of torment different from, yet kindred to, that Gehenna of fire which was viewed by them as the final abode of the lost. Now, the purpose of the Saviour in this parable was to illustrate the truth that this rich man, having proved unfaithful to his trust in the use of his money, had no friend to receive him after death into the everlasting habitations of heaven; and he very naturally ran his illustration into the mould of the conception of Hades which was current among the people at the time. It would not have been intelligible to them otherwise; but just because of this, we now are apt to misunderstand its meaning. The beggar is carried — not in body, of course, but in spirit — by the angels to Abraham's bosom; and the rich man finds himself in the place of torment. So far all is plain. But when it is said that "he lifted up his eyes, and saw Abraham afar off, and Lazarus in his bosom," we see at once that the literal has passed into the figurative, that the place has given place to him after whom it was named, and what follows is simply designed to show that this rich man had made no friends who could stand him in good stead in his extremity, and was left unrelieved to bear his doom. His cry to Abraham, and Abraham's conversation with him, do not warrant us in drawing the conclusion that the saved and the lost will be in sight of each other in the disembodied state, or that they will have any communication of any sort with each other. The residuum of truth which remains to us out of this part of the parable is, that whereas if this wealthy man had been a faithful steward of God's trust, he would have had in Lazarus and all the others whom, as God's servant, he had assisted, so many friends to welcome him, he found himself, because of his unfaithfulness, left to hapless torment. He let Lazarus lie uncared-for outside of his door on earth; and now he is left outside of heaven, with the sad reflection that no one either can or will relieve his misery, even by so much as a drop of water would cool a burning tongue.

The moral of the story follows in the conversation between Abraham and the once rich man. The latter asks that Lazarus may be sent to relieve him: but receives for answer, first, that such a request was unreasonable, inasmuch as he had made his own choice of what his good things would be when he was on earth, and now he must abide by the results of that choice; even as Lazarus, who from his name, which signifies "God is my help," must be understood as having made God his portion, was now enjoying the blessed consequences of that wise determination. But, second, while it was thus unreasonable in him to ask that Lazarus should be sent to his relief, it was impossible for Lazarus to go even if he wished; for there was no passing

to and fro between the saved and the lost. No one
could cross the gulf which God had fixed between the
two. Now, of course, here is much of figure. The
flame and the gulf may not be literal. The one is the
symbol of a spiritual anguish as intense to the soul as
the pain of fire is to the quivering flesh; and the other
is the material emblem of that Divine decree which shall
forever separate the saved from the unsaved. The letter
is figure. But the unreasonableness of the request of
the lost man, and the impossibility of complying with
it on the part of the saved, — these are the spirit
in the letter, and these are real, so that if we reject them
the whole parable becomes unmeaning.

Again, when we learn that this rich man proceeds to
plead for his five brothers, we almost begin to feel that
his punishment has tended to soften his spirit, and to
make him thoughtful for others; but when we read on,
we discover that his design is rather to vindicate himself than to save them. It was as much as to say, "If
I had been properly warned I never would have been
here." But Abraham's answer was sufficient to silence
all such God-upbraiding words: "They have Moses and
the prophets: let them hear them." "If you had obeyed
Moses in your life, and sought to carry out all his precepts, you would have been with me; and though you
think that 'if one went unto them from the dead, they
would repent,' you are entirely at fault; for those who
repudiate Moses will always find some plausible reason
for rejecting the testimony even of one who rises from
the dead." Here again, you see, the form, which is that
of a dialogue between Abraham and the rich man, is
figurative; but the substance, which is that every man
has sufficient light for the discharge of the duties which
God requires at his hand, is reality, — true for the Jew,

true for the heathen, and true for the Christian, in every age, and for all time.

Such is our analysis of this story; and if it be correct, you will see at once that this is not an allegory in which the rich man represents one spiritual class, and the beggar another, as, in the parable of the sower, the different kinds of ground stand for different sorts of gospel hearers. Rather it is simply an illustrative story told to give emphasis to the importance of making to ourselves friends out of the mammon of unrighteousness, that when it fails they may receive us into everlasting habitations. We have had similar instances in the parables of the friend at midnight, the good Samaritan, and the unjust steward; and when we view it in this way, as illustrative and not symbolical, it becomes amazingly clear and suggestive.

Moreover, if our analysis of the story be correct, we can have no difficulty in separating the merely figurative and dramatic from the truths of permanent importance which it was intended to teach. Thus, with the key which I have given you for the unlocking of its meaning, you will be in no danger of falling into the mistake of supposing that it lends any countenance to the ideas that the rich man will be condemned simply on account of his riches, and that the poor man will be saved simply because of his poverty. It is not the having of riches that is here condemned, but the neglect to use them for God and in his service. And poverty, in and of itself, is not a virtue. There is as much iniquity among the poor as among the rich. Not what a man has, but what a man is, counts before God. Riches test character in one way, poverty tests it in another; and the character that stands the test in either condition will be approved. If the rich man esteems the

favor of God above all wealth, and uses his money as
God requires, he will be accepted; if the poor man,
hardened by his poverty, turns away from God, and becomes a regardless, scoffing, impious man, he will be
rejected. Our relation to God in Christ is the deciding
element. If we keep that close, despite the temptations that come from the deceitfulness of riches, we
shall be eternally with God, no matter though on earth
we may have been immensely wealthy; but if we repudiate that relation, and live in defiance of God, we
shall be forever with the lost, no matter though here
we may have been the poorest of the poor.

But now, leaving these expository details, let me, in
the light of the results at which we have arrived, gather
up the lessons of the parable, under these three heads:
the sin, the inexcusableness, and the punishment of this
rich man.

I. Let us inquire, then, first, wherein consisted the sin
of this rich man. It is frequently asserted, that we have
here an arbitrary condemnation of one whose sole fault
was that he was wealthy; but those who speak thus
only reveal that they have failed to see the great truth
which here the Redeemer purposed to illustrate. No
doubt the rich man was not positively vicious. He is
not charged with drunkenness or adultery or open immorality. He did not put his riches, so far as appears,
to an injurious use. All that is implied is, that he
failed to employ them as God's trustee, for the benefit
of his fellow-men, and for the glory of Him to whom,
of right, they belonged. He kept them to himself, and
spent them simply and only on his own enjoyment. He
was himself the centre of all his efforts; and that which
was another's, intrusted to him for a special purpose,

he regarded as his own, and used as such. The beggar that sat neglected at his gate is the little feature which indicates his great unfaithfulness. He did no more for the outlying world than he did for the poor diseased Lazarus. He was like the wicked servant in the other parable, who kept his talent to himself; with this difference, that instead of hiding it in a napkin, and burying it in the earth, he spent it on his own table and attire. He was like the lady of whom Thomas Hood has sung, who was surrounded by all the comforts of affluence, and had in her hands the means of providing for the orphan, and making glad the widow's heart, but who never thought of doing such beneficent work until when in her dream, confronted with death and beholding the many sufferers in this world of woe, she soliloquized thus, —

> "For the blind and the cripple were there,
> And the babe that pined for bread;
> And the homeless man, and the widow poor
> Who begged to bury her dead, —
> The naked, alas! that I might have clad,
> The famished I might have fed.
>
> "Each pleading look, that long ago
> I scanned with a heedless eye,
> Each face was gazing as plainly there
> As when I passed it by.
> Woe, woe, for me if the past should be
> Thus present when I die!
>
> "The wounds I might have healed,
> The human sorrow and smart, —
> And yet it never was in my soul
> To play so ill a part.
> But evil is wrought by want of thought,
> As well as want of heart."

He was a type of those to whom it shall be said at last, "Inasmuch as ye did it not to one of the least of these, ye did it not to me." And the lesson of his history, as here recorded, is that to live for one's self alone is to lose one's self. Wondrous paradox, yet sober truth! The most enlightened self-interest is that which crucifies self. "He that loveth his life shall lose it; but he that willeth to lose it for Christ's sake, shall keep it unto life eternal."

II. But now let us look at the inexcusableness of this rich man. When he wished that Lazarus should be sent to his five brothers, to warn them lest they also should come to the place of torment, there was an implied assertion that if he had known, he would not have lived as he had done. It was as if he wished to cast the blame on God; but when Abraham said, "They have Moses and the prophets; let them hear them;" and again, "If they believe not Moses and the prophets, neither will they be persuaded though one rose from the dead," — he furnished a satisfactory reply. God gives every man enough light for the performance of the duties which he requires at his hand. He "doth not exact day-labor, light denied;" and no one will be condemned at last for not doing that which he never could have known he was to do. Responsibility is for each man proportioned to his opportunity. If one does not perform that which the little light he had might have made clear to him, the reason for his neglect is not the want of light, but the want of will; and that, no amount of extra light would have removed. Here, again, it is true that "he that is faithful in that which is least is faithful also in much, and he that is unjust in the least is unjust also in much." This man had the writings of Moses and the prophets in his hands. Very probably he was a regular worshipper in the synagogue, and heard them statedly read there. In any case he had the means of becoming acquainted with them, if he had chosen to avail himself of them. And though they contained little about the future life, they said as much regarding it as, if it had referred to his worldly business, would have made him take precautionary measures. Moreover, though they said little comparatively about the future state, they were exceedingly full and clear about the duties which, as laid upon them by God, the rich owed to the poor in the present life. There was in them the clearest light in that department of morality, and to that light he had closed his eyes; therefore he was righteously condemned. He knew what God required; he knew also that he was responsible to God for the doing of that; and nothing more was needed, if he had chosen, to set him on its diligent performance: therefore he was without excuse.

But if this was the case with him, who had only the Jewish scriptures, how much more will it be so with us, if, having the complete revelation of the new covenant, we should still thoughtlessly live to ourselves, and disregard alike our responsibility to God, and our duties to our fellow-men! For to us now, One has come even from the dead, and sealed, as indubitably true, all the statements which his gospel contains. Nay, more: by his own pure, divine, unselfish life, during which "he went about doing good," — healing the sick, cleansing the lepers, feeding the hungry, instructing the ignorant, shedding joy and happiness everywhere around him, even while he was bearing the sins of the world, — until at length, in solemn self-sacrifice, he offered himself to the death of the cross, he has left us an example, that we should follow his steps. Shall it be, then, that with such a pattern before us we shall seek to live for ourselves, and lose our entrance into the everlasting habitations, for the poor, paltry ambition to amass a fortune which we must leave behind us, or to make a position which we must give up at last, or to enjoy the amusements and pleasures and luxuries of the world, which perish in the using? There is no fortune so noble as that which is made in doing good; no position so exalted as that which is reached by him who belongs to the peerage of benevolence; no pleasure so pure as that which is enjoyed by him who, imbibing the spirit of the Lord Jesus, seeks to mitigate the miseries of his fellow-men, and finds his life-work in the lessening of human suffering and the salvation of immortal souls. Up, then, and give yourselves to this Christ-like labor. Live every day for God, in the service of his people, and the promotion of his cause. So shall you escape the corrupting and down-dragging influences of the world, and find your place at last by the side of your Redeemer. But if with such a clear revelation before you, and such a glorious ensample above you, all your thought is still about yourselves, then your guilt is deeper than that of Dives, and your doom will be heavier than that which fell on him.

III. But now, finally, let us glance solemnly at the rich man's punishment. Now, here, as I have said, we must beware of supposing that in the future life things will be literally as they are here described. I do not believe that it is possible, in our present speech, to portray exactly what the future state will be; and most certainly our Lord does not here make the attempt to do any thing of that kind. What he has done is, under the guise of this story, to convey to us truthful impressions, though the mode in which he has done that may be — nay, from the very nature of the case, must be — figurative. But, stripping away all mere figure and embellishment, two things about this man's doom seem to me to be positively certain. These are, the intensity of its agony, and the eternity of its duration. This is an awful subject, and I do not wish to dwell upon its dread details: nevertheless, the truest, tenderest kindness is to set the meaning of this parable, in this regard, fairly and fully before you. The anguish of this man is implied in his use of the word "flame." Now, as he was then in the state of disembodied spirits, we cannot understand that he was in material fire. But it is a mistake to suppose that by taking this figuratively we thereby deprive it of its terror. No! to a rightly constituted mind, we only increase that thereby; for the figure is always less than the reality, and in the union of memory perfectly unsealed, with conscience fully awakened, we have all that is needed to produce in the soul such distress as is here figuratively described.

But there is further revealed here, the eternity of the duration of this punishment. I cannot see how else the fixity of that gulf is to be understood. It is as true that no change of place is possible to those who are here described, as it is that if Moses and the prophets be not heard, the mission of one from the dead will be in vain. For both of these announcements stand on the same plane. I know that it is said that this is in Hades, — the state of disembodied spirits, — intervening between this life and the general resurrection and judgment. Be it so. I accept the representation. But that completely explodes the modern notion of Dorner and others, that probation continues through that state, and is only terminated at the resurrection and the final judgment. For, how can there be probation, with this impossibility of passing from one place to the other? There is here no possible probation in the intermediate state; and there is not a single word in all the Scriptures which indicates that there will be probation after the judgment, — not one. That ought to be enough, and with that I leave the subject to stand before you in its own dread and awful solemnity.

But I cannot conclude my discourse without reminding you, that if you live faithfully and lovingly for God in Jesus Christ, then, no matter how lowly your lot may have been upon the earth, you shall have everlasting blessedness and glory in heaven. Lazarus was not saved because he was poor, any more than the rich man was condemned because he was wealthy. But in his mean and pitiful estate he had served his God, finding his help in Jehovah; and lo! at death he is carried by angels to Abraham's bosom. Courage, then, ye humble ones. God will not forget your work of faith and labor of love. No matter what be your lot here, if you can say with Paul, "For me to live is Christ," you will be with Christ at last. And He who did not spurn the meanest of the people from him on earth, will himself receive you into the fellowship of his glory.

XXVI

THE PLOUGHING SERVANT
Luke 17:7-10

THIS parable has not received from Christians generally the measure of attention to which it is entitled. Few of us are conscious of having derived spiritual inspiration from the study of it; and in some of the best expository works on the parables of our Lord, as, for example, in the recent valuable one of Goebel, it is entirely omitted. This neglect may be owing, in some degree, to the superior attractiveness of many of the Saviour's other allegories, the lessons from which are more palatable to most of us than those which are here enforced; but it is due perhaps, most of all, to the difficulty which has been universally felt in its interpretation. Still, the view which, under any feasible exposition, it gives of the exactions of the Christian life, and the spirit in which these are to be met by us, is so important, that, no matter what our success may be in its explanation, we may profitably spend a little time in its examination.

Whether the context furnishes any key to the solution of its meaning, is a question on which the most opposite opinions have been maintained. On the one hand, it has been held by some, that, as the sayings which precede it have been introduced in other connections by Matthew and Mark, they are here grouped together by Luke on no other principle than that he wished to preserve them, and might as well bring them in at this point as at any other; and even such a writer as Godet, who is in this instance followed by Bruce, calls them, as I think, somewhat irreverently, "a remnant scrap at the bottom of the portfolio," which the Evangelist has here delivered to us without any introduction. Others, however, with much greater probability have alleged, that, although used by our Lord on other occasions, these utterances form one discourse here. Now, as there are some undeniable instances in which the Saviour repeated, under new circumstances, sentiments which he had already expressed in other relations, I have no hesitation in believing that here we have a new and distinct address, though the separate portions of which it is composed had been before employed by him at different times and for other purposes. This view is confirmed by the fact that we can easily trace at least *some* links of association between its several parts. Thus the opening verses deal with the causing of others to stumble, and these are followed by precepts as to how his disciples should act towards those who should trespass against them. Now, we can easily see that we have in these two sections both sides of the same subject presented; for the one relates to the giving, and the other to the taking, of offence. The injunction to forgive a penitent brother, even if he should trespass against them seven times in a day, evoked from the disciples the prayer, "Lord, increase our faith," because they felt that only through the possession of a larger measure of that grace, could they attain to the obedience of such a command. Their prayer, again, led to the answer, "If ye had faith as a grain of mustard-seed, ye might say unto this sycamore-tree, Be thou plucked up by the root, and be thou planted in the sea; and it should obey you." Then, lest they should be puffed up with pride at the very idea of their accomplishing such great things, he goes on in this parable to impress upon them the arduous and unceasing nature of the service which was required of them as his disciples, and the spirit and temper in which that should be rendered.

This being the main purpose of the parable, the illustration is taken from the state of things then actually existing upon the earth. The relation between master and servant was not one of contract, but of ownership. The slave was not hired to do just so much and no more; but he actually belonged to his master, who had an absolute right to all his time and all his exertions. But the Lord, in using this relation for the purpose of making plain the point which he desired to enforce, says nothing whatever of its propriety or lawfulness. That was not the matter which was then before him; but taking it just as it was, without pausing to discuss the question of the rightfulness of slavery, he employs it to impress upon the minds of his hearers the truth which he wished particularly to emphasize. Such a bond-servant, then, who belonged to his master, is described as having just returned from out-door labor in the field, where he had been following the plough, or keeping the sheep; and the question is asked, whether his master would say to him, "Come at once, and sit down to meat," or whether he would not rather address him after this fashion: " Make ready wherewith *I* may sup, and gird thyself, and serve *me* till *I* have eaten and drunken, and afterward *thou* shalt eat and drink." Then the further question is raised, "Doth the master thank the servant because he did the things that were commanded?" and in some manuscripts the answer, "I trow not," is inserted; but whether we follow the Authorized Version in retaining these words, or the Revised Version in rejecting them, it is equally clear that a negative answer is expected, and is the true one; so that the moral follows, as an inference from the whole: "Even so ye also, when ye shall have done all the things that are commanded you, say, We are unprofitable servants: we have done that which it was our duty to do."

Now, it is undeniable that we have in this parable much that is startling, and apparently inconsistent with the Saviour's teaching: for example, the haughty bearing of the master toward his tired slave, and the unappreciative spirit in which he receives the services rendered to him, are not at all in keeping with the representations elsewhere made of the kindness shown by God to those who sincerely and lovingly seek to do his will. Accordingly, I am not surprised that many commentators have shrunk from any interpretation which would even seem to admit that this master is in any sense the representative of God. To escape from that, therefore, some have maintained that we have here simply an exposure of the spirit of legalism; that, as one has said,[1] "Christ descends to the moral plane of his auditors, and seeks to convict them, not by proving their principles to be wrong, but by apparently accepting and using them. He addresses himself to the Pharisees, or to the spirit of Phariseeism in his own disciples, of which the essence was, and is ever, a *claim* to be received and rewarded by God for work's sake. And he says in effect something like this: 'You claim to be the servant of God?'—'Yes.'—'A faithful servant?' —'Yes.'—'On that ground entitled to a seat at the

[1] Abbott, *in loco.*

table of the King?'—'Yes.'—'Do you treat your servants thus? When they come in from the field, do you make haste to welcome them? to serve them? or to thank them? I trow not. But if you are a *servant*, you must be content with a *servant's recompense.*' And so the moral of the parable, in this view of it, is not that the Christian is to say, 'We are unprofitable servants,' but rather that he is not a servant at all, but a son, and is to serve for love's sake, and not for reward." Now, all this is a true description of the case as between the Christian and his God, and we may ourselves come out to a result not very different in the end; but it does seem to me, that in making the inference from the whole parable that the Christian is not a servant, but a son, such a view of the teaching takes all the force out of the words, "Even so ye also, when ye shall have done all the things which are commanded you, say, We are unprofitable servants." Besides, while the Christian is a son, it is not to be forgotten that he is also, in a very important sense, a servant. Repeatedly in the parables of our Lord, he is represented by a laborer and a servant; and Paul in all his epistles styles himself "the bond-servant of the Lord Jesus Christ:" so that there must be some appropriateness in bringing that side of the truth into view. We are not prepared, therefore, to accept this interpretation.

Others have supposed that the parable, instead of setting forth how God actually deals with any one individual, describes how he might have dealt with all men. But neither can we rest in that theory of the case; for Christ is dealing with actualities, and guarding his hearers specially against a spirit of pride and self-congratulation, and the one thing on which he wishes to concentrate our attention is not the spirit in which God deals with his servants, but rather the spirit in which we should serve God, — not what God thinks of our work, but rather how we should regard it ourselves. The Christian belongs to God. He is bought with a price. Whatever doubt there may be about the legality of any one man's title to property in his fellow-man, — and to me there is no question of its absolute injustice, — there can be none about God's title to all that the Christian is and has, and can do. He is the "possession of God's purchase." Nay, he himself admits that he is "not his own;" he has not only been "bought with a price" by God, but he has by his own voluntary act consecrated himself to God. Therefore God has a right to all the service he can render. And, when he has rendered it all, he may not indulge in self-complacency as if he had done any thing extraordinary, or had deserved any special commendation; for even at the best he has done no more than he ought to have done, since soul, body, and spirit, in all places and in all cases, everywhere and at all times, he is the property of God.

This, in my judgment, is the simple significance of the parable. It tells the Christian how he is to think of himself, but it says nothing of what his Lord thinks of him. The portion of the story which tells of the gruffness and thanklessness of the master belongs to what I may call "the blind side" of the parable. It belongs to what may be styled the drapery of the parable, and is not to be pressed into significance. The story has no typical meaning Godward. Its entire teaching is on the human side. It looks earthward, not heavenward. It draws an inference for the servants, but it says nothing of the Lord. And though the servants are to regard their work and themselves with humility, as unprofitable, that does not imply that God will not give them both commendation and reward. This is only one side of the matter, — the side which is true to our experience in this world, and which gives us the advice that is appropriate thereto.

But there is another side to the case, the heavenly; and in order to complete the presentation of the subject we must take that in also. It is set before us in Luke xii. 35-37: "Let your loins be girded about, and your lights burning; and ye yourselves like unto men that wait for their lord, when he will return from the wedding; that when he cometh and knocketh, they may open unto him immediately. Blessed are those servants whom the lord, when he cometh, shall find watching: verily I say unto you, that he shall gird himself, and make them to sit down to meat, and will come forth and serve them." What a contradiction! do you say? Nay, there is no discrepancy: for the parable before us shows us the Christian toiling on earth, and gives us what should be his own estimate of himself and of his work; while the words which I have just read describe the Christian's welcome into heaven, where he shall be waited upon by his Lord, in token of gratitude and affection.

Having thus, as I trust, made the meaning of our parable perfectly clear to you, let me only now detain you for a few minutes, while I seek to bring out some profitable hints which are suggested by this method of interpretation.

I. There is, first of all, the continuous obligation of the Christian life. This servant had been *all day* in the field. He had returned weary and hungry, needing rest and food; but instead of being permitted to satisfy his wants, and lie down to enjoy repose, he must forthwith address himself to another sort of labor. He must make ready his master's repast, and gird himself, and wait on him at table while he eats and drinks. Now, arduous as this lot of his surely was, there are aspects of the Christian life in which it appears to be no less exacting. The slave could not say with truth that his work was ever done. He had to keep himself always at the call of the master, by night as well as by day; and whensoever that call might come, at evening or midnight, at cock-crowing or in the morning, he had to rise, and do what was commanded him. But it is the same with the Christian and his Lord. At no moment is he absolved from obligation to serve; and even when he has been exhausted by some heavy and protracted labor, he is still under obligation as heavy as ever to live the Christian life. His day is not one merely of twelve hours; but throughout the twenty-four he must be ready for any emergency, and must meet that at the moment when it rises. Always he is under obligation to his Lord; and "without haste," but also "without rest," he must hold himself absolutely at the disposal of his Master. When the physician, on his return from his daily round of visits, with mind exhausted and body fatigued, is met at his door by an urgent summons to the bedside of one who has been suddenly stricken by severe illness, he feels himself constrained to set out at once, and give what help he may to the man who has thus called him. So the Christian is to be always at the call of his Lord; and no matter though the command may come at the most inconvenient time, he is to be willing to comply with it. This is the exaction of his calling. He belongs altogether to the Lord; and when *He* needs him, every thing else must be set aside in order that *His* will may be done. It seems hard; and yet there are many of us who must admit that this is an exact description of our own experience. Our labor is never done. The workingman, so called, sticks out for his ten, or perhaps eight, hours a day; and when these have been put in, the rest of the evening and the night are his own; or, if he is required to give any portion of that reserved season up, a new contract is entered into, and he is paid so much for "overtime." But as between the Christian and his Lord there is no "overtime;" for all his time he is his Lord's, and he never can allege that any portion of himself or of his day is absolutely his own. He can never have "a day off." There are no holidays in Christ's service; and, no matter how weary we may be in it, our weariness is no reason why we may not be required to do something else. This applies to the regular work of the Christian life: for, wherever a believer is, his work is to be a Christian; to manifest the graces of character which the situation requires; to do the precise thing which the case demands; to preserve, in the midst of all temptations, loyalty to his Lord; to act in every thing as it becometh the gospel of Christ, — in one expressive phrase, "whatsoever he does, in word or in deed, to do all in the name of the Lord Jesus Christ, giving thanks to God and the Father by him."

Other servants may have some respite. The very slave is almost always sure of his sleep, and may be free in his dreams; the soldier is "mustered out" after the war; the man of business retires after he has made his competency; the professor may become "emeritus," and live on his annuity: but the Christian is to be a Christian, and to hold himself at the disposal of his Lord, while he lives. His fight continues while life lasts; his obligation to attend his Master's call abides till he hears that last call of all, "Come up hither." He is to be always waiting and watching, until death.

Now, this may seem a hard saying; but it is true, and it is well that we should look it fairly in the face. The Christian vocation is no holiday affair. It is, on the contrary, a most arduous and exacting thing; a thing that has no attractions for human indolence; a thing loftier in its ideal than any standard of duty which men may set up for themselves. It demands our *all*, at *all* times, for Christ, and that we hold ourselves by day and by night at his disposal, for the doing of his will.

II. Now, with this view of our calling clearly before us, observe, in the second place, what light the parable throws on the spirit in which such demands ought to be met by us. And here it is pertinent to say, first of all, that we must meet them with patience. There must be no murmuring or whimpering over our lot, as if it were tremendously hard, and as if we were undergoing a species of martyrdom. We are not to pity ourselves as if we were being oppressed or overborne, but to go forward to that which is required of us, courageously, patiently, and perseveringly.

And then, on the other side, we are not to stroke ourselves down complacently after we have met the demand upon us, as if we had done something extraordinary. Pride after toil is just as much out of place here as murmuring under toil. As one[1] has well said, "There is no enemy to all high attainment so deadly as self-satisfaction." We are not to think about ourselves at all, but of God, of what he has been to us and what

[1] Bruce: Parabolic Teaching of Christ, p. 171.

he has done for us, and of what we owe to him, and then, when we get to a right and proper estimate of that, our most arduous efforts and our most costly sacrifices will seem so small in comparison, that we shall be ready to exclaim, "We are unprofitable servants! All that we have done does not begin to measure the greatness of our indebtedness to Him for whom we have done it." Thus, though the language which the parable puts into the mouth of a Christian is that of a servant, one must be something higher than a mere servant before he will use it. For, to quote again from Bruce,[1] "It is true of slaves, that they *are* unprofitable; but it is not true of them that they confess themselves to be so. . . . It is only the free man who makes such a confession, and in the very act of making it he shows himself to be free."

Thus, in order to comply with the exactions of the Christian life, in the spirit which this parable recommends, we have to become reconciled to God through Jesus Christ. It is the sense of redemption and the consciousness of regeneration whereby we have become no longer servants, but sons, alone, that will impel us to reckon ourselves as not our own, and to do without a murmur, and without the least self-complacency, all that God requires at our hands. The man whose idol is duty will say, after he has satisfied its demand, "I have done my duty, and my work is finished." But he whose impulse is love will never be satisfied with what he has accomplished, but will go on to new efforts and new sacrifices, just to give expression to that affection. Only, therefore, when we get to the apprehension of the love of God to us in Christ, can we rise to the height whereon a man is disposed to count duty too small, and, disparaging his doing of that, to start off, and

[1] Ibid, p. 176.

climb a steeper and loftier hill, at the impulse of gratitude. Conscience will urge to duty, and will be content with that, nay, will be complacent over that; but love will constrain to something more than duty, and will never cease its exertions while they are needed or while it endures. And so, although the parable at first sight may seem to present God to us in a repulsive light, as a mere slave-master, we see, now that we have got to the end of it, that we can comply with its requirements only when we attain to the apprehension of his love. Thus the allegory has as its unseen foundation, all the while, the very grace which it appears to ignore. I cannot say, " I am an unprofitable servant," until I am a redeemed man; and when I am a redeemed man, I am no longer a mere servant, but a son, working for love, and not simply from a sense of duty. The Christian calling requires that we shall do more than others; but then it gives us, in the love of Christ, a motive which will not allow us to be content with doing just as others do. To get that motive, therefore, we must open our hearts to receive Christ's love. We must freely accept him and his salvation, and then that will enkindle in our souls a gratitude that will emancipate us from the thraldom of legal service, and impel us to offer unto God the constant devotion of a child.

When the life of a beloved son is hanging in the balance, no one can persuade his mother to take rest. You may tell her that others are watching, that every thing is being done that can be done, that it is her "duty" to take a respite; but you might as well speak to the deaf, for she is his mother, and her mother-love will not let her be content with less than her own personal ministry to her boy. But does she think then of doing merely her duty to him? Is she measuring her conduct then by any standard of rectitude? Nothing of the kind! She has risen above all standards and all duty. She does just what her love impels her; and all she does is so little able to content her, that she is only sorry she can do no more. Now, it will be the same with us and the service of God, if only we attain to love of him for what he is to us, and for what he has done for us in Christ. It will lift us above legalism, and make the mere doing of duty seem but meagre and unprofitable. It will keep us from murmuring, and preserve us from self-complacency; for duty can be satisfied with its doings, but love can never do enough. "Thank God," said one in dying, "I have done my duty." "Alas!" says the expiring Christian, after all he has done, "I am an unprofitable servant." *There* is the difference between the two. Let us, then, get to this love of God in Christ, and the exactions of the Christian life will not appal us, while the meeting of them will not puff us up; for we shall have the courage to go forward to them, and the humility not to be complacent over them. And when our life on earth is done, just as here we felt all through that we could never do enough for Christ, we shall discover hereafter that Christ can never do enough for us; that, as we have sought to serve him here, he will serve us there; and that, as we constantly strove to honor him here, he will do immortal honor to us there. "For" — I revert to the other side, and quote again the words, and wonderful words they are — "he will gird himself, and make us to sit down to meat, and will come forth and serve us."

XXVII

THE IMPORTUNATE WIDOW, AND THE PHARISEE AND THE PUBLICAN
Luke 18:1-14

THE parable of the importunate widow was designed to enforce the lesson that "men ought always to pray, and not to faint." But in order to see what these words specially refer to, we must go back upon the discourse which is summarized in the latter portion of the chapter which immediately precedes. That discourse, as you will at once perceive, treats of the second personal appearance of the Lord Jesus upon the earth; and while dwelling upon the certainty of that event, it particularly emphasizes these two things concerning it: namely, that it should be long delayed, and that it should occur when it was least expected. There would be many times in the history of the church, when, contending with adversaries, and suffering injustice at the hands of their persecutors, its members should "desire to see one of the days of the Son of man," and should not see it; but they were not to cease to expect or to pray for that great deliverance, because of its being so long deferred. It would surely come, and when it came it would bring a speedy issue out of all their troubles: therefore, at all times, and in all circumstances, they were to keep that great event in mind, and make its coming the object of their earnest supplication.

This being the primary purpose for which the parable was spoken, we can see that the "praying always" here is a different thing from that which Paul had in his mind when he enjoined his readers to "pray without ceasing." That referred to the constant maintenance of a devotional spirit, so that the habitual attitude of the soul toward God should be one of prayer. But this describes the case of one who has been long making request for that which has not yet been granted, and it encourages him to continue in the presentation of his petition, in spite of its apparent uselessness. As Edersheim has said, "The word 'always' must not be understood as if it meant continuously, but in the sense of under all circumstances, however apparently adverse, when it seems as if an answer could not come, and we are therefore in danger of 'fainting' or becoming weary."[1] It is not that we should never be doing any thing else than praying for the coming of the Lord; but that we should not allow any influences however depressing, or any delay however long, to keep us from continuing to pray for the appearing of our Lord and Saviour Jesus Christ. The Church on earth must never allow herself to become so hopeless and unbelieving, in regard to the second coming of her Lord, as to give up praying for that great consummation, when all her wrongs shall be redressed, and all her troubles shall be brought to a blessed and everlasting end. That is the great lesson of the parable, and it is to that the Saviour reverts when, as he concludes, he says, "Nevertheless, when the Son of man cometh shall he find *that* faith?" for in the original, the article is used, and the reference is to such faith as will continue to the end looking and praying for the coming of the Son of man "upon the earth."

[1] Life and Times of Jesus the Christ, vol. ii. p. 286.

Now, with this clear comprehension of the design of the parable in our minds, let us proceed to its interpretation. We have here a widow, deprived of her natural protector, and made the victim of an unscrupulous man's injustice. In her extremity she applies to the judge, but he too is without any principle. He is not only known by others as one who neither fears God nor regards man, but he absolutely glories in these things himself as if they constituted a title to greatness. He did just as it pleased him; and it pleased him most to serve his own interests, to promote his own aggrandizement, and to take his own ease. There was small hope, therefore, that he would care to right this widow's wrongs. She could bring no influence to bear upon him that was likely to move him, and she had no gold wherewith to bribe him. But she held at him with the persistence of one who was apparently determined not to let him go until he did her justice. And at length she conquered; for he said, "Because this widow troubleth me, I will do her justice, lest by her continual coming she weary me." This last phrase has been rendered in the Revised Version, "lest she wear me out by her continual coming;" and by the American Revisers, "lest at last by her coming she wear me out." But it is questionable, to me, if either of these expressions conveys the full force of the original. The word rendered "weary," or "wear," is literally "to strike under the eyes,"[1] and seems to indicate that this judge felt that if he did not attend to the case of the widow, she would ultimately be tempted to violence. It was as if he had said, "She'll come to blows by and by;"[2]

[1] The Greek is ὑπωπιάζῃ, and the verb signifies to give one a black eye, to disfigure the face.
[2] This is the view of Meyer.

and it is not unlikely, as Godet suggests, that there is a touch of humor in the term. In any case, the widow gains her cause at last through that very love of ease in the judge which at first prevented him from examining into her case.

Now, from this analysis of the parable, it is at once apparent that we have here not an allegory proper, but a simple story from which an argument is drawn. We must not say that the judge in any sense represents God, or that the widow is a type of what a suppliant should be. The very reverse is true; and the force of the argument drawn by our Lord from the parable lies in the unlikeness of God to this unjust judge, and in the unlikeness of the true Christian suppliant to this widow. It is here just as it was in the case of the parable of the friend at midnight, with which this one has so much in common; and the argument is not so much from the less to the greater, as from the worse to the better. It may be amplified into these words: "Hear what the judge of unrighteousness saith; and shall not God — the Judge of righteousness, and the Father of his people — do justice to his elect, who cry to him night and day, not to tease and worry him by their entreaties, but out of their love to him and confidence in him, though he delay long to interfere in their behalf? I tell you that he will do justice to them, and when he begins he will do it speedily; for the day of the Lord will make short work with all who are his adversaries, and who have been the oppressors of his people." You observe that I have carried this argument through; and that I have pointed a contrast between the widow, and the elect of God, as well as between the unjust judge, and God himself. I do not think that we are warranted to take this woman's importunity with the judge as a pattern for our praying, any more than we are to take the judge's yielding to her at last as a type of God's answering of prayer. This woman was not a model suppliant. Her plan was to "browbeat" — for that is the exact idiomatic equivalent to the original word — the judge into giving her what she wanted. But that is no right spirit to cherish when we pray to God; and the argument of the parable is, that if she succeeded by that plan, with such a judge, much more God's people, praying to him in filial love and reverence and confidence, will receive from him at length that which he has promised.

I am the more particular to insist on this, because I am persuaded that multitudes among us have an entirely erroneous idea about this matter of what they call importunity in prayer. They imagine that if they will only *hold at* God, as a foolish child does at an indulgent parent, they will at last receive what they want, whatever it may be. They give the impression that they believe that the Lord is unwilling to bless them, and that they must wring favors out of him by force of importunity. They think, in other words, that they will be heard for their persistence in speaking to him. Now, the success of our prayers does not depend on any thing of that kind, and it is a libel on God to cherish the notion that he is reluctant to bless his children. Moreover, it is an entire perversion of the purpose of this parable, to take it as if meant to teach us that we shall get from God that which we want, provided only we "browbeat" him into giving it by our persistence. The inference from the parable is not that we shall be heard because we persevere in prayer; but, rather, that we should persevere in prayer even when the answer appears to be long delayed, because it is God to whom we are praying, and we know that he is always willing to bless, and will ultimately give to us that which is best.

The primary reference of this parable, as we have seen, is to the second coming of Christ, which would be so long delayed that the Church would be tempted to cease praying for it altogether; but its principle is equally applicable to all cases in which believers, seeking for that which God has promised, are in danger of growing faint through weariness in waiting, or through unbelief. "Wait on God." Let him take his own time; and while you wait for that time, solace yourselves with devout and loving dependence on him as expressed in prayer. That is the true spirit of filial piety, and that will succeed with God far, far better than the widow's method did with the unjust judge. The delay in answering prayer does not imply that God has forgotten either you or his promise; therefore be not tempted by that delay to give up prayer altogether, or to lose your faith in God as the hearer of prayer. He has not overlooked you, and in his own time the answer will come in such a way as to convince you that all through he has been planning for your highest good.

Such is the bearing of this parable on the subject of prayer. It admits that God may delay answering prayer, and it tells us what our demeanor should be under such an experience; but it gives no explanation of the delay. Still, with the light which is thrown on the subject from other parts of the Scripture, we may see that oftentimes answers to prayer are deferred, in order that God's forbearance may be shown a little longer to those who are oppressing his people, if haply they may be led to repentance. Sometimes, too, the purpose of the delay, as in the cases of Jacob and of the Syrophœnician woman, is to foster and develop the faith and holiness of the suppliant; while occasionally, as in the case of Job, it may be due to the fact that God designs, through the demeanor of the suppliant himself, to show how powerful his grace is to sustain, under the most trying circumstances, all who trust in him. But whatever may be the explanation of the delay, it is not either in God's lack of love to us, or in his unwillingness to bless us, or in his unfaithfulness to his promises; and therefore it should never tempt us to give up praying to him. His delay should not destroy our faith in him, but rather quicken it into livelier exercise; and we should continue to pray, not because we shall be heard for our continuance, but because, in spite of his apparent indifference, we are sure that he continues to love us, and will certainly bless us. Not because we trust in our importunity, so called, but because we know his love and faithfulness, we should pray in all circumstances, and never faint.

But all is not prayer which calls itself by that name; and in order to guard us against mistake in a matter of so much importance, the Lord proceeds to show what true prayer is, by letting us overhear two men at their devotions. The first is a Pharisee, who, like so many of his class, trusted in himself that he was righteous, and despised others. He took his position by himself in the temple; but his prayer, if so we may call it, was merely a self-complacent soliloquy. He expressed no wants. He framed no petition. He simply rehearsed the number of his religious observances, and recounted his good qualities. He thanked God indeed, in words: yet even while he was doing that, we can perceive that he was merely congratulating himself. But there was no consciousness of need, and none of the urgency of one who felt that unless God supplied his need he would be eternally undone. It was thus he spake: "God, I thank thee that I am not as other men are, extortioners, unjust, adulterers, or even as this publican. I fast twice in the week, I give tithes of all that I possess." Here was nothing of devotion, or dependence, or any other religious emotion, — nothing but a trusting in himself, and a despising of others.

The other suppliant was a publican, who, abashed in the presence of the Great Supreme, "stood afar off, and would not lift up so much as his eyes unto heaven, but smote upon his breast." His attitude was not assumed for effect, like that of the Pharisee, but was the natural expression given by his whole body to the feelings which were vibrating within him. For it is a mistake to suppose that a man speaks only by the tongue. His eyes, his face, his hands, all have been endowed with the power of expression; and, when his heart is profoundly moved, the very posture which his body intuitively and unconsciously assumes is an indication of the emotions which stir his soul. Hence the attitude and action of the publican, his bowed head, the smiting of his breast, as well as the place on which he stood, were just so many indices — all the more sincere because they were unstudied — of his profound humility.

Equally apparent is his earnestness. Here was no playing at prayer. Here was no attempt, either, at making a prayer by elaborate phrase-mongering. This entreaty was born out of the emergency in which the man felt himself to be. It came forth, as one might say, of itself, without any thought on his part of how he would shape it; and just because of that, it took the best possible shape. There was no circumlocution about it. He went at once to the heart of the matter, and condensed into one brief utterance the whole need of his soul, "God be merciful to me, the sinner." No one but a man in earnest could have done that. The general on a review day, when he and his troops are to go through all the manœuvres of a military parade, may harangue his soldiers in a style of florid and high-sounding rhetoric; but when they are on a real battle-field with the enemy in front of them, he can utter only a few burning words, yet these few are genuine, simple, direct, and therefore eloquent. When the heart is stirred, it speaks in telegrams. Its words then are winged; and the more thoroughly it is stirred, the more arrowy do its exclamations become. "Lord, save me, I perish!" "Lord, help me!" "Lord, I believe, help thou mine unbelief!" such are specimens of its panting ejaculations in its times of agony; and such also was the fervid utterance of the publican in the case before us. One may say a great deal, and yet have little real prayer in his words; and again, as here, one may be hardly able to utter a sentence, but there may be in that sentence the condensation of a whole liturgy.

These are the characteristics of the two prayers in this parable, so far as they appear upon the surface. Indeed, that of the Pharisee was altogether on the surface, and therefore we need not trouble ourselves further about it; but if we would really comprehend all that the publican's implied, we must go a little deeper, and when we do so we may learn how it came that he "went down to his house justified rather than the other."

I. For, in the first place, when we come to examine it, we find that it sprang out of deep conviction of sin.

"God — me the sinner." These are the words which indicate the workings of the man's conscience; and when we place them thus, side by side, we see how serious a thing in his view sin really was. Many would restrict that term to the designation of flagrant offences, and such deeds as affect a man's respectability in society; others, reading the law of God as having reference only to outward acts, imagine that sin consists merely in overt wickedness; while, in the view of not a few, sin is a mere misfortune, — a thing to be regretted as a calamity, but not involving personal blame. And there are some who, comparing themselves with their neighbors, think that there is little wrong with them at all. But when one has been enlightened in the knowledge of himself and of God's law, by the Holy Ghost, he has but one idea of the matter, and one estimate of himself. Behold it here! Sin, in this man's eyes, is rebellion against God. It is so, else why does he call on God at all? He does not invoke society to wipe away the reproach which it had written against the publican. He does not beg his fellow-men to receive him into their confidence and esteem. But he asks mercy from God, and he does so because he knows that it is against God that he has sinned, — against God, who had done more for him than ever earthly father did for a son; against God, who had crowned him with his tender mercies and loving-kindnesses. The essence of sin, to him, is that it has dishonored God by outraging his law and insulting his love. And in so regarding sin he does not restrict it to actions. He sees God's law to be exceeding broad, including his thoughts and desires and disposition, as well as his outward conduct; nay, such is his sense of the enormity of his own guilt, that he has nothing to say about his neighbors. The Pharisee, when he had exhausted his panegyric upon himself, could not conclude without a horizontal fling at the publican; but the publican is so overwhelmed with his own sin, that he has no thought at the moment for others. It is almost with him as if he were the only guilty one in the world; for he says, "God be merciful to me *the* sinner." Brethren, when a man is convinced thus of sin, he cannot but be abased; when, in his guiltiness and ingratitude, he confronts himself thus with God in His purity and love, he cannot but exclaim, "Woe is me, for I am a man of unclean lips!" "Behold, I am vile, and what shall I answer?" "God be merciful to me the sinner!"

II. But, in the second place, this prayer sprang out of a sense of helplessness. Observe, it is a cry for *mercy*. Now let us see what is implied in that. Very clearly it evinces that in the suppliant's estimation there was nothing about himself, on the ground of which he could claim forgiveness. He does not ask for justice. He does not seek that any thing should be done for him, or given to him, as a debt or of right. He presumes not, like the Pharisee, to speak of his own merit. His cry is for mercy. He acknowledges the justice of his condemnation. He admits, besides, that there is in him no cause or ground why the sentence under which he lies should not be executed upon him. He sues alone for mercy. Now, it is the same with every one of us: and the sooner we come to see that, it will be the better for us; for if we ever obtain deliverance from God, it will not be because of any thing about ourselves, but simply from the free, unmerited favor of the Most High. We are to accept it as a gift, but we cannot claim it as a right. It is "not of works, lest any man should boast." This is a humbling doctrine, but it is the doctrine of

God's book; and it puts us all on a level, for, as Paul says, "There is no difference, for all have sinned and come short of the glory of God."[1] Before him every one of us deserves to perish; and when we come to him each of us must renounce merit, and plead for mercy. Just here many falter. They want to have some of the credit of their own deliverance. They wish something to be allowed for their liberality to good objects, something for their activity in benevolent enterprises, something for the restraint which they have tried to put on their evil principles; and then they will be content to receive the balance as a gratuity from God. But all such claims must be disavowed. "'Tis from the mercy of our God that all our hopes begin." Now, merit and mercy are altogether incompatible : as Paul has put it, and we never can put it better, "if it be by grace, then it is no more of works, otherwise grace is no more grace ; but if it be of works, then it is no more grace, otherwise work is no more work."[2] "Not by works of righteousness which we have done, but according to his mercy he saved us."[3] To that mercy, then, we must make our plea; for that we must cry in the spirit of these simple lines, —

> "Mercy, good Lord! mercy I crave,
> This is the total sum;
> For mercy, Lord, is all my suit:
> Lord, let thy mercy come."

III. But now, finally, this prayer was a cry of faith. So much is evident from the statement of the Lord that the publican went down to his house justified; but in the petition itself, there is, to the reader of the original, a striking proof of the same thing. For, the term ren-

[1] Rom. iii. 22, 23. [2] Rom. xi. 6. [3] Tit. iii. 5.

dered "be merciful" has in it a reference to atonement.[1] It is a form of the same word which is used when the reconciliation of sinners to God, on the ground of sacrifice, is referred to throughout the Scriptures. It is the verb of which the Greek name which designated the blood-besprinkled "mercy-seat" is the cognate noun. It is allied to the word which is translated "propitiation" in the well-known passage,[2] "whom God hath set forth to be a propitiation;" and also to that occurring in the First Epistle of John,[3] "He is the propitiation for our sins, and not for ours only, but for the sins of the whole world." Now, the use of this term by the publican shows that he had in his mind a reference to sacrifice, and to the promises which God had made to the Jews in connection with the sprinkling of the blood of the victim upon the mercy-seat. Besides, we must not forget that his prayer was offered in the temple, from the court of which every day there ascended the smoke of sacrifice both morning and evening. Doubtless, therefore, to Jehovah as he had there revealed himself, to Jehovah as dwelling between the cherubim and over the mercy-seat, this prayer was addressed. Whether the supplicant had any clear idea of the typical nature of these animal sacrifices; whether he had even a glimpse of the great atonement that was to be made by Him "who was wounded for our transgressions, and bruised for our iniquities," — may be exceedingly doubtful; but the peculiarity of his language seems to prove that his faith took hold of the promises which God had made in connection with sacrifice. Now, it has to be the same with us yet: only, instead of the typical sacrifice and the typical mercy-seat, we have the true atonement, and the true

[1] It is ἱλάσθητί.   [2] Rom. iii. 25.   [3] 1 John ii. 2.

throne of grace; and when we come seeking mercy,
we must come through Jesus Christ, grounding our
hope of acceptance on the atonement which he has
made on our behalf. We have no claim even on God's
mercy, except in Christ. It is written, "God was in
Christ reconciling the world unto himself, not imputing
unto men their trespasses;"[1] and if we would obtain
that reconciliation, we must go into Christ to secure
it. "In Christ," that is the common ground, if I may
so express it, whereon God and the sinner meet in
reconciliation. All that way in the direction of men,
God has come to meet us; all that way in the direction
of God, we must go to meet him; and when we meet
him thus "in Christ," we have "redemption through his
blood, even the forgiveness of sins."[2] Indeed, nowhere
save in Christ has God revealed mercy to those who
have violated law. In this regard the aspect of nature is often very terrible. There is nothing there
but hard, remorseless, inflexible law, which comes
down on every transgressor with unpitying penalty.
Fire burns, even though it be a martyr that is in the
flames. The tide flows remorselessly in, even though
a maiden testifying to Jesus is chained to a stake far
within the flood-mark. Everywhere we look, there is
law, and penalty for its violation, but not a trace of
mercy to those by whom law is broken. You cannot
see that in the evening sky, or on the face of ocean,
or anywhere on the surface of the dry land. Nature
may and does unfold God's power and wisdom; but not
until he revealed himself "in Christ" could we learn
any thing of his mercy. At the cross of Calvary we
see his justice and his mercy; his law, and his tenderness to the law-breaker, equally conspicuous; justice

[1] 2 Cor. v. 19.   [2] Eph. i. 7.

satisfied to be merciful, and mercy exercised in justice. Here we understand fully the meaning of the mystic name proclaimed to Moses as he stood in the cleft of the rock:[1] "Jehovah, Jehovah, God merciful and gracious, long-suffering, and abundant in goodness and truth, keeping mercy for thousands, forgiving iniquity, transgression, and sin; and that will by no means clear the guilty." Yea, over that cross of agony, we may read in characters of light, all the brighter for the gloom out of which they shine, another inscription than that which Pilate wrote; and it is this: "God so loved the world, that he gave his only begotten Son, that whosoever believeth in him should not perish, but have everlasting life."[2] Here, then, O sinner, is the ground on which thy hope must rest. God hath spoken to thee in mercy, and promised thee forgiveness through the giving-up of his own Son on thy behalf. Come and take him at his word. Come and seek his mercy in this the way of his appointment. And come now, so that thou too, like this publican, mayst go down to-night to thy house justified, accepted, saved.

It has not been possible, even in this brief and comprehensive manner, to treat the publican's prayer, without preaching the gospel from it to sinners generally. But we must not forget, that as it stands here contrasted with the self-laudation of the Pharisee, it is, in a sense, a model for ourselves; and we must for just a moment or two return to look at it in that aspect, and see what we may learn from it as to how we are to pray. The attitude and words of the Pharisee warn us against pride, self-confidence, and arrogant boasting of ourselves over others, in our approaches to

[1] Exod. xxxiv. 6.   [2] John iii. 16.

God. These things are not prayer at all. They have nothing in them that is devotional. They are simply and only sins, and, as such, must be an abomination to God. But if we would pray aright, we must draw near to God as sinners, with humility and earnestness; we must seek those things which we feel we need; and we must in seeking them make our appeal to God's mercy, as that has been revealed to us through the sacrifice of his Son on our behalf, and expressed in the promises which his Word contains. That will be true prayer; and though the answer may be at times delayed, we must not lose our faith in God's love and fidelity, but wait in patience, because we know that we are waiting upon God. Pray like the publican, and wait like Abraham, whose whole life was one great, patient, prayerful expectation; and who died "not having received the things promised," but seeing them and saluting them from afar. That is the lesson which we are to learn from the two parables of this evening's study.

XXVIII

THE POUNDS

Luke 19:12-27

RIGHTLY to understand this parable, and give their due significance to those features in it which differ from that of the talents, to which it has a general resemblance, it is essential that we give good heed to the circumstances in which, and the purpose for which, it was spoken. Our Lord had just been entertained by Zacchæus, one of the chief of the publicans in the city of Jericho, and was about to proceed to Jerusalem on the occasion of that passover to which he had so often referred as destined to be the crisis of his earthly career. He was attended by a crowd, the members of which were differently affected by these movements on his part. The Pharisees, of course, were utterly out of sympathy with his treatment of the tax-gatherer. They were indignant that he had accepted the hospitality of one who belonged to a class which they despised; and, whoever might be disposed to accept him as a king, they utterly repudiated his claim to royalty over them, and gave him to understand that they would never own his authority.

On the other hand, his own disciples were looking forward with high hopes to his visit to Jerusalem at this time. They trusted that it was he who should redeem Israel, and eagerly anticipated that he would now unfurl his standard, and gather round him those by whose means he would deliver the chosen people from a foreign yoke, and restore the kingdom of David to its ancient glory. Their idea of the kingdom of God was that of a splendid temporal dominion, and they had the belief that now it was immediately to appear.

Round these two parties, the units in the multitude mainly ranged themselves; while there were, perhaps, a few in the crowd, who were there merely out of curiosity, and did not concern themselves at all either about Jesus or his work.

It was to meet these various states of mind among his hearers, that the Lord spake the parable before us. The story is one which a well-known event in their recent national history would help them all to appreciate. Indeed, it may have been in part suggested to the mind of the Redeemer by his proximity to the palace of Archelaus, which was in the neighborhood of Jericho; for, on the death of Herod the Great, that prince went to Rome to obtain from Augustus the ratification of his father's will, and was followed thither by an embassy from Judæa, appointed by the citizens, who, wearied of a dynasty of adventurers, desired of the emperor that their country might be converted into a Roman province. Now, every one can see that in these historical incidents we have much that is parallel to the framework of this story. In the parable, however, the new feature is introduced, that the nobleman intrusted certain of his servants with sums of money, which they were to trade with on his account in his absence; and then, on his return, he held a reckoning with them similar in almost every respect to that which we have already had before us in the parable of the talents.

Now, in the light of the statements which we have made, it is not difficult to perceive the peculiar pertinence of some of the points in this beautiful but solemn allegory. The nobleman is the Lord Jesus Christ himself; the far country is heaven, to which Christ has gone to await the consummation of that kingdom which he receives from his Father; the pound is the common privilege of the gospel, which is conferred alike on all those to whom it is proclaimed; and the return of the nobleman is the second coming of the Lord, when he shall at the final judgment take account of all to whom his Word has been preached. These are the main lines of exposition; but, as we dwelt at sufficient length on most of them in our enforcement of the lessons taught by the parable of the talents, we shall not linger over them now. We content ourselves, rather, with bringing out some of the distinctive features which belong to this of the pounds.

Now, here, in the first place, the departure of the nobleman to the far country, and his sojourn there until he should receive his kingdom, intimate that the second coming of the Lord was not to be immediate. The whole trend of the story is in the direction of the idea that a long while was to elapse before his return to earth as King of kings and Lord of lords. It is, therefore, somewhat marvellous in our eyes, that after the repeated references to that fact, which the Lord had made, the early Christians should have fallen into the very mistake of those here mentioned, who thought that the kingdom of God was immediately to appear. But so it was: and the error led them into two different — I might almost say opposite — evils. On the one hand, expecting the speedy re-appearance of the Lord, and yet disappointed by his lengthened delay, some were tempted to break through all restraint, and to act as if he would never come at all. Like the disloyal servant, who began to say, "My lord delayeth his coming," and proceeded to "smite his fellow-servants, and to eat and drink with the drunken," they gave themselves to excesses of every sort, and virtually threw off their allegiance to him. Just as those who have taken up the erroneous opinion that God has promised to answer literally every prayer presented in Christ's name, are stumbled when they do not obtain what they request, and sometimes rush to the extreme of unbelief, alleging that there is no efficacy in prayer at all; so, their anticipation of the immediate re-appearance of Christ being frustrated, they went on to the denial that he would ever come, saying, "Where is the promise of his coming?" It was against these, as you remember, that Peter wrote his second epistle, in which he re-affirmed with great positiveness, that "the day of the Lord should come as a thief in the night." On the other hand, there were those whose belief in the immediate re-appearance of Christ was so strong, that they could do nothing either in the way of self-culture, or of work, whether secular or sacred, because of their constant outlook for his approach. This was the case with some of the Thessalonians, who actually gave up laboring for their own support, in the expectation that there would be no need for any such action on their part, since the Lord was just at the door.

But both of these classes might have been preserved from their eccentric courses if they had been careful to mark what the Lord's teaching on this subject precisely was; for, while he always spoke most unqualifiedly of the act of his coming again as certain, he invariably indicated that the time of it would be uncertain, only he made it clear, as in the case of this parable, that it would *not* be immediate.

Thus the history of the early Christians in regard to this matter is strikingly suggestive, as showing the connection between erroneous doctrinal belief and laxity of life in one respect or other. They first misunderstood the Lord, and then, as the result, dishonored him; and if we mean to adorn his doctrine, we must make sure first that what we believe is precisely what he taught. Extravagant expectations of him or from him, for which there is no warrant in his Word, have often led to utter disbelief in him, or to conduct which he most emphatically condemns. And in these days, when so much that is utterly unwarranted is said regarding answers to prayer, it is well that this truth should be kept in mind by all; for I greatly fear that the exaggerated assertions that are made by many, in regard to healing by prayer, and so called faith-cures, will yet be responsible for an amount of infidelity that will startle the apostles of this new anomaly. Be sure, therefore, that what you believe as the doctrine of Christ is that which he really taught; and especially, in regard to his second coming, be on your guard against either attempting to fix its date, or to prescribe its manner, for neither of these has he thought proper to reveal.

We may note, again, that in the light of this parable the true preparation for the coming of the kingdom of the Lord is that of character. The disciples, at this time, had the idea that their Lord was to be a mere literal successor to the throne of David. They had no notion whatever of the spirituality of his kingdom; but dreamed that he was to be an earthly monarch, and that they were to be the members of his cabinet. Now, the fact that the nobleman in this parable is represented as giving to each of his servants a pound to trade with on his account was well calculated to rectify their views on this important subject. For, by that trading these servants would reveal of what sort they were, and show their fitness or the reverse for positions in the kingdom of their master. They all received the same sum; and the different degrees of improvement which they made of that would indicate the qualities which they severally possessed, while the very use of these qualities would develop them into larger excellence. The things they did in their lord's absence would not be the same as those which they would be set to do when he returned, but in their larger and more important field they would need the very same characteristics which were required in the smaller; and the fact that such qualities as prudence, faithfulness, energy, and activity, and not the military virtues of drill, manœuvre, and the like, would be required there, proves that the kingdom itself was not to be of an ordinary sort. As Bruce has well said here, the end contemplated by this nobleman "is not money-making, but character-making, the development in his servants of a hardihood of temper and a firmness of will which can be turned to good account when the obscure traders shall have been transformed into distinguished rulers."[1] So the design of Christ, during his absence from the earth, is that his followers shall be trained in character for the future that is before them when he shall come in his kingdom. For this purpose he has given each a *pound;* that is, the common blessing of the gospel and its opportunities. The talents were **different**

---

[1] Parabolic Teaching of Christ, p. 220.

for each, but the pound is the same for all; and so it aptly symbolizes that gospel which preaches the same truth to the rich and to the poor, to the learned and to the ignorant, to the old and to the young; which tests the character of all to whom it is proclaimed; and which wherever it is believingly received, and in the proportion in which it is obeyed, is the great educator of the soul for eternal excellence in the heavenly kingdom. In the interval between his disappearance and his re-appearing, Christ has given us his Word; and our work is to make the best of that Word for the formation of ourselves, so that he may know what we shall be most aptly fitted for at the consummation of his coming.

Now, bearing these things in mind, we shall find in this parable, when we examine it minutely, four different ways of dealing with this pound, and the lord who gave it.

I. First of all, there is that illustrated by the good and faithful servant who made his one pound into ten. He took it, small as it was, and made the very best possible improvement of it, so that he increased it tenfold. So, when his lord returned, he received this commendation and reward: " Well, thou good servant; because thou hast been faithful in a very little, have thou authority over ten cities." Now, this symbolizes the conduct and blessedness of those who make the most of their enjoyment of the gospel blessings. They do not despise the day of small things. They do not trifle away their time in idleness, or waste it in sin; but finding salvation in the gospel, through faith in Jesus Christ, they set themselves to turn every occupation in which they are engaged, and every providential dispensation through which they may be brought, to

the highest account, for the development in them of
the Christian character. They " exercise themselves to
keep a conscience void of offence toward God and
toward men;" they make strenuous efforts after godliness; they give all diligence to "add to their faith
courage, and to their courage knowledge, and to their
knowledge temperance, and to their temperance patience, and to their patience godliness, and to their
godliness brotherly kindness, and to their brotherly
kindness charity."[1] They labor not for their own
sanctification merely, but for the welfare of their fellow-
men. And they do all these things in humble dependence on the help of the Holy Spirit; so that at last, with
their one pound multiplied to ten, they have ministered
to them an entrance abundantly into the everlasting
kingdom of their Lord and Saviour Jesus Christ.
These are the "choice" specimens of the Christian character and life; believers like Paul and saints like John,
who, having filled up their lives with devotion to their
Lord, receive at last the highest measure of reward at
his hands. This servant obtained authority over ten
cities; but the form of the reward in the parable is
determined by the fact that the nobleman went to
receive an earthly kingdom, and we get no light from
it as to the nature of the reward which Christ will
give at last to those whom he delights to honor. All it
tells us is that the degree of the reward, whatever be
its nature, will be determined by the fidelity of the
disciple in his present sphere, and the result of that
upon his character and work. Perhaps full often this
noble one had bemoaned his shortcomings and infirmi-
ties, his lack of energy and his slowness of heart, saying, "Alas, I am an unprofitable servant." But his

[1] Acts xxiv. 16; 1 Tim. iv. 7; 2 Pet. i. 5-7.

master did not so depreciate him. Nay, rather, he greeted him with heartiest congratulation, saying, "Well, thou good servant." What a blessing if we shall be found worthy to be thus addressed!

II. But another way of dealing with the common blessing of the gospel is illustrated in the case of him who had increased his pound to five. He had been a real servant; but his diligence had been less ardent, his devotion less thorough, his activity less constant, and so the lord simply said to him, "Be thou also over five cities." Here, you observe, were no special words of commendation. He is not called a "good servant." It is not even said that he had done well. It was good that he had done so much, but if he had chosen he might have done much more; and so he becomes the representative of the easy-going disciple, who is admitted to be a true disciple, but has not felt, to the same degree as "first-rate" Christians feel, the constraining influence of the love of Christ. He had not kept such close watch over himself as they had done. He had not given the same diligence to the great work of character-making as they had devoted. He had not so concentrated himself on the one thing of following after Christ as they had done. And so he had less to show for his labor. He had made less of his opportunities, therefore he received a smaller reward.

Here, as I have already hinted, is the great distinction between the teaching of this parable, and that of the parable of the talents. In the latter, we are taught that equal improvement of unequal talents shall have an equal proportionate reward; but in this we are informed that unequal improvement of the same trust shall have an unequal reward. So he who had made the one pound into ten may be held as symbolizing those who receive an "abundant entrance;" this one who made the one pound into no more than five may be regarded as representing such as receive merely an entrance, without any thing of the "abundantly" connected therewith. There are some who will be saved yet so as by fire, and others who shall have salvation in fulness;[1] some who shall have little personal holiness on which to graft the life of the future, and who shall thus be in a lower place in heaven for evermore, enjoying its blessedness as thoroughly as they are competent to do, yet having there a position analogous it may be, though of course not at all identical, with that occupied by the Gideonites of old in the promised land.

On that drizzly morning when the corn-ship stranded on the Maltese shore, all the passengers and crew got safely to land; they had all an entrance into Malta: but there was little of abundance in that entrance, for some of them floated ashore on broken pieces of the wreck. How different such a landing, from that given to a prince when he goes to visit a loyal portion of his dominions! Amid the enthusiastic cheers of the multitude, accompanied by the thunder of cannon and the stirring strains of martial music, he is welcomed by the greatest of the place, and led by them through streets festooned with flowers, and gay with fluttering flags, to the banqueting-house that has been prepared for his reception. That is an "abundant" entrance. Such, and so different, will be the welcomes given to those servants who have done their very best for Christ, and those, who, while truly his disciples, have built wood, hay, and stubble, instead of precious

---

[1] See Binney's great sermon so entitled, in Weigh-House Sermons.

stones, into the fabric which they have erected on the one great foundation.

This man who had the five pounds was not so low down in the scale as many. Perhaps he was higher than any one of us. Yet let the difference between his Lord's words to him, and to the servant who had the ten pounds, stir us up to renewed diligence in the cultivation of the spiritual life, and the furtherance of the gospel of Christ, both in ourselves and in the world. There is a wrong humility, which indeed is not humility at all, but slothfulness, in many, concerning this matter. "Oh," say they, "it will be enough for us, if we but get within the door of the celestial mansion;" and no doubt that will be eternally better than to be shut out entirely. But the choicest Christians are those who desire to be nearest Christ; and if we would get such places, we must not be content with a bare increase of our pound, but must seek to multiply it manifold. Ah! but that is a serious matter; and those who start out to attain that end had need to ponder well the question put by the Lord to the sons of Zebedee, when they sought similar honor, "Can ye drink of the cup that I shall drink of, and be baptized with the baptism that I am baptized with?"[1] Only thus and thereby can we make the one pound into the largest possible sum, and so secure the "well done," and the seat on the right hand.

III. But the third mode of dealing with the common privilege of the gospel is illustrated by the servant who hid his pound in the earth, after he had carefully sought to keep it from being injured, by wrapping it in a napkin. As one has said, "He thought it was enough, to do no

[1] Matt. xx. 23.

harm. He lost every thing by an unbelieving anxiety to lose nothing. He was so afraid of doing any thing amiss, that he did nothing at all. He would make no venture, and run no risk, even when his master bade him. His was not a case of over-conscientiousness: it was an instance of sloth and selfishness taking the threadbare dress of superior prudence."[1] To add to his folly, though it was also the explanation of it, he gave as his excuse, that he feared the austerity of his master, who, he alleged, "took up that which he had not laid down, and reaped that which he did not sow." Now, as we saw when treating the parable of the talents, that statement, even if it had been true, would not avail; for then his prudence ought to have impelled him to secure interest for the pound. But it was not true, and therefore he only added insult to unfaithfulness by making such a plea. So he stands as the representative of the great multitude of hearers of the gospel, who simply do nothing whatever about it. They do not oppose it; they do not laugh at it; they do not argue against it; their worst enemies would not call them immoral: but they "neglect the great salvation," and think that because, as they phrase it, they have done no harm, therefore they are in no danger. But Christ requires positive improvement of the privileges which he bestows. He gives the seed, not to be hoarded in the granary, but to be scattered over the field that it may be multiplied many-fold; and though it may not seem so at first, yet the keeping of it in the granary is as really a disobedience of him, as would be the emptying of it out into the sea.

Negative excellence, even if that were ours, is not positive obedience. Innocence is not virtue. Virtue is

[1] The Parables of Jesus, by Rev. James Wells, p. 352.

innocence tempted yet triumphant, tried and so proved; and therefore, when Christ seeks virtue, it will not be enough to give him innocence. But, alas! who are we, that we should talk of giving him innocence? That we are guilty, is the very reason why he has come to us with the gospel. What folly, therefore, on our part, to neglect that by which alone we can be saved from guilt, and built up in holiness, and then think to excuse ourselves by saying that we have done no harm! Oh, if there be any here to-night, who have been acting in this way, let them see how utterly irrational their conduct is, and let them dig up their buried pound, and shake it out of their napkin, and proceed at once to use it for the glory of their Lord. Study these Gospels. Get faith in Him of whom they tell. Accept his principles. Obey his precepts. Build your lives after his example. And then, if you may not get the reward of him who had the ten pounds, you may perhaps attain to that of him who had the five; and, at all events, you will escape the doom of him who, stripped of his hidd trust, was thrust out into disgrace.

IV. But now, finally, we have a fourth mode of dealing with the gospel and its Lord, symbolized in the conduct of those citizens who hated the nobleman, and said, "We will not have this man to reign over us." These were the open enemies of him who went to receive his kingdom; and they represent those who defy the Lord Jesus, and set themselves against his cause. They make a merit of their frankness. When you speak to them of the claims of Christ upon them, they reply that there is nothing of the hypocrite about them. They do not pretend to be what they are not; they will have nothing to do with our Christ, and they will **go** their own way in spite of him. Who is he, that he should demand their obedience? Thus they are very decided, and very pronounced; and they think that they are better than he was who took the pound, and hid it. But are they? In the light of this parable we must say, No. For the man with the one pound was punished by the forfeiture of that pound, while these enemies were slain. A man is not the less Christ's enemy because he is an open and armed enemy. The avowal does not change the enmity into friendship. He is an enemy, and defies Christ. That is the simple truth. And here is the result: "Those mine enemies which would not that I should reign over them, bring hither, and slay them before me;" the meaning of which is thus resolved by Paul: "They that obey not the gospel of Christ shall be punished with everlasting destruction from the presence of the Lord, and from the glory of his power, when he shall come to be glorified in his saints, and to be admired among all them that believe."[1] Oh, why will you recklessly rush, my unbelieving and disobedient friend, on such a doom? Consider your ways, I entreat you, and let your enmity to Christ give place forthwith to simple trust in him and sincere love for him. And thus you will secure at length an entrance into his kingdom.

We have come to-night to the end of our study of the Redeemer's parables. For twenty-eight sabbath evenings we have been engaged together in the pleasant and profitable work; and as we have gone on, we have had deeper insight into the heart of our Master, and glimpses into regions of truth, which, perhaps, were

[1] 2 Thess. i. 8-10.

heretofore unknown by us. When I began, I feared that the way had been so frequently trodden, that little freshness would be found in it by us. I thought of my work as that of a belated gleaner in a well-raked field. But it has been far otherwise; and I know not if from any of our winter studies in the word of God, whether of the Old Testament or the New, we have gathered in so many sheaves of golden grain as we have done during these past months from the exposition of these exquisite stories. It is an affecting thought, to me, that some of those who began the investigation of them with us are now no longer in this earthly sphere, but have gone into that region which awaits us all. They have now the key to much that is still mysterious to us here; and their removal is a loud warning to us all to improve the passing opportunities so that we may gain at last the "well done," with which, as I trust, they have been greeted. Do not let us forget that these studies have increased our responsibilities, and that if we are not the better for them we must inevitably be the worse. We have been very near the Saviour all the while. Have we learned thereby to love Him more? or must it be with any of us as with that disciple, who heard all the parables at the first, and yet went "to his own place" at last? "Now unto Him that is able to keep you from falling, and to present you faultless before the presence of his glory with exceeding joy, to the only wise God our Saviour, be glory and majesty, dominion and power, both now and ever. Amen."

www.ingramcontent.com/pod-product-compliance
Lightning Source LLC
Chambersburg PA
CBHW022055150426
43195CB00008B/151